MARK TWAIN

101-16

TWENTIETH CENTURY VIEWS

The aim of this series is to present the best
in contemporary critical opinion on major
authors, providing a twentieth century perspective on their changing status in an era
of profound revaluations.

Maynard Mack, *Series Editor*
Yale University

MARK TWAIN

A COLLECTION OF CRITICAL ESSAYS

Edited by

Henry Nash Smith

A SPECTRUM BOOK

Prentice-Hall, Inc., *Englewood Cliffs, N.J.*

Table of Contents

MARK TWAIN

Introduction

by Henry Nash Smith

I

Twentieth century criticism of Mark Twain has followed the general course of American criticism. It has been influenced by the impressionism of the years before the First World War, the search for a usable past during the 1920's, the cult of realism and of social significance during the 1930's, the emphasis on technique that became fashionable in the later 1930's and 1940's, and the interest in symbolism, often involving psychological speculation, that has rather paradoxically flourished along with formalism in recent years. But Mark Twain poses special problems. He was a humorist, and criticism is notoriously helpless in the presence of writing that is really funny. Furthermore, he was and is immensely popular, whereas in our day it is usually taken for granted that writers of any consequence are alienated from society.

Since humor is so difficult to analyze, Mark Twain's strongest attraction for most of his readers has been very little discussed in print. On the other hand, the fact of his astonishing hold on a vast unliterary public has been a central concern for critics almost from the beginning of his career. The extent of his popularity during his own lifetime can best be conveyed by an anecdote. In 1878 a ne'er-do-well named Jesse M. Leathers got on a train in Cincinnati bound for Washington, D.C. As he wrote Clemens in a begging letter some years later, he had no money to pay his fare, and when the conductor discovered this fact he was "furious." But Leathers was not without resources. In lieu of a ticket he produced a brief note addressed to him by Clemens (whom he had not met and never would meet). The conductor looked at the signature and the monogram on the notepaper, smiled, and said, "That will do. I like Twain." Leathers continued:

> He took me to Chillicothe, the end of his route, where I stopped over night. Here I made the acquaintance of a gifted Irishman who, when he saw your letter, put up the drinks for the house, and invited me to dine with him. He proved to be a boss workman on the Baltimore & Ohio R. R. and learning my embarrassed condition by degrees offered to settle my Hotel bill and presented me a pass over the Road which carried me to Parkersburg, Va.

The next conductor, even in Virginia, was unmoved by the sight of a letter from Jefferson Davis introducing Leathers to Judah P. Benjamin, but the note from Clemens melted his resistance.

> "Ah!" he exclaimed "this is from Mark Twain. Good! My wife is a great admirer of Mr. Clemens—give me his autograph, or signature and I will pass you through safe and sound." The bargain was struck at once and he tore off your "fist" and the monogram and carefully placed the preacious [sic] relic in his pocket, handing me back the rest of the letter. . . .

This is the kind of veneration that railway conductors and gifted Irishmen in bars might feel for generals or prizefighters; it is not their usual attitude toward men of letters. The fact is that in the popular conception Mark Twain was not a man of letters. If he had to be classified he was a humorist, but with the possible exception of Artemus Ward, who had died in 1867, no other humorist had this kind of hold on the general public. The name Mark Twain meant more than telling jokes. It designated the narrative voice that spoke in *The Innocents Abroad* and *Roughing It,* and the picturesque figure on the lecture platform with the dead-pan manner described by an admirer as that of innocence beleaguered by the world and the devil. Mark Twain's readers and lecture audiences felt themselves to be in direct communication with a personality whose tastes and attitudes seemed identical with their own, a voice that spoke for them as well as to them.

This personality was in large part a fictional construction, neither identical with the actual Samuel L. Clemens nor fully under his control, but rather the product of a collaboration between him and his audience. Mark Twain could for that reason readily come to seem an embodiment of the typical American character. Clemens did what he could to help the process along. The contemporary reviewer of *The Innocents Abroad* who remarked that "the eyes with which [the narrator] sees are our eyes as well as his . . . the book becomes a transcript of our own sentiments" was merely echoing the author's claim that his purpose was "to suggest to the reader how *he* would be likely to see Europe and the East if he looked at them with his own eyes rather than with the eyes of those who traveled in those countries before him." When Howells, much later, called Mark Twain "the Lincoln of our literature" he meant not only to confer a title of greatness but to emphasize this capacity for entering into the attitudes of the vast majority of the American people. Clemens' official biographer Albert B. Paine set forth an accepted axiom when he declared him to be "the man most characteristically American in every thought and word and deed."

Hostile observers also took Mark Twain to be representative of dominant American attitudes. Matthew Arnold, for example, identified him in the 1880's as the most conspicuous among the vulgar funny men who were second only to the newspapers as a force making against "distinction" in America, and Mark Twain in his annoyance accepted the charge, claiming to have no interest in the cultivated minority but to be a writer solely for the uncultivated masses.

In 1890, when Mark Twain made this declaration, the ferment of the populist movement was revealing a widespread hatred of England in this country that recalled the rancors of the opening decades of the century. Reviewers of *A Connecticut Yankee* welcomed the strain of Anglophobia in the book. But with the passage of time populism tended to dramatize the issue of West versus East more vividly than that of America versus England. Frederick Jackson Turner's frontier hypothesis, first announced in 1893, expressed this attitude in a form that appealed strongly to historians and eventually to students of literature. The shift in emphasis was subtle, and was masked by Turner's contention that the frontier— popularly understood to be a synonym for the West—had shaped the American character and had given rise to the characteristic American values. Thus without ceasing to be the typical American, Mark Twain could become pre-eminently the typical Westerner, a spokesman for the frontier in literature.

II

In bare outline, this was the accepted view in 1920, when Van Wyck Brooks published his immensely influential *The Ordeal of Mark Twain*. Brooks had attained the status of spokesman for the new generation of American intellectuals with his *America's Coming of Age* (1915). The collapse of Wilsonian idealism after the war strengthened the impulse of these men to repudiate the official goals of a society that had in their opinion made business its god. In the circumstances, Mark Twain was an almost inevitable target. Brooks's disciple Waldo Frank had begun the attack in 1918, and two years later Brooks spelled out the indictment in full.

Although the ensuing debate, extending through the 1920's and even into the 1930's, was ostensibly about a writer and his career, the real issue was a reassessment of the prevalent American system of values. In depicting Mark Twain as a potentially great artist turned into a mere funny man by the repressive forces of Puritanism and the frontier, Brooks was attempting to exorcise pernicious elements of the American tradition in order to clear the ground for the creation of the kind of civilization he desired. When he spoke (in an essay in the *Dial*) for the discovery of a "usable past," he apparently had in mind a process like the rehabilitation of Melville that began with the publication of Raymond Weaver's biography in 1921. The Melville of the enthusiasts in this period was an almost exact counter-symbol to Brooks's Mark Twain: an alienated artist who, defying the pressures of conformity, had shouted "No!" in thunder and then had withdrawn into silence rather than tailor his writing to the measure of perverted popular tastes.

Brooks's hostility to a business civilization was clear, but he was rather vague about what he wished to affirm. Despite his air of modernity, he fell back on the decadent post-Romantic cult of ideality that George Santayana had already labelled "the genteel tradition." Much of Brooks's case against Mark Twain is a mere restatement of charges that had been made a half-century earlier by such genteel critics as Josiah G. Holland. When Brooks maintains, for example, that the "sole and willful purpose" of the oesophagus hoax in *A Double-Barrelled Detective Story* was "to disturb the contemplation of beauty" he is equating beauty with the outworn cult of the natural sublime that had blighted whole acres of nineteenth century American prose. Brooks also objects to Mark Twain's satire of the spurious raptures of American tourists in *The Innocents Abroad,* and even defends the Tennysonian mirage of medieval chivalry that is burlesqued in *A Connecticut Yankee.* He was attempting to make Arnold's case without Arnold's clear conception of culture as a force capable of transforming society. Arnold would have been astonished by Brooks's acknowledgment that Clemens had great native gifts as an artist, but otherwise the two critics were in full agreement. Both were disturbed by the combination of vast and growing economic power in the United States with an indifference to art and the free play of ideas. And both saw Mark Twain as a symptom, a mouthpiece through which American philistinism had made itself articulate.

Bernard DeVoto, whose *Mark Twain's America* (1932) was by far the most vigorous reply to Brooks, was able to point out numerous errors of fact in *The Ordeal of Mark Twain,* and his identification of himself with the frontier freed him from the kind of residual gentility that hampered Brooks. But in his eagerness to champion the West against the East— which he presented as an oversimplified antithesis to Brooks's equally oversimplified image of the frontier—he often became an advocate rather than an interpreter. To say of Mark Twain that "He was the frontier itself" was to add all the ambiguities of Turner's hypothesis to a discussion already well provided with irrelevancies.

The controversy over Brooks's *Ordeal* dominated the first phase of twentieth century Mark Twain criticism. It ramified into side issues and generated a voluminous discussion that Lewis Leary has recently collected in an anthology, with a historical introduction making it unnecessary to retrace the ground here. The topic is also dealt with in considerable detail by Roger Asselineau in the introduction to his bibliography of *The Literary Reputation of Mark Twain from 1910 to 1950* (1954).

Asselineau, in fact, has so thoroughly documented the development of critical opinion about Mark Twain during the first half of this century that the present collection may appropriately concentrate on the period since 1950. Aside from Brooks's chapter on Mark Twain's humor and DeVoto's "The Symbols of Despair," to which I shall return presently, the only other essay included here that was published before that date is Maurice Le Breton's "Appreciation." I have chosen it because it is the most accurate and perceptive European interpretation of Mark Twain that I know of. At the same time, this study published in the mid-1930's is a judicious summary of the best work that had been done on Mark Twain down to that date. Le Breton illustrates in its most useful form the notion of realism as a guiding principle of criticism, yet suggests the shortcomings that have led to its gradual abandonment during the last quarter of a century on both sides of the Atlantic. I must confess that the essay attracts me also by its skeptical attitude toward the strain of chauvinism in the American cult of Mark Twain.

The other essays in this collection are all in effect contemporary. I have arranged them not in the order of their composition but according to the chronological order of the works of Mark Twain they deal with. From the abundance of materials at my disposal I have allowed the choice of items to be guided by a desire to include discussions of all Mark Twain's major works. The result is a compromise among three principles of selection: choosing the best recent criticism, representing a variety of critical methods and approaches, and providing a commentary on successive phases of his career.

III

The posture in which interpretation of Mark Twain was left by the controversy over Brooks's *Ordeal* was summed up in Henry S. Canby's review of *Mark Twain's America*, published in the *Saturday Review of Literature* for 29 October 1932 under the significant title "Mark Twain Himself." Canby deplored the violence of DeVoto's attack on Brooks and maintained that "a complete estimate of Mark Twain will not be content to rest everything on the West." Nevertheless, he concluded that "Mr. DeVoto has the right key to Mark Twain. For Clemens was essentially a Western democratic man." In fact, "Twain *was* democracy, even while his mind sorted and satirized it."

Whether these statements are true or false—and they are so vague they can hardly be either proved or disproved—they have only a distant relation to Clemens' achievement as a writer. Preoccupation with broad cultural issues apparently made it difficult at that period to deal with actual texts. Although DeVoto announces that he wishes to "restore discussion of a man of letters to what he wrote," when he approaches specific books he shifts gears into a kind of eloquence that makes analysis impossible. What he is really talking about is the state of affairs that could make the display of a note from Clemens in a barroom good for a round of drinks. Of *Huckleberry Finn* he asserts: ". . . here is America." The details he cites from the book are marshaled in support of this thesis: Huck's story is "American life formed into great fiction"; Mark Twain "wrote books that have in them something eternally true to the core of his nation's life."

Thirty years later one is disposed not so much to challenge these propositions as to place them in a genre other than literary criticism. We have grown accustomed to a critical method which—for better or for worse—avoids such sweeping statements and is more concerned with what individual books are actually like. We are inclined to ask, *How* is American life formed into great fiction?

In tracing the most recent phase of Mark Twain criticism it will be convenient to set out from Canby's summary of the point of view prevalent during the 1920's. The main effort of the past two or three decades has been directed toward analysis of propositions that Canby and his contemporaries took for granted. The question of what Mark Twain actually was, for example, has been drastically reformulated. Beginning with the recognition that Mark Twain was in any case not identical with Clemens, the critics have gone on to probe the writer's shifting identification with his first-person narrators. They have continued to be interested in Clemens' relation to American culture, but they have tried to determine the precise meaning of the diverse notions linked together under such rubrics as "the West" and "the frontier" and "democracy." The critics have also distinguished the value judgments implicit in Canby's statement that "Twain *was* democracy" from the historical facts concerning the writer's use of elements drawn from popular culture. In short, they have put into practice the program announced but only partially carried out by DeVoto: they have restored discussion of a man of letters to what he wrote.

The achievement proved to be surprisingly difficult. In *Mark Twain: The Man and His Work* (1935) Edward Wagenknecht attempted to free himself from the obsessive concern with biography by adopting a topical arrangement, with chapters devoted to the writer's experience, his temperament, his conceptions of technique, and so on; but the man is still more prominently displayed than his work, and there is virtually no effort to deal with specific books. As late as 1943, DeLancey Ferguson could point out with justice in the preface to his *Mark Twain: Man and Legend* that "no one has tried to write Mark Twain's life as a man of letters." Ferguson produced what is still the best one-volume study of Mark Twain's life and writings, but the plan of giving approximately equal emphasis to both these topics prevents him from dealing adequately with literary questions. Even his most original contribution—his pioneer examination of the *Huckleberry Finn* manuscript in the Buffalo Public Library—shows the continuing influence of the debate over *The Ordeal of Mark Twain,* for he uses this fresh material primarily to disprove Brooks's thesis that Mark Twain's work was subjected to "blighting censorship" by his wife and his friend Howells.

Nevertheless, by 1943 Mark Twain criticism was quite a different affair from what it had been ten years earlier. The most obvious change is indicated by Ferguson's note of acknowledgments, which mentions an impressive amount of factual research published during the previous decade: biographical studies such as Minnie M. Brashear's *Mark Twain, Son of Missouri* (1934) and Ivan Benson's *Mark Twain's Western Years* (1938); edited texts of additional letters by Clemens and of his early writings for newspapers; and Walter Blair's anthology of *Native American Humor* (1937), with its monographic introduction. Mark Twain had been taken over by the professors. This shift of jurisdiction has proved a mixed blessing, but it has tended to inhibit the vagaries of speculation that Brooks's rather autocratic treatment of fact had encouraged.

The accumulation of verified data does not automatically advance critical insight; it can become as much of a distraction to the critic as the earlier tendency to talk vaguely about cultural issues. Both the opportunities and the risks attending the effort to make critical use of fresh information become clear if one compares DeVoto's *Mark Twain's America* (1932) with his *Mark Twain at Work,* published ten years later. DeVoto was not then a professor, but he had been one, and in leaving the academy he had taken with him a scholar's regard for evidence. His appointment to succeed Albert B. Paine as literary editor of the Mark Twain Estate in 1937 opened a new era in Mark Twain scholarship, for DeVoto not only began himself to explore the thousands of pages of unpublished manuscript in the Mark Twain Papers but opened the archive for the first time to other qualified scholars. In *Mark Twain at Work* he makes brilliant use of the materials to which he had gained access. Although he throws much new light on the composition of *Tom Sawyer* and *Huckleberry Finn,* the most novel and ambitious section of the book is the essay "The Symbols of Despair" which is included in the present collection.

As DeVoto announces at the outset, he is writing biography rather than literary criticism. He has abandoned his polemic against Brooks (whom he does not even mention); indeed, his subject is the psychic wound that Brooks had said was inflicted on Clemens by a philistine culture. On the basis of an impressive body of evidence drawn from unpublished manuscripts he maintains that what crippled Clemens was a series of personal disasters suffered in the 1890's. This hypothesis is not incompatible with the notion that during the most productive decades of Mark Twain's career, the 1870's and 1880's, he had been an exuberant spokesman for the frontier. But DeVoto does not return to his earlier thesis, and the description of an aging writer struggling to conclude "an armistice with fate" leaves an impression vastly different from the radiant panoramas of *Mark Twain's America.* Something like a tacit accommodation with Brooks has occurred: Mark Twain is no longer a symbol of either the artist's ordeal in a business civilization or the fresh energies of the West, but a man and a writer facing his own special trials and frustrations.

The essay is equally notable for the critic's compassionate identification with Clemens and the care with which he documents an analysis he acknowledges to be partly speculative. The psychological concepts DeVoto uses are more sophisticated than those of Brooks, and if he is writing biography, it is emphatically the biography of a writer, centered about the problem of how to recover from artistic impotence. Later critics have inevitably returned to the topic, revealing misplaced emphases and loose ends in DeVoto's treatment of it. James M. Cox and Tony Tanner, in quite different ways, show that DeVoto took for granted too simple a connection between biographical events and the treatment of them in fiction. DeVoto's version of Clemens' later career postulates a peak of achievement in *A Connecticut Yankee* (1889) followed by a paralysis of the writer's imagination brought on by the calamities of the 1890's and then an ascent to the "minor masterpiece" of *The Mysterious Stranger,* which DeVoto believed to have been written about 1905. Cox discovers in *A Connecticut Yankee* inner tensions similar to those DeVoto found in the later unfinished narratives, resulting in a perceptible loss of control over the materials of the story. Yet this book was published before Clemens' personal disasters came upon him. The causes of his despair are therefore deeper, they are part of a development that can be traced from early in his career. *The Mysterious Stranger* can now also be recognized as a basically chaotic work. Leslie Fiedler's disparagement of it in his essay on *Pudd'nhead Wilson* is perhaps excessive, but as Tanner's references to it indicate, the book has a much lower standing in contemporary criticism than DeVoto assigns to it. DeVoto's contention that *The Mysterious Stranger* is an act of self-healing on the writer's part has been made untenable by new evidence concerning its date of composition presented by John S. Tuckey in a study still unpublished. The book was almost certainly written between 1897 and 1900, during the period which DeVoto regards as the darkest phase of Clemens' psychic block. DeVoto's hypothesis about the cause of Clemens' pessimism is also called in question by Tanner's parallel between Mark Twain and Henry Adams. That two men of such strikingly different backgrounds and temperaments should have reached nearly identical conclusions about American society creates a strong presumption that Clemens' despair was not primarily personal, but had an objective basis in his observation of historical change in the world around him.

The effort to place Mark Twain within the context of American culture as a whole, particularly within the main stream of American literature, is carried even farther in Fiedler's study of *Pudd'nhead Wilson*. Yet this undertaking too has its dangers. Just as DeVoto's thesis about Clemens' psychic state led him to minimize or ignore structural defects in both *A Connecticut Yankee* and *The Mysterious Stranger,* Fiedler's discovery in *Pudd'nhead Wilson* of archetypal images and myths characteristic of American culture impels him to overvalue this book. An entirely satisfactory technique for analyzing the relation of Mark Twain's work to American culture has evidently not yet been found. Fiedler's method of treating all fiction as "dream" is an improvement over Brooks's marshaling of evidence chosen indiscriminately from biographical records and imaginative writing to support a preconceived thesis, or DeVoto's uncritical use of the frontier hypothesis, but depth psychology can also give rise to dogmatisms that distort critical judgment. Fiedler is on firmer ground when he relates Mark Twain's work to that of other American writers from Cooper and Melville to Faulkner. Perhaps a new literary history using thematic analysis to establish its continuities will prove to be the most reliable method for placing a writer in his cultural context.

IV

As we have seen, in their exploration of Clemens' psyche Cox and
Fiedler are developing one of the principal lines of inquiry opened up
by the Brooks-DeVoto controversy. Kenneth Lynn also uses psychological
concepts in his *Mark Twain and Southwestern Humor*. But as his title
indicates, his main emphasis is on Mark Twain's relation to the native
tradition of humor. Such historical inquiry likewise has antecedents in
the earlier period of Mark Twain criticism; it is an analytical extension
of the older notion of Mark Twain as a spokesman for the frontier and
thus ultimately of the long-established preoccupation with his relation to
American culture. In his chapter on *Roughing It* Lynn brushes aside
DeVoto's Turnerian stereotypes in order to get at precisely what the Far
West means in the book. Here, as always in dealing with Mark Twain's
ostensibly autobiographical writings, valid historical insight depends on
the recognition that the narrative is not a "realistic" recital of fact but
a work of the imagination.

Mark Twain's relation to democracy has also been subjected to analysis
in recent criticism. At the level of explicit statement, his political views
turn out to have been, like many of his abstract ideas, somewhat confused.
He can be quoted on both sides of almost any controversial issue of his
day. Even his most ambitious imaginative treatment of political and
economic themes, *A Connecticut Yankee,* has held contradictory meanings for its readers. Howells called the book "an object-lesson in democracy," and it was welcomed by various radical groups because its satire of
feudal tyranny was taken to be a thinly veiled attack on nineteenth century abuses. Yet as Roger Salomon has recently pointed out (in *Twain
and the Image of History,* 1961), the protagonist undergoes a bitter disillusionment concerning the ability of the common people to govern
themselves which the author seems to share. Whatever Mark Twain's intention may have been, the ending of the story suggests a despair of
democracy.

On the other hand, there can be no doubt that Mark Twain was an
artist of the people. His fresh handling of the materials and techniques
of backwoods story-tellers is the clearest example in our history of the
adaptation of a folk art to serious literary uses. Here is another area where
historical inquiry has merged imperceptibly into evaluative criticism.
Building upon the work of DeVoto, Walter Blair, and others, Leo Marx
analyzes in "The Pilot and the Passenger" the stages of Mark Twain's
development toward the creation of a narrative prose based on American

vernacular speech. The topic presents one of the most promising avenues of further inquiry in Mark Twain studies.

Yet another aspect of Mark Twain's relation to popular culture is examined by Daniel G. Hoffman in his essay on the use of folklore in *Huckleberry Finn*. Hoffman's emphasis on the intimations of disaster and death that are added to the narrative in this fashion is particularly valuable as a corrective for the current tendency to read the book as a moralistic celebration of Huck's natural goodness. To mention only one other example, Franklin R. Rogers has shown in his *Mark Twain's Burlesque Patterns* (1960) that practice in burlesquing popular novels and plays gave the writer ideas of structure which he later used in his own books. This study establishes a link between Mark Twain and the commercialized "sensation novels" and melodramas produced for a mass audience that is quite distinct from his reliance on the tradition of native humor.

Rogers points out that the literary burlesque was an international genre: Thackeray, for example, was a leading practitioner of it and a model carefully imitated by Mark Twain as well as by Bret Harte and other California writers. The fact that these journalists in Nevada and California were reading London humorous magazines under the tutelage of self-conscious Bohemians recently arrived from New York provides further qualification of what is usually meant by calling Mark Twain a spokesman for the West. Once this motion is disentangled from the doctrinal requirements of the frontier thesis, it is revealed as only a half-truth, and a very complicated one at that. For even the tradition of native humor was not a Western monopoly. One of Mark Twain's clearest direct borrowings from the newspaper funny men was his modeling of Tom Sawyer's Aunt Polly on Mrs. Partington, a celebrated character created by Benjamin P. Shillaber of Boston; and George W. Harris, creator of Sut Lovingood, whom Mark Twain correctly regarded as the best among his predecessors, was a fire-eating Tennessean, emphatically Southern in his regional loyalty.

Calling Mark Twain a product of the frontier implied, a generation ago at least, that his outlook was formed by first-hand experience of life rather than by reading and that he was, if not illiterate, at least decidedly un-bookish. The revisionist case for a bookish Mark Twain can be overstated, as for example in Miss Brashear's *Mark Twain, Son of Missouri*, but it is nevertheless true that he read widely if unsystematically and made frequent use in his books of what he had read. Documentation of this thesis has required long and patient labor, most of it performed by Walter Blair. Blair's *Mark Twain & Huck Finn* (1960), from which the chapter on *Tom Sawyer* is included in this collection, documents Mark Twain's borrowings from scores of writers, both American and European. Although information of this sort does not of itself settle any critical question, it tends to alter the pervasive tone of Mark Twain criticism by undermining the tendency to approach his work as if it were written by a slightly older Huck Finn. The critic who knows he is reading the work of a man with a normal amount of knowledge about the world, past and present, is in a better position to understand Mark Twain than is the critic who assumes he is dealing with a spokesman for the strong uneducated inhabitants of the Great West.

The contemporary critics represented here have highly diverse points of view and sometimes reach contradictory conclusions, but they share a number of unstated assumptions: that Mark Twain's work, even the "personal books" that bear the outward semblance of autobiography, is best treated as fiction; that the "I" who speaks in the first-person narratives is a character deliberately projected by the writer for artistic purposes, even though the technique of the projection may falter and drift into confusions; and finally that the celebrated style, whether in the explicitly vernacular mode of *Huckleberry Finn* or in the apparently colorless, straightforward prose of the later works, is, like Mark Twain's narrative technique, a careful and conscious construction, not a spontaneous "natural" utterance. These assumptions are now commonplaces, but they have gained acceptance in Mark Twain criticism only recently. His frequent use of his own experience as material for fiction made it peculiarly difficult for critics to rid themselves of the notion that his books were simply unedited transcripts of reality; and the deliberate artlessness of his manner—the literary equivalent of the humorous lecturer's dead-pan mask—compounded the difficulty by suggesting that the writer was quite simple-minded. With the overcoming of these confusions, Mark Twain criticism has begun to attain the penetration and richness of themes that the subject deserves. His very shortcomings as a writer present a stimulating challenge. At its best, his work is so radically original that it defies classification and makes nonsense of critical dogmatisms. Its staggering unevenness imposes a constant need for discrimination. And however naïve we may now find the once current notion of Mark Twain as the representative American, the man and his career do undoubtedly constitute an essential part of our past.

Mark Twain's Humor

by Van Wyck Brooks

"To be good is noble; but to show others how to be good is nobler and less trouble."

Pudd'nhead Wilson's New Calendar

And now we are ready for Mark Twain's humor. We recall how reluctant Mark Twain was to adopt the humorist's career and how, all his life, he was in revolt against a role which, as he vaguely felt, had been thrust upon him: that he considered it necessary to publish his *Joan of Arc* anonymously is only one of many proofs of a lifelong sense that Mark Twain was an unworthy double of Samuel Langhorne Clemens. His humorous writing he regarded as something external to himself, as something other than artistic self-expression; and it was in consequence of pursuing it, we have divined, that he was arrested in his moral and aesthetic development. We have seen, on the other hand, that he adopted this career because his humor was the only writing he did in Nevada that found an appreciative audience and that, as a result of his decision, he obtained from the American public the prodigious and permanent approval which his own craving for success and prestige had driven him to seek. Here, then, are the facts our discussion of Mark Twain's humor will have to explain. We must see what that humor was, and what produced it, and why in following it he violated his own nature and at the same time achieved such ample material rewards.

It was in Nevada and California that Mark Twain's humor, of which we have evidences during the whole of his adolescence, came to the front; and it is a notable fact that almost every man of a literary tendency who was brought into contact with those pioneer conditions became a humorist. The "funnyman" was one of the outstanding pioneer types; he was, indeed, virtually the sole representative of the Republic of Letters in the old West. Artemus Ward, Orpheus C. Kerr, Petroleum Nasby, even Bret Harte, sufficiently remind us of this fact. Plainly, pioneer life had a sort of chemical effect on the creative mind, instantly giving it a humorous cast. Plainly, also, the humorist was a type that pioneer society required in order to maintain its psychic equilibrium. Mr. Paine* seems to have divined this in his description of Western humor. "It is a distinct product," he says. "It grew out of a distinct condition—the battle with the frontier. The fight was so desperate, to take it seriously was to surrender. Women laughed that they might not weep; men, when they could no longer swear. 'Western humor' was the result. It is the freshest, wildest humor in the world, but there is tragedy behind it."

Perhaps we can best surprise the secret of this humor by noting Mark Twain's instinctive reaction to the life in Nevada. It is evident that in many ways, and in spite of his high spirits and high hopes, he found that life profoundly repugnant to him: he constantly confesses in his diary and letters to the misery it involved. "I do *hate* to go back to the Washoe," he writes, after a few weeks of respite from mining. "We fag ourselves completely out every day." He describes Nevada as a place where the devil would feel homesick: "I heard a gentleman say, the other day, that it was the 'd——dest country under the sun'—and that comprehensive conception I fully subscribe to. It never rains here, and the dew never falls. No flowers grow here, and no green thing gladdens the eye. . . . Our city lies in the midst of a desert of the purest—most unadulterated and uncompromising—*sand.*" And as with the setting, so with the life. "High-strung and neurotic," says Mr. Paine, "the strain of newspaper work and the tumult of the Comstock had told on him": more than once he found it necessary—this young man of twenty-eight—"to drop all work and rest for a time at Steamboat Springs, a place near Virginia City, where there were boiling springs and steaming fissures in the mountainside, and a comfortable hotel." That he found the pace in California just as difficult we have his own testimony; with what fervor he speaks of the "d——n San Francisco style of wearing out life," the "careworn or eager, anxious faces" that made his brief escape to the Sandwich Islands —"God, what a contrast with California and the Washoe!"—ever sweet and blessed in his memory. Never, in short, was a man more rasped by any social situation than was this young "barbarian," as people have called him, by what people also call the free life of the West. We can see this in his profanity, which also, like his humor, came to the front in Nevada and remained one of his prominent traits through life. We remember how "mad" he was, "clear through," over the famous highway robbery episode: he was always half-seriously threatening to kill people;

* Albert B. Paine, author of *Mark Twain: A Biography*, 3 vols., New York, 1912. [Ed.]

he threatened to kill his best friend, Jim Gillis. "To hear him denounce a thing," says Mr. Paine, "was to give one the fierce, searching delight of galvanic waves"; naturally, therefore, no one in Virginia, according to one of the Gillis brothers, could "resist the temptation of making Sam swear." Naturally; but from all this we observe that Mark Twain was living in a state of chronic nervous exasperation.

Was this not due to the extraordinary number of repressions the life of pioneering involved? It was, of course, in one sense, a free life. It was an irresponsible life, it implied a break with civilization, with domestic, religious, and political ties. Nothing could be freer in that sense than the society of the gold-seekers in Nevada and California as we find it pictured in *Roughing It*. Free as that society was, however, scarcely any normal instinct could have been expressed or satisfied in it. The pioneers were not primitive men, they were civilized men, often of gentle birth and education, men for whom civilization had implied many restraints, to be sure, but innumerable avenues also of social and personal expression and activity to which their natures were accustomed. In escaping responsibility, therefore, they had only placed themselves in a position where their instincts were blocked on every side. There were so few women among them, for instance, that their sexual lives were either starved or debased; and children were as rare as the "Luck" of Roaring Camp, a story that shows how hysterical, in consequence of these and similar conditions, the mining population was. Those who were accustomed to the exercise of complex tastes and preferences found themselves obliged to conform to a single monotonous routine. There were criminal elements among them, too, which kept them continually on their guard, and at best they were so diverse in origin that any real community of feeling among them was virtually impossible. In becoming pioneers they had, as Mr. Paine says, to accept a common mold; they were obliged to surrender their individuality, to conceal their differences and their personal pretensions under the mask of a rough good-fellowship that found expression mainly in the nervously and emotionally devastating terms of the saloon, the brothel and the gambling-hell. Mark Twain has described for us the "gallant host" which peopled this hectic scene, that army of "erect, bright-eyed, quick-moving, strong-handed young giants—the very pick and choice of the world's glorious ones." Where are they now? he asks in *Roughing It*. "Scattered to the ends of the earth, or prematurely aged or decrepit—or shot or stabbed in street affrays—or dead of disappointed hopes and broken hearts—all gone, or nearly all, victims devoted upon the altar of the golden calf." We could not have a more conclusive proof of the atrophying effects upon human nature which this old Nevada life entailed.

Innumerable repressions, I say, produced the fierce intensity of that life, which burnt itself out so quickly. We can see this, indeed, in the fact that it was marked by an incessant series of eruptions. The gold-seekers had come of their own volition, they had to maintain an outward equilibrium, they were sworn, as it were, to a conspiracy of masculine silence regarding these repressions, of which, in fact, in the intensity of their mania, they were scarcely aware. Nevertheless, the human organism will not submit to such conditions without registering one protest after another; accordingly, we find that in the mining-camps the practical joke was, as Mr. Paine says, "legal tender," profanity was almost the normal language, and murder was committed at all hours of the day and night. Mark Twain records that in Virginia City murders were so common that they were scarcely worth more than a line or two in the newspaper, and "almost every man" in the town, according to one of his old friends, "had fought with pistols either impromptu or premeditated duels." We have just noted that for Mark Twain this life was a life of chronic nervous exasperation. Can we not say now that, in a lesser degree, it was a life of chronic exasperation for all the pioneers?

But why? What do we mean when we speak of repressions? We mean that individuality, the whole complex of personal desires, tastes, and preferences, is inhibited from expressing itself, from registering itself. The situation of the pioneers was, humanly speaking, an impossible one. But, victims as they were of their own thirst for gold, they could not withdraw from it, and their masculine pride prevented them even from openly complaining of it or criticizing it. In this respect, as I have already observed, their position was precisely parallel to that of soldiers in the trenches; and, like the soldiers in the trenches, they were always on the verge of laughter, which philosophers generally agree in calling a relief from restraint.

We are now in a position to understand why all the writers who were subjected to these conditions became humorists. The creative mind is the most sensitive mind, the most highly individualized, the most complicated in its range of desires: consequently, in circumstances where individuality cannot register itself, it undergoes the most general and the most painful repression. The more imaginative a man was, the more he would naturally have felt himself restrained and chafed by such a life as that of the gold-seekers. He, like his comrades, was under the necessity of making money, of succeeding—the same impulse had brought him there that had brought everyone else; we know how deeply Mark Twain felt this obligation, an obligation that prevented him from attempting to pursue the artistic life directly because that life was despised and because the pursuit of it would have required just those expressions of individuality that pioneer life rendered impossible. On the other hand, sensitive as he was, he instinctively recoiled from violence of all kinds and was thus inhibited by his own nature from obtaining those outlets in practical jokes, impromptu duels, and murder to which his companions constantly resorted. Mr. Paine tells us that Mark Twain never "cared for" duels and "discouraged" them, and that he "seldom indulged physically" in practical jokes. In point of fact, he abhorred them. "When grown-up people indulge in practical jokes," he wrote, forty years later, in his autobiography, "the fact gauges them. They have lived narrow, obscure and ignorant lives, and at full manhood they still retain and cherish a job-lot of left-over standards and ideals that would have been discarded with their boyhood if they had then moved out into the world and a broader life. There were many practical jokers in the new Territory." After all those years he had not outgrown his instinctive resentment against the assaults to which his dignity had had to submit. To Mark Twain, in short, the life of the gold-fields was a life of almost infinite repression: the fact, as we have seen, that he became a universal butt proves in itself how large an area of individuality he was obliged to subject to the censorship of public opinion if he was to fulfill his pledge and win success in Nevada.

Here we have the psychogenesis of Mark Twain's humor. An outlet of some kind his prodigious energy was bound to have, and this outlet, since he had been unable to throw himself whole-heartedly into mining, had to be one which, in some way, however obliquely, expressed the artist in him. That expression, nevertheless, had also to be one which, far from outraging public opinion, would win its emphatic approval. Mark Twain was obliged to remain a "good fellow" in order to succeed, in order to satisfy his inordinate will-to-power; and we have seen how he acquiesced in the suppression of all those manifestations of his individuality—his natural freedom of sentiment, his love of reading, his constant desire for privacy—that struck his comrades as "different" or "superior." His choice of a pen name, as we have noticed, proves how urgently he felt the need of a "protective coloration" in this society where the writer was a despised type. Too sensitive to relieve himself by horseplay, he had what one might call a preliminary recourse in his profanity, those "scorching, singeing blasts" he was always directing at his companions; and that this in a measure appeased him we can see from Mr. Paine's remark that his profanity seemed "the safety-valve of his high-pressure intellectual engine.

. . . When he had blown off he was always calm, gentle, forgiving and even tender." We can best see his humor, then, precisely as Mr. Paine seems to see it in the phrase, "Men laughed when they could no longer swear"—as the expression, in short, of a psychic stage one step beyond the stage where he could find relief in swearing, as a harmless "moral equivalent," in other words, of those acts of violence which his own sensitiveness and his fear of consequences alike prevented him from committing. By means of ferocious jokes—and most of Mark Twain's early jokes are ferocious to a degree that will hardly be believed by anyone who has not examined them critically—he could vent his hatred of pioneer life and all its conditions, those conditions that were thwarting his creative life; he could, in this vicarious manner, appease the artist in him, while at the same time keeping on the safe side of public opinion, since the very act of transforming his aggressions into jokes rendered them innocuous. And what made this a relief to him made it also popular. According to Freud, whose investigations in this field are perhaps the most enlightening we have, the pleasurable effect of humor consists in affording "an economy of expenditure in feeling." It requires an infinitely smaller psychic effort to expel one's spleen in a verbal joke than in a practical joke or a murder, the common method among the pioneers, and it is vastly safer—a fact that instantly explains the function of the humorist in pioneer society and the immense success of Mark Twain. By means of those jokes of his—("men were killed every week," says Mr. Paine, of one little contest of wit in which he engaged, "for milder things than the editors had spoken each of the other")—his comrades were able, without transgressing the law and the conventions, to vent their own exasperation with the conditions of their life, to vent the mutual hatred, the destructive desires that were buried under the attitude of good-fellowship imposed by the exigencies of their work. And as for Mark Twain himself, the protective coloration that enabled him to maintain his standing in pioneer society ended by giving him the position which he craved, the position of an acknowledged leader.

For, as I have said, Mark Twain's early humor was of a singular ferocity. The titles of his Western sketches reveal their general character: *The Dutch Nick Massacre, A New Crime, Lionizing Murderers, The Killing of Julius Cæsar "Localized," Cannibalism in the Cars.* He is obsessed with the figure of the undertaker and his labors, and it would be a worthy task for some zealous aspirant for the doctor's degree to enumerate the occasions when Mark Twain uses the phrase "I brained him on the spot" or some equivalent. "If the desire to kill and the opportunity to kill came always together," says Pudd'nhead Wilson, expressing Mark

Twain's own frequent mood, "who would escape hanging?" His early humor, in short, was almost wholly aggressive. It began with a series of hoaxes, "usually intended," says Mr. Paine, "as a special punishment of some particular individual or paper or locality; but victims were gathered wholesale in their seductive web." He was "unsparing in his ridicule of the Governor, the officials in general, the legislative members, and of individual citizens." He became known, in fact, as "a sort of general censor," and the officials, the corrupt officials—we gather that they were all corrupt, except his own painfully honest brother Orion—were frankly afraid of him. "He was very far," said one of his later friends, "from being one who tried in any way to make himself popular." To be sure he was! He was very far even from trying to be a humorist!

Do we not recall the early youth of that most unhumorous soul Henrik Ibsen, who, as an apothecary's apprentice in a little provincial town, found it impossible, as he wrote later, "to give expression to all that fermented in me except by mad, riotous pranks, which brought down upon me the ill-will of all the respectable citizens, who could not enter into that world which I was wrestling with alone"? Any young man with a highly developed individuality would have reacted in the same way; Mark Twain had committed the same "mad, riotous pranks" in his own childhood, and with the same effect upon the respectable citizens of Hannibal: if he had been as conscious as Ibsen and had not been obliged to make terms with his environment, his antagonism would ultimately have taken the form, not of humor, but of satire also. For it began as satire. He had the courage of a kind heart, the most humane of souls: to that extent the poet was awake in him. His attacks on corrupt officials were no more vehement than his pleas on behalf of the despised Chinese, who were cuffed and maltreated and swindled by the Californians. In these attacks and these pleas alike he was venting the humane desires of the pioneers themselves: that is the secret of his "daily philippics." San Francisco was "weltering in corruption," and the settlers instinctively loathed this condition of things almost as much as did Mark Twain himself. But they could not seriously undertake to reform it because this corruption was an inevitable part of a social situation that made their own adventure, their own success as gambling miners, possible. The desire to change and reform the situation was checked in the individual by a counter-desire for unlimited material success that throve on the very moral and political disorder against which all but his acquisitive instincts rebelled. And satire, a true campaign of satire, would naturally have tended towards a reorientation of society that would have put an end to the conditions under which the miners flourished, not as human beings, but as seekers of wealth. Consequently, while they admired Mark Twain's vehemence and felt themselves relieved through it—a relief they expressed in their "storms of laughter and applause"—they could not permit it beyond a certain point. Mark Twain had been compelled to leave Nevada to escape the legal consequences of a duel. He had gone to San Francisco, where he had immediately engaged in such a crusade of "muck-raking" that the officials "found means," as Mr. Paine says, "of making the writer's life there difficult and comfortless." As a matter of fact, "only one of the several severe articles he wrote criticizing officials and institutions seems to have appeared," the result being that he lost all interest in his work on the San Francisco papers. When, on the other hand, he wrote about San Francisco as a correspondent for his paper in the rival community in Nevada, it was, we are told, "with all the fierceness of a flaming indignation long restrained." His impulse, his desire, we see, was not that of the "humorist," it was that of the satirist; but whether in Nevada or in California, he was prohibited, on pain of social extinction, from expressing himself directly regarding the life about him. Satire, in short, had become for him as impossible as murder: he was obliged to remain a humorist.

In a pamphlet published in the Eighties, a certain phrenologist, "Professor" Beall, found the trait of secretiveness very strongly indicated in Mark Twain's "slow, guarded manner of speech." Such testimony perhaps has little value, yet it seems to throw some light on the famous Mark Twain "drawl," which he had inherited indeed, but which people say he also cultivated. Perhaps we can understand also why it is that half the art of American humor consists in "keeping one's face straight." These humorists of ours do not know themselves how much they are concealing; and they would be as surprised as anybody to learn that they are a kind of social revolutionists who lack the audacity to admit it.

Mark Twain, once committed to the pursuit of success, was obliged, as I say, to remain a humorist whether he would or no. When he went East to carry on his journalistic career, the publishers of *The Galaxy*, to which he became a regular contributor, specifically asked him to conduct a "humorous department"; and after the success of *The Innocents Abroad* his publisher, Bliss, we find, "especially suggested and emphasized a humorous work—that is to say, a work humorously inclined." We have already seen, in a previous chapter, that whatever was true of the pioneer society on the Pacific slope was essentially true also of the rest of the American population during the Gilded Age, that the businessmen of the East were in much the same case as the pioneers of the West. The whole country, in fact, was as thirsty for humor as it was for ice-water.

Mark Twain's humor fulfilled during its generation a national demand as universal in America as the demand fulfilled in Russia by Dostoievsky, in France by Victor Hugo, in England by Dickens; and we have at last begun to approach the secret of this fact.

I have spoken of the homogeneity of the American people during the Gilded Age. Howells has already related this to the phenomenon of Mark Twain's humor. "We are doubtless," he says, "the most thoroughly homogeneous folk that ever existed as a great nation. In our phrase, we have somehow all 'been there.' When [our humor] mentions hash we smile because we have each somehow known the cheap boarding-house or restaurant; when it alludes to putting up stoves in the fall, each of us feels the grime and rust of the pipes on his hands." We smile *because!* In that "because" we have the whole story of Mark Twain's success. The "cheap boarding-house," where everyone has to pretend that he loves all his neighbors, is the scene of many restraints and many irritations; and as for the grime and rust of stovepipes, that is a sensation very far from pleasant. Sensitive men, constrained by love and duty to indulge in these things, have been known more than once to complain about them; they have even been known, if the truth were told, to cry bloody murder. That was Mark Twain's habitual reaction, as we can see from the innumerable sketches in which he wades knee-deep in the blood of chambermaids, barbers, lightning-rod men, watch-makers, and other perpetrators of the small harassments of life. Mark Twain was more exasperated by these annoyances of everyday life than most people are, because he was more sensitive; but most people are exasperated by them also, and, as Howells says, all the American people of Mark Twain's time were exasperated by the same annoyances. They were more civilized individually, in short, than the primitive environment to which they had to submit: and Mark Twain's humor gave them, face to face as they were with these annoyances, the same relief it had given the miners in the West, afforded them, that is to say, the same "economy of expenditure in feeling." We "smile because" that humor shows us that we are all in the same boat; it relieves us from the strain of being unique and solitary sufferers and enables us to murder our tormentors in our imaginations alone, thus absolving us from the odious necessity of shedding the blood our first impulse prompts us to shed. Howells says that "we have somehow all 'been there,'" a phrase which he qualifies by adding that the typical American of the last generation was "the man who has risen." The man who has "risen" is the man who has become progressively aware of civilization; and the demands of the typical American of Mark Twain's time, the demands he made upon his environment, had become, *pari passu*, progressively more strin-

gent, while the environment itself remained, perforce, just as barbarous
and corrupt and "annoying" as ever. But why perforce? Because it was
"good for business": it was the environment favorable for a regime of
commercial exploitation. Was not the "man who has risen," the typical
American, himself a businessman?

Now, we have already seen that this process of "rising in the world,"
of succeeding in business, is usually attained at the cost of a certain suppression of individuality. The social effect of the stimulation of the acquisitive instinct in the individual is a general "levelling down," and this
is universally conceded to have been characteristic of the epoch of industrial pioneering. The whole nation was practically organized—by a sort
of common consent—on the plan of a vast business establishment, under
a majority rule inalterably opposed to all the inequalities of differentia-
tion and to a moral and aesthetic development in the individual that
would have retarded or compromised the success of the business regime.
We can see, therefore, that if Mark Twain's humor was universally popular, it was because it contributed to the efficiency of this regime, because
it helped to maintain the psychic equilibrium of the businessman,
throughout the United States, precisely as at first it had helped to maintain the psychic equilibrium of the Western pioneer.

As a matter of fact, Mark Twain has often been called the "businessman's writer." In that humor of his, as in no other literature, the "strong,
silent man," who is the arch-type of the business world, sees an aid rather
than a menace to his practical efficiency. But why does he find it an aid
and not a menace? Let us put the question the other way and ask why,
in other forms of literature, he finds a menace and not an aid? The acquisitive and the creative instincts are, as we know, diametrically opposed, and, as we also know, all manifestations of the creative spirit require an emotional effort, a psychic cooperation, on the part of the
reader or the spectator. This accounts for the businessman's proverbial
dislike of the artist. Every sort of spiritual expansion, intellectual interest, emotional freedom implies a retardation of the businessman's mental
machinery, a retardation of the "strenuous life," the life of pure action;
and the businessman shuns everything that distracts him, stimulates him
to think or to feel. Such things are bad for business! On the other hand,
he welcomes everything that simplifies his course, everything that helps
him to cut short his impulses of admiration and sympathy, everything
that prevents his mind from opening and responding to the complications and the implications of the spiritual and intellectual life. And this
is precisely what Mark Twain's humor does. It is just as "irreverent" as
the Boston Brahmins thought, when they gave Mark Twain a seat below

the salt: it degrades, "takes down," punctures, ridicules as pretentious and absurd everything of a spiritual, aesthetic, and intellectual nature the recognition of which, the participation in which, would retard the smooth and simple operation of the businessman's mind. Mark Twain, as we shall presently see, enables the businessman to laugh at art, at antiquity, chivalry, beauty and return to his desk with an infinitely intensified conceit of his own worthiness and well-being. That is one aspect of his humor. In another aspect, he releases, in a hundred murderous fantasies of which I have mentioned several, all the spleen which the business life, with its repression of individuality, involves. Finally, in his books about childhood, he enables the reader to become "a boy again, just for a day," to escape from the emotional stress of maturity to a simpler and more primitive moral plane. In all these respects, Mark Twain's humor affords that "economy of expenditure in feeling" which, as we now perceive, the businessman requires as much as the pioneer.

Glance, now, at a few examples of Mark Twain's humor: let us see whether they corroborate this argument.

In *A Tramp Abroad,* Mark Twain, at the opera in Mannheim, finds himself seated directly behind a young girl:

> How pretty she was, and how sweet she was! I wished she would speak. But evidently she was absorbed in her own thoughts, her own young-girl dreams, and found a dearer pleasure in silence. But she was not dreaming sleepy dreams,—no, she was awake, alive, alert, she could not sit still a moment. She was an enchanting study. Her gown was of a soft white silky stuff that clung to her round young figure like a fish's skin, and it was rippled over with the gracefullest little fringy films of lace; she had deep, tender eyes, with long, curved lashes; and she had peachy cheeks, and a dimpled chin, and such a dear little dewy rosebud of a mouth; and she was so dove-like, so pure, and so gracious, so sweet and bewitching. For long hours I did mightily wish she would speak. And at last she did; the red lips parted, and out leaped her thought,—and with such a guileless and pretty enthusiasm, too: "Auntie, I just *know* I've got five hundred fleas on me!"

This bit of humor is certainly characteristic of its author. What is its tendency, as the psychologists say? Mark Twain has, one observes, all the normal emotions of a man confronted with a pretty girl: he has them indeed so strongly that he cannot keep his mind on the "business in hand," which happens to be the opera. He finds himself actually, prevented as he is from expressing himself in any direct way, drifting into a rhapsody about this girl! What does he do then? He suddenly dashes a pailful of cold water over the beautiful vision, cuts it short by a turn of the mind so sharp, so vulgar indeed, that the vision itself evaporates in a sudden jet of acrid steam. That young girl will no longer disturb the reader's thoughts! She has vanished as utterly as a butterfly under a barrel of quicklime. Beauty is undone and trampled in the dust, but the practical man is enabled to return to the "business in hand" with a soul purified of all troubling emotions.

Another example, the famous "oesophagus" hoax in the opening paragraph of *A Double-Barrelled Detective Story:*

> It was a crisp and spicy morning in early October. The lilacs and laburnums, lit with the glory-fires of autumn, hung burning and flashing in the upper air, a fairy bridge provided by kind nature for the wingless wild things that have their home in the tree-tops and would visit together; the larch and the pomegranate flung their purple and yellow flames in brilliant broad splashes along the slanting sweep of woodland, the sensuous fragrance of innumerable deciduous flowers rose upon the swooning atmosphere, far in the empty sky a solitary oesophagus slept upon motionless wing; everywhere brooded stillness, serenity, and the peace of God.

We scarcely need Mr. Paine's assurance that "the warm light and luxury of this paragraph are facetious. The careful reader will note that its various accessories are ridiculously associated, and only the most careless reader will accept the oesophagus as a bird." Mark Twain's sole and willful purpose, one observes, is to disturb the contemplation of beauty, which requires an emotional effort, to degrade beauty and thus divert the reader's feeling for it.

To degrade beauty, to debase distinction, and thus to simplify the life of the man with an eye single to the main chance—that, one would almost say, is the general tendency of Mark Twain's humor. Mr. Ludwig Lewisohn is of another opinion. This humor, he says, is "directed against pretentiousness and falseness. It 'takes them down a peg.' " But it "takes down" real superiority, too. In almost every one of Mark Twain's sallies, as anyone can see who examines them, he burns the house down in order to roast his pig—he destroys, that is to say, an entire complex of legitimate pretensions for the sake of puncturing a single sham. And, as a rule, even the "shams" are not shams at all; they are manifestations of just that personal, aesthetic, or moral distinction which any but a bourgeois democracy would seek in every way to cherish. Consider, for example, the value assailed in Mark Twain's famous speech on General Grant and his big toe. The effect of this humorous assault on the dignity of Grant was to reduce him not to the human but to the common level, to puncture the reluctant reverence of the groundlings for moral elevation in itself, and the success of that audacious venture, its success even with General Grant himself, was the final proof of the universal acquiescence of a race of pioneers in a democratic regime opposed, in the name of business, to the recognition of any superior value in the individual. And we may add that it would hardly have been possible if Grant himself had not gone the way of all flesh and become a businessman.

The supreme example of Mark Twain's humor in this kind is *A Connecticut Yankee.* "It was another of my surreptitious schemes for extinguishing knighthood by making it grotesque and absurd," says the Yankee. "Sir Ozana's saddle was hung about with leather hat-boxes, and every time he overcame a wandering knight he swore him into my service and fitted him with a plug and made him wear it." Mark Twain's contemporaries, Howells among them, liked to imagine that in this fashion he was exposing shams and pretensions; but unhappily for this argument knighthood in the classic sense had long been extinct when Mark Twain undertook his doughty attack upon it, and it had no modern equivalent. To exalt the plug above the plume was a very easy conquest for our humorist; it was for this reason, and not, as mark Twain fancied, from any snobbish self-sufficiency, that the English public failed to be abashed by the book. In this respect, at least, *A Connecticut Yankee* was an assault, not upon a corrupt social institution, but upon the principle of beauty, an assault, moreover, committed in the very name of the shrewd pioneer businessman.

How easy it is now to understand the prodigious success of *The Innocents Abroad,* appearing as it did precisely at the psychological moment, at the close of the Civil War, at the opening of the epoch of industrial pioneering, at the hour when the life of business had become obligatory upon almost every American! How easy it is to understand why it was so generally used as a guidebook by Americans travelling in Europe! Setting out only to ridicule the sentimental pretensions of the author's pseudo-cultivated fellow-countrymen, it ridiculed in fact everything of which the author's totally uncultivated fellow-countrymen were ignorant, everything for which they wished just such an excuse to be ignorant where knowledge would have contributed to a personal development that was incompatible with success in business, a knowledge that would have involved an expenditure in thought and feeling altogether too costly for the mind that was fixed upon the main chance. It attacked not only the illegitimate pretensions of the human spirit but the legitimate pretensions also. It expressly made the American businessman as good as Titian and a little better: it made him feel that art and history and all the great, elevated, admirable, painful discoveries of humankind were not worth wasting one's emotions over. It exempted the Holy Land, to be sure. But the popular biblical culture of the nineteenth century was notoriously, as Matthew Arnold pointed out, the handmaid of commercial philistinism; and besides, ancient Palestine was hardly a rival, as Europe was, of modern America. There was something to be said, it is true, for *The Innocents Abroad.* "I find your people—your best people, I suppose they are—very nice, very intelligent, very pleasant—only talk about Europe," says a travelling Englishman in one of Howells' novels. "They talk about London, and about Paris, and about Rome; there seems to be quite a passion for Italy; but they don't seem interested in their own country. I can't make it out." It was true; and no doubt Mark Twain's dash of cold water had its salutary effect. The defiant Americanism of *The Innocents Abroad* marked, almost as definitely as Whitman's *Leaves of Grass,* the opening of the national consciousness of which everyone hopes such great things in the future. But, unlike *Leaves of Grass,* having served to open this national consciousness, it served also to postpone its fruition. Its whole tendency ran precisely counter to Whitman's, in sterilizing, that is to say, instead of promoting, the creative impulses in the individual. It buttressed the feeble confidence of our busy race in a commercial civilization so little capable of commanding the true allegiance of men that they could not help anxiously asking every travelling foreigner's opinion of it. Here we have the measure of its influence both for good and for evil. It was good in so far as it helped to concentrate the American mind on the destinies of America; it was evil, and it was mainly evil, in so far as the book contributed to a national self-complacency, to the prevailing satisfaction of Americans with a banker's paradise in which, as long as it lasts, the true destinies of America will remain unfulfilled.

So much for the nature and the significance of Mark Twain's humor. I think we can understand now the practical success it brought him. And are we not already in a position to see why the role of humorist was foreign to his nature, why he was reluctant to adopt it, why he always rebelled against it, and why it arrested his own development? For obviously the making of the humorist was the undoing of the artist. It meant the suppression of his aesthetic desires, the degradation of everything in his own nature upon which the creative instinct feeds. How can a man forever check his natural impulses without in the end becoming the victim of his own habit?

I have spoken of *A Connecticut Yankee.* We know how Mark Twain loved the tales of Sir Thomas Malory: they were to him a lifelong passion and delight. As for "knightly trappings," he adored them: think of his love for gorgeous costumes, of the pleasure he found in dressing up for charades, of the affection with which he wrote *The Prince and the Pauper!* When, therefore, in his valiant endeavor to "extinguish knighthood," he sent Sir Ozana about the country laying violent hands on wandering knights and clapping plug hats on their heads he was doing something that was very agreeable indeed to the complacent American businessman, agreeable to the businessman in himself, but in absolute violation of his own spirit. That is why his taste remained infantile, why he continued to adore "knightly trappings" instead of developing to a more advanced aesthetic stage. His feeling for Malory, we are told, was one of "reverence," but the reverence which he felt can be justly measured by the irreverence with which he acted. One cannot degrade the undegradable, one can actually degrade only oneself; and the result of perpetually "taking things down" is that one remains "down" oneself, and beauty becomes more and more inaccessibly "up." That is why, in the presence of art, Mark Twain always felt, as he said, "like a barkeeper in heaven." In destroying what he was constrained to consider the false pretensions of others, he destroyed also the legitimate pretensions of his own soul. Thus his humor, which had originally served him as a protective coloration, ended by stunting and thwarting his creative life and leaving Mark Twain a scarred child.

He had, to the end, the intuition of another sort of humor. "Will a day come," asks Satan, in *The Mysterious Stranger,* "when the race will detect the funniness of these juvenilities and laugh at them—and by laughing at them destroy them? For your race, in its poverty, has unquestionably one really effective weapon—laughter. Power, money, persuasion, supplication, persecution—these can lift at a colossal humbug—push it a little—weaken it a little, century by century; but only laughter can blow it to rags and atoms at a blast. . . . As a race, do you ever use it at all? No; you lack sense and the courage." It was satire that he had in mind when he wrote these lines, the great purifying force with which nature had endowed him, but of the use of which his life had deprived him. How many times he confessed that it was he who lacked the "courage"! How many times we have seen that if he lacked the courage it was because, quite literally, he lacked the "sense," the consciousness, that is to say, of his own powers, of his proper function. Satire necessitates, above all, a supreme degree of moral maturity, a supreme sense of proportion, a free individual position. As for Mark Twain, by reacting immediately to every irritating stimulus he had literally sworn and poked away the energy, the indignation, that a free life would have enabled him to store up, the energy that would have made him not the public ventilator that he became but the regenerator he was meant to be. Mr. Paine speaks of his "high-pressure intellectual engine." Let us follow the metaphor by saying that Mark Twain permitted the steam in his system to escape as fast as it was generated: he permitted it to escape instead of harness-

ing it till the time was ripe to "blow to rags and atoms" that world of
humbug against which he chafed all his life. But he had staked everything upon the dream of happiness; and humor, by affording him an endless series of small assuagements, enabled him to maintain that equilibrium. "I am tired to death all the time," he wrote in 1895, out of the
stress of his financial anxieties. With that in mind we can appreciate the
unconscious irony in Mr. Paine's comment: "Perhaps, after all, it was
his comic outlook on things in general that was his chief life-saver."

Mark Twain: An Appreciation

by Maurice Le Breton

Mark Twain's work is a panorama of the West in all its variety. He has observed everything: landscapes, environments, physical characteristics of the inhabitants, ways of life, customs, beliefs, superstitions. Through him we know the little Missouri town, asleep on the banks of the river, with its houses rising in steps from the levee, surrounded by its circle of wooded hills terminating near the Mississippi in sheer cliffs pierced by caves. He has described for us the river itself, with its rapids and its half-submerged logs feared by the navigators, the wooded isles and dismal cotton plantations of the South. With him we cross the desert in the emigrant's wagon, along a trail marked by the skeletons of animals; clumps of sagebrush are scattered here and there, and at night coyotes roam about the camp. We follow him into the isolated Arkansas farm minutely described in *Huckleberry Finn,* with its clean rooms, its floors covered with rugs, the hearth framed in well-scrubbed red brick, the naïve knickknacks on the mantelpiece, and the popular prints on the wall. Elsewhere, it is Washoe, the country of the prospector, the hut of the lumberjack, the encampment in the snow, the saloon where two months' earnings are gambled in one night. The entire West files past us in a succession of precise, faithful images.

Mark Twain's realism does not stop at externals. He knows admirably how to convey the special atmosphere of each characteristic environment. On the river, in the pilot's cabin, we observe the struggle of man against the force of capricious and changing nature. The level of the waters, the configuration of the bends, the location of isles and harbors, these are the whole life of the pilot; the river is his whole horizon. In the somnolent village we see various social forces at work: society shows a tendency to organize itself into rigid classes, spirits are blunted, the inhabitants submit to a dull conformity, religion grows narrow, public opinion is stern and restrictive: men have settled down, have lost the drive of the pioneers.

"Mark Twain: An Appreciation" by Maurice Le Breton. From *Revue Anglo-Américaine*, XII (October 1934), 401-418. Translated by Myra Jehlen. Reprinted by permission of the author.

But the spirit of freedom and of adventure has not completely disappeared. It survives among the children, for whom the Indian fights of their ancestors are still alive; it survives among the Negroes, so numerous and so much a part of everyday life, in the melancholy songs which express all the terrors of superstitious Africa, and an impassioned feeling for primitive nature. Generations of children nursed by Negroes carry into their own lives something of the rhythms of these songs, the childish fears, the African black magic, and the nostalgia of vague, naïve, and mystical aspirations. In these children reveries and superstitions mingle with the atavism of the emigrant to keep alive a great desire for freedom and for the primitive life. When a troup of actors passes through, or a wagon train on its way West, or a meager circus, a crowd gathers and then gazes long after the departing travelers. The atmosphere of Nevada and California is altogether different: there a harsh reality must be faced. Men live alone, miserably, in boredom and despair, a prey to disease, with every faculty straining toward a specific but elusive goal: the precious metal, gold or silver. Men work and speculate; here the dream can be measured, it is expressed in dollars. There is little in the way of social life: everyone is a fierce individualist with raw nerves, and there is little comradeship even in the camps. If men must laugh together in order to forget their hardships, the laughter is loud, rough, and nervous, with overtones of disillusionment and bitterness: the humor of the Far West.

Thus different temperaments correspond to different environments and social patterns. Mark Twain conveys this realization to us quite clearly. His picture of the West, far from sharing the conventional uniformity of too many such portrayals, has remarkable variety and great documentary value. No doubt Mark Twain fails to tell everything. He is not conducting an investigation, he is evoking memories. Many things happened on the Mississippi and on the boats themselves of which a pilot would not be ignorant and which Mark Twain does not mention.[1] He could also have written at length about the administration of Nevada, about the mining communities. His purpose is not to say everything, nor even to present everything in an objective way. His realism is not the modern photographic realism of Dreiser. Mark Twain allows himself to pursue his inquiries into reality with varying intensity, to support his observations with a wider or a narrower range of evidence. He does not have his model before his eyes while he is describing it. Since he draws from memory, he interprets reality, to a certain extent he colors it. But despite his love for this Western society, he does not hide its ugly aspects

[1] On this point see Bernard DeVoto, *Mark Twain's America* (Boston, 1932), pp. 108-110.

or its stains. When the occasion demands it, he stigmatises the brutality of masters toward their slaves, the narrow-mindedness of the small towns, or the exploits of Western desperadoes who terrorize whole populations.

Nevertheless, the presentation of the West in all its aspects is not Mark Twain's principal object. Though he captures it so vividly and conveys it so skillfully, the mere picturesque is not the greatest concern of the author. More faithful to truth in this respect than the realist, Mark Twain always seeks the deeper reality beneath appearances. Viewed from without, the West is a multicolored chaos: contrasts and contradictions are so abundant that it is difficult to perceive general characteristics. But Mark Twain is not satisfied with the role of a superficial observer. *Roughing It* was published in 1871, *Tom Sawyer* in 1876, and *Huckleberry Finn* in 1884. He had left the West in 1865. He had had time to reconsider his impressions, to classify them, to distinguish between the lasting, essential elements, and the passing, secondary ones. It was the characteristic traits of the West, which the passage of time had allowed him to define more precisely by simplifying them, that Mark Twain attempted to set down in his books. In emphasizing the most representative traits of character, he attempted to create original types having a truth to life so specific that they would not be met with elsewhere, and at the same time general enough to be admitted to the family of mankind.

He takes his heroes from the strange and motley world between the Mississippi and the Pacific. Lowly heroes indeed, but what a variety! Among the children: Tom Sawyer, Huckleberry Finn, Joe Harper, and the whole gang of urchins in St. Petersburg and Dawson's Landing; among the Negroes: the good, devoted Jim, and Roxy, the mulatto of *Pudd'n-head Wilson,* so crafty and so painfully human; wandering actors, who are at the same time tragedians, charlatans, preachers, doctors, teachers— and whatever they may be doing, complete rascals; dreamers and sober townspeople, postmasters, coach-drivers, inn-keepers, bandits. Each has his own individuality and acts in his own way, no one is like another, and yet Mark Twain is able to distinguish certain common traits in the crowd. These diverse characters have in common the fact that two strong contradictory tendencies attract them by turns. They are not new tendencies, they are as old as mankind, but they take on a peculiar character in the West, a unique sharpness. The emigrants who have set out to conquer new lands or yet unexploited wealth are greedy realists who demand a tangible reward for their efforts. Living an emancipated life, far from social conventions, with the future open before them, they are given to dreams and fantasies. Among them realism will take many forms: they are above all observers; they have the trained vision of the Indian, they know how to see: not one of the thousand movements and noises in nature escapes them. They know the ways of wild animals, the dangers of the river, the signs which foretell the coming of a storm. Their minds are as acute as their senses: perspicacious and shrewd, they never lose their bearings. Their practical common sense excels in resolving every difficulty. Hopeful, greedy for results, they always have some material profit in view. Ready for action as they are, they find a small supply of general ideas sufficient. Fantasy serves to balance this realism; it provides sport, relaxation. Both for his own benefit and for that of others, the Western man enjoys embellishing the reality which he perceives so clearly. Although Tom Sawyer has read *Don Quixote,* his imagination alone would have been enough to cause him to transform a group of children on an outing into a caravan of rich Arab merchants. In the West this trait of character is not limited to the children. To substitute fantasies for reality is the favorite game of the West, and it is a game by which the player himself is often taken in. The sun is certainly not enough of an explanation for this transformation of reality, this mirage. To it must be added the tenacity of the dreamer who has been disappointed by reality but refuses to admit it to himself. Mark Twain's visionaries living in their castles in the air, these characters who are always ready to tell you a story more extraordinary than the one you have just heard, are not lying to themselves and are not lying to you; they are of as good faith as are the men of Tarascon. It is only that they love the grandiose, the unique, the sensational, and that for them the limits of possibility and probability have been rolled back toward infinity. Exorbitant exaggeration is the essence of Western humor. Realism, however, does not surrender its jurisdiction here; in order to be really complete, humor must not be merely a morbid exaggeration born of fantasy, it must also spring from the conflict of realism and fantasy; there must be counter-thrust of common sense to burst the soap bubbles, deflate the pretensions, and leave man incorrigible, no doubt, but for the moment humbled.

Mark Twain was able to perceive these "eternal truths" about America —particularly evident in the West of 1840-1870—and to translate them into fiction, because he bore them within himself. This temperament, at once realist and visionary, was to a great extent the same as his own. In his personality as in his works, one finds the contradictory currents of realism and of idealism, of common sense and of fantasy, and his humor itself seems less a special talent over and above the various elements which constitute his personality, than the result of these elements in combination.

As a visionary, Mark Twain himself easily surpasses all the characters he has created. The nervous child of a father who himself tended to live in illusions, made superstitious by his education, enjoying besides a certain gift for divination and having complete faith in his star, he was ruled by his imagination to such an extent that he never drew a clear line between the real and the unreal, between the wish and the reality. Imagination urged him to action, reflection came afterwards. Near the end of his life he recalled how, having set out to find his fortune at the headwaters of the Amazon, he was seduced by the beauty of the Mississippi into becoming a pilot on that river. "That was more than fifty years ago," he said. "In all that time my temperament has not changed, by even a shade. I have been punished many and many a time, and bitterly, for doing things and reflecting afterward, but these tortures have been of no value to me: I still do the thing commanded by Circumstance and Temperament, and reflect afterward." [2] It is thus that he paints for his sister Pamela a bewitching picture of the West, land of plenty, and urges her to join him there. Then in a sudden about-face, he reconsiders. He had not meant to say that. He had made plans, obviously hopeful ones, but of what value are human plans? "Don't you know that I have only *talked,* as yet, but proved nothing? Don't you know that I have expended money in this country but have made none myself?" [3] All of which does not prevent him, two lines later, from judging himself a shrewd businessman. He has grand visions; he is dazzled by large numbers, whether it is a question of calculating the distance from the earth to the stars, or the profits to be derived from an invention; by a curious need to give his dream material substance, he scribbles these astronomical sums on paper or estimates the weight of the money he will earn: "If these chickens should really hatch according to my account," he writes while weighing in advance the profits from the publication of Grant's *Memoirs,* "General Grant's royalties will amount to $420,000, and will make the largest single check ever paid an author. . . . If I pay the General in silver coin at the rate of $12 per pound, that will weigh seventeen tons." [4] As a matter of fact, his calculations were completely valid, and the Grant heirs received $450,000. But his addiction to large numbers and great names would lead him to his ruin. Not only numbers seduced him, but everything large and great. At home he led the life of a nobleman: he liked generous living, a superabundance of delicate dishes,

[2] "The Turning-Point of My Life," in *What Is Man? and Other Essays* (New York, 1917), pp. 134-135.

[3] Albert B. Paine, *Mark Twain: A Biography* (New York, 1912), p. 191.

[4] *Ibid.,* p. 811.

well-trained servants. During his years of prosperity, he spent $100,000 a year; as a widower with a reduced household, he still needed $50 a day. What impressed him most about Paige's composing machine, in which he sank a fortune, was first the fabulous profits to be derived from it, and also the prospect of dazzling the whole world.

He is also sentimental, and has a great need to be either enthusiastic or indignant. He must be passionately for or against something. His support or his opposition immediately take on the appearance of a crusade and he often engages in battles against windmills. To a large extent this explains his attitude toward Europe. In 1860, the democratic and humanitarian ideals of the eighteenth century were still very much alive in the West, where they had acquired the added nuances of a Protestantism and an American particularism which was clearly hostile to a Europe thought of as a land of obscurantism. As Miss M. Brashear has pointed out, Mark Twain had read Voltaire and Tom Paine early in his life. Urged on by his passionate nature, he needed no further motive to throw himself completely into a crusade against the special privileges and the abuses which afflicted a Europe submerged in the darkness of the Middle Ages. Mark Twain does not worry, any more than does Don Quixote, whether or not the objects of his indignant opposition do indeed really exist. He is hostile to the idea of abuses, the idea of privileges, the idea of tyranny. If he thus flatters American pride he does not do so consciously, but because he is himself an American of the West, a democrat, jealous of his freedoms and full of contempt for a backward Europe. One should not, however, see in such works as *A Connecticut Yankee in King Arthur's Court* or *The Prince and the Pauper* a general condemnation of the past by an American who is infatuated with the modern age. His democratic indignation in no way prevents Mark Twain as an artist and a visionary from savoring the displays, the elaborate feasts, all of the luxury and the color of royal pomp, the picturesque variety of medieval cities; and he has a real veneration for the remote past. Ancient civilizations move him deeply. The man who at the age of eighteen, standing beside the blocks of stone at a construction site in Philadelphia, said he had been transported by his imagination to the ruined monuments of ancient Babylonia,[5] when he stands at Baalbec before the Temple of the Sun is amazed by the enormity of the work and its perfection, and finds it "an eloquent rebuke unto such as are prone to think slightingly of the men who lived before them." [6] The Sphinx inspires him to write a

[5] *Ibid.*, p. 100.
[6] *The Innocents Abroad* (Definitive Edition, New York, 1922), Vol. II, Chap. XVI.

beautiful meditation on the passage of time and the succession of em-
pires.[7] Viewing the Acropolis by moonlight, he is penetrated by delight
in the beauty of antiquity, and with masterful artistry expresses the unforgettable emotion aroused by the contrasts of shadow and light. It is
not the enormous size of the monument which moves him here: the word
which comes to his mind to convey the fulfillment of his yearning for
an ideal of beauty is the word "perfection." [8]

Nevertheless, this feeling for the great or the beautiful, which is more
frequent in Mark Twain than one would think, in no way implies conformity to rules or canons. It is purely the emotion of an imaginative
man who, dissatisfied with the commonplace, takes refuge in the unique.
It is a moment of happiness, not the goal of a patient and rational search.
Mark Twain demands freedom without limits for his imagination and his
sensibility. His art, purely anecdotal and discursive, ignores rigid categories. This rather wild freedom, this flavor of adventure exists in all
of his work. It is rare that he finds an Acropolis about which to focus
his vague aspirations. They float about in the air and are embodied in
his favorite heroes, picaresque figures animated by the nomadic instinct
which, "after thirty centuries of steady effort, civilization has not edu-
cated . . . entirely out of us. . . ." [9] They are in more than one sense at
the frontiers of civilization and yearn to escape its laws. "The children,"
he says in *Tom Sawyer*, "went off grieving that there were no outlaws any
more, and wondering what modern civilization could claim to have done
to compensate for their loss." [10] And when the current carries off their
raft leaving them on an uninhabited island in the river, the loss only
gratifies them, "since its going was something like burning the bridge
between them and civilization." [11]

This horror of convention is the trait common to Mark Twain's idealism and to his realism. If he accepts the most nonsensical fantasy, he does
so as the Westerner does, on condition of finding in it a game and a relaxation, a symbol of freedom. If he twists the truth it is for fun, to put
everyone in a good humor. He is suspicious, however, of fantasy which
takes itself seriously, of systematic distortions of the truth, of literary in-
sincerity, of social hypocrisy.

As a writer, he is entirely sincere. He describes without embellishments.
He sees the desert as monotonous and depressing, Washoe as sinister and
cheerless. Even California elicits no shouts of admiration from him. He
marks the lack of variety in the vegetation, the smell of turpentine, the

---

[7] *Ibid.*, Vol. II, Chap. XXVII.   [8] *Ibid.*, Vol. II, Chap. I.   [9] *Ibid.*, Vol. II, Chap.
XXVIII.   [10] Chap. VIII.   [11] Chap. XIV.

needles of conifers littering the ground, the scarcity of grass and foliage. The landscape of the East, generally less admired, seems to him incomparably superior in its variety of aspects, its freshness, the delicate coloring of its autumns which more equable climates do not enjoy. He has a vivid feeling for nature, with no taint of bookishness; one senses the man who has lived in forests, on the great river, in the desert, who reports what he has seen and sometimes what he has felt, always without affectation. He speaks with simplicity and truth about settlers, Negroes, Indians, as if neither Mrs. Stowe nor Fenimore Cooper nor Bret Harte had ever written. He describes what exists without the affectation of either romanticism or realism. He detests all snobbery, false sensibility, sentimental commonplaces. Conventional literature he makes the target of a most bitter satire: he is scornful of popular fiction with its gentlemen pirates, its hidden treasures, its naïve vicissitudes of plot, as well as of the novels of Walter Scott or the funereal genre admired in the Middle West. In his aversion for primitivism, which he does not understand, there is a great deal of this obstinate resistance to compulsory admiration; he rebels against imposed attitudes. He is not satisfied with generalized protests, he is specific: in *Tom Sawyer* he exposes to ridicule a novel then widely popular in the West. In *The Innocents Abroad* he attacks the authors of books of travel in the Holy Land. He wants to place honest pictures before the eyes of the American reader accustomed to travel narratives in which false sensibility is given free rein. He looks at the Orient with the eyes of a Westerner and tries to picture the life of Christ as it must have been in this poor and sad country without legends, without embellishments: he would like to substitute true emotion for conventional admiration.

He handles didactic literature just as roughly. He never tires of scoffing at those "moral" stories in which the good, virtuous, and obedient child rises by force of circumstances to the presidency while his turbulent and somewhat skeptical friend invariably ends up in poverty or on the gallows. Mark Twain's realism is indignant at these fairy tales. His heroes all cultivate as their most precious possession a robust virility which refuses to conform. Tom Sawyer, Huckleberry Finn are rascals, but they have in themselves the stuff of brave and sincere men. All hypocrisy exasperates Mark Twain. The sight of St. Petersburg after a "revival" saddens Tom Sawyer: "He found Joe Harper [another scamp] studying a Testament, and turned sadly away from the depressing spectacle. He hunted up Ben Rogers, and found him visiting the poor with a basket of tracts." [12] In

---

[12] Chap. XXII.

fact the burden of conformity in the village is hard to throw off: Mark Twain shows us these communities along the Mississippi oppressed by narrow-minded customs and maintaining in their children a religion of mere form which finds expression in Sunday-school exercises where the prize goes to the pupil who has been able to learn two thousand verses by heart. His realism and his idealism join forces here to plead the case for greater freedom and spontaneity. If he has not worked out very clearly for himself his ideas about man and God, his skepticism—everywhere apparent, although not explicit—clings mercilessly to reality and emphasizes his persistent concern with truth in defiance of public opinion.

Whether it be enthusiasm or indignation, in studying Mark Twain one always comes back at the end to the element of passion in him. Perhaps these are not the most favorable conditions for the development of humor, which would seem to require more detachment and coolness. The palmists who examined Mark Twain's hand at the age of seventy without being told his name all declared that it was the hand of a man who lacked a sense of humor! [13] A recent theory even maintains that he forced himself to play the role of a humorist all his life to please the tastes of his public. On this point the truth seems to have been stated by the author himself: "I value humor highly," he wrote to the publisher McClure, "& am constitutionally fond of it, but I should not like it as a steady diet. . . . Of the twenty-three books which I have written eighteen do not deal in humor as their chiefest feature, but are half & half admixtures of fun & seriousness. I think I have seldom deliberately set out to be humorous, but have nearly always allowed the humor to drop in or stay out, according to its fancy." [14]

There are in fact two trends in the humor of Mark Twain: one pure fantasy, completely spontaneous; the other more thoughtful and tinged with seriousness. Mark Twain had no need to make an effort to diffuse his work with fantasy; his temperament impelled him naturally in that direction, and besides he never sought a true originality in this genre. In his themes as in his techniques, he limits himself to following the well-established tradition of the Western humorists. We know, thanks to Mr. DeVoto, that many of his jokes were already current, that whatever genre he might choose, such as the macabre or the truculent, he was working in the line of his predecessors. He contributes simply his irresistible verve, his boisterous high spirits, and his superior handling of language. But this humor is still at heart the rough laughter of the West, the vast joking of the miners' camp which relaxes the nerves after a hard day, a humor

---

[13] Paine, *Mark Twain*, p. 1255.　　[14] *Ibid.*, p. 1100.

which is often too exclusively verbal, in any case always transient; a contest of absurdity in which the participants display their ingenuity in spinning fantastic yarns.

The other trend is altogether different. It is not superficial, it emerges indeed from the very depths of his personality. Fantasy then becomes only a comic mask for common sense. Here common sense dominates and imposes its rules on the imagination. It is no longer a matter of rough farce, but the amusing apologue which invokes laughter to castigate manners and morals. Such humor already partakes of satire. There is subtlety in it, and sometimes bitterness. One recognizes in it the complex and impassioned personality of Mark Twain. In certain passages one seems to be reading Sterne: there is the same knowledge of the human heart, the same feeling for nuances. Again, and perhaps more often, we are reading Swift. Here Mark Twain has not been able to restrain his generous indignation. He is still joking, but the laughter grows more bitter, indeed almost sarcastic. One understands then how such divergent judgments could have been passed on him. Depending on whether the critic emphasizes one or the other of the two aspects of his humor, Mark Twain will appear either an overgrown child who amuses himself in the simplicity of his heart with enormous lies, or an embittered sentimentalist who barely hides his deep pessimism beneath the mask of humor.

Twenty-five years after his death, far from falling into the unjust and temporary obscurity which is often the fate of the most popular writers immediately after their deaths, Mark Twain remains one of the great figures of American literature, and his fame seems to be in no danger. The place he occupies in that literature is out of proportion to the rather modest artistic effort which he made. His natural talent, a pleasant way of telling a story interlarded with amusing anecdotes, is almost the whole of his art. Even the personality of the man is not enough to explain the favor with which he is regarded by the public today: if critics impatiently await the publication of the last unedited manuscripts of Mark Twain in order to be able to form their opinions in full possession of the facts, this is a problem of little interest to the public. The general reader has already made his choice among the works of Mark Twain. Optimist or pessimist, dupe of his own emotions or coerced by his audience, Mark Twain does not appear to the American reader as a man of letters imprisoned by the demands of his vocation, but rather as a free spirit to whom one turns in order to breathe the virile, joyous, healthy atmosphere of an America which has disappeared. He survives as the evocator, the poet of a unique phase of American experience. There is an understanding between him and his public, just as there was during his life-time. He continues to have an almost seductive charm for his readers. The reasons for his success are sentimental; America sees him, with real affection, as the first of her writers to draw from the American soil the material for an original and lasting work.

Roughing It

by Kenneth S. Lynn

Roughing It, the author's prefatory note announces, is a "personal narrative." The adjective is to be understood in an etymological sense. For the narrator who tells us in the first chapter of the book that he is about to go West as the secretary to the Secretary of Nevada Territory is "young and ignorant," and "never had been away from home," a description which hardly fits the seasoned steamboat pilot and erstwhile Confederate Army officer who, not quite twenty-six years old, made his separate peace in the summer of 1861. The character called "Mark Twain" who is the narrator of *Roughing It* is a persona, as the "Mark Twain" of *The Innocents* had been. The narrators of the two travel books are, in fact, the same literary character, and *Roughing It* represents a continuation of this innocent's adventures, albeit the continuation has taken us backward in time. In the second installment of Mark Twain's imaginative projection of himself, his hero—significantly enough—has grown younger.

Exactly how old he now is cannot be determined with any precision. During an audience that his brother, the Secretary, has been granted with Brigham Young, the narrator tells how the Mormon chief "put his hand on my head, beamed down on me in an admiring way and said to my brother: 'Ah—your child, I presume? Boy or girl?' " This, however, would seem to be what Huck Finn would call a "stretcher," not only because Orion Clemens never met Brigham Young in his life, but because throughout most of the book the narrator clearly behaves like an adult. That he is a younger man than either the narrator of *The Innocents* or the actual Mark Twain who went West in 1861 is nevertheless unmistakably established, and it is done so primarily by the style. For if the prose in *Roughing It* has a disciplined fluidity and an incisiveness that mark how much more accomplished a writer Twain now was as compared to when he wrote *The Innocents,* the literary sophistication of the style is slyly masked by a tone of youthful naïveté:

> I envied my brother. I coveted his distinction and his financial splendor, but particularly and especially the long, strange journey he was going to make, and the curious new world he was going to explore. . . . Pretty soon he would be hundreds and hundreds of miles away on the great plains and deserts, and among the mountains of the Far West, and would see buffaloes and Indians, and prairie dogs, and antelopes, and have all kinds of adventures, and maybe get hanged or scalped, and have ever such a fine time.

These are, indeed, the accents of a tenderfoot who has never been away from home before. In *Roughing It,* Twain has not yet fully responded to the magnetic pull of childhood, but he has clearly felt the tug.

Entering, in the second installment of his hero's adventures, the realm of memories now a decade old, Twain evokes at the outset of *Roughing It* an almost pastoral vision of the West. The trip to Nevada represents for his narrator an escape from all the cares and obligations of the contemporary world:

> By eight o'clock everything was ready, and we were on the other side of the river. We jumped into the stage, the driver cracked his whip, and we bowled away and left "the States" behind us. It was a superb summer morning, and all the landscape was brilliant with sunshine. There was a freshness and breeziness, too, and an exhilarating sense of emancipation from . . . the years we had spent in the close, hot city, toiling and slaving.

That Mark Twain in 1861 had not been toiling and slaving in a close, hot city only points up the deliberate effort of this passage to contrast the workaday reality of American society to the fabulous play-world of the Western frontier. To a people publicly committed to the frantic hustle of the American Way of Life, the idea of quitting work, of simply walking out, suddenly and without explanation, on all responsibilities, has been a haunting one; in American literature, the idea can be traced from "Rip Van Winkle" to *Walden,* from Walt Whitman to Sherwood Anderson. Of all American writers, however, Mark Twain is the principal celebrant of the escape dream. There was, of course, the Mark Twain who was a go-getter, who liked the friendship of millionaires and schemed to become one himself, who could write enthusiastic letters to the unsuccessful Orion in praise of energy and single-minded purpose, even as Lincoln had once written to his shiftless stepbrother, John D. Johnston. On the other hand, there was a side of Lincoln's personality that was drawn very strongly toward the slower, easier rhythms of drifting along and taking things easy, and this was also true of Mark Twain. Laziness to William

Byrd was a horrid and appalling temptation; but to the heroes of Mark Twain, thoroughly unconcerned with keeping up a gentlemanly front, loafing is very Heaven. Thus as the trip West gets under way, the narrator of *Roughing It* tells us that the stagecoach in which he and his brother are traveling is loaded with mail sacks; when rearranged, the sacks fill up the seats to make a wonderful "lazy bed." And so they go bowling westward, lying down, luxuriously stripped to their underclothing, over a land that is as level as a calm sea. The resemblance of this stagecoach to a raft is unmistakable.

Set aside for a time—for the opening chapters of *Roughing It* compose a kind of overture in which many themes are introduced—the laziness theme is reintroduced and given its fullest development in the narrator's account of his journey to Lake Tahoe with his friend Johnny. If Hannibal had not existed, Tahoe would have been the great good place of Twain's imagination. Whenever Europe was pressing his patriotism hard, the narrator of *The Innocents* had only to think of Tahoe to be reassured of America's superiority. In *Roughing It,* the lake and its surrounding countryside come to us in the terminology of Paradise: Tahoe's air "is the same the angels breathe." In the "delicious solitude," Johnny and the narrator loll in the sand, smoke their pipes, and sleep. But "we seldom talked. It interrupted the Sabbath stillness, and marred the dreams the luxurious rest and indolence brought." Mocking the world they have left behind, they act out a parody version of the American success myth. They will get rich, they decide, by developing a certain forested area which is theirs for the asking if only they will fence the property and build a house on it. After an enthusiastic start, however, the work proves troublesome and they abandon it to return to the "business" of drifting around the lake in a boat, soaking in impressions. The decision looks forward to the narrator's comic career as a miner who dreams of making a fortune without doing any physical labor, and who lets a fabulous property slip through his fingers when he goes off in pursuit of some other interest and fails to develop the claim in time. Like the narrator of *Walden,* the hero of *Roughing It* finds the work involved in getting rich too expensive an outlay of time and energy. Quite obviously, he prefers his own drifting rhythm to the hustle of the money-getters, a fact which makes the Parrington-Van Wyck Brooks criticism that the values of *Roughing It* are vulgarly materialistic seem somewhat mysterious. Twain's young man has come to the West for "adventures," of which the possibility of getting rich quick is only one.

As was true of his European trip, the narrator is determined to see the frontier clearly, and not in the manner ascribed by Twain to Fenimore

Cooper—"through a glass eye, darkly." In *Roughing It,* however, this determination confronted Twain with a serious artistic problem. Reporting the facts of life in Virginia City, where the first twenty-six graves contained the corpses of murdered men, was a rather different proposition from simply refusing to blink at the existence of poverty in the Holy Land. William T. Porter's humorists had faced up with brutal frankness to the violence of the frontier, but the *Spirit of the Times* had been a magazine for gentlemen only. As both William Dean Howells and H. H. Boyesen testified, women in post-Civil War America came to compose an enormous bloc of the reading population to whom book publishers and magazines of national circulation appealed. How was it possible to talk about eyeball-gougers to *this* audience? And if it was not possible to do so, how could one be honest about the West?

Bret Harte got around this problem via the redemption formula. The first author to deal with the Western mining camps, Harte described a life which, as the *Atlantic* put it, was "vulgar and vicious"; in the words of a *Century* critic, Harte's stories had a "kind of devil's humor suited to the diabolism of the surroundings." What made such fiction go down with a Victorian and quasi-female audience was Harte's inevitable revelation that beneath the rough exterior of the miners of Roaring Camp or the outcasts of Poker Flat there existed what *Putnam's* sobbingly described as "the purest and loveliest feelings and influence that can touch a human heart." By glossing over the disturbing truths of his Western materials, Harte—and his imitators—pandered to a readership that wished to be titillated by roughness and then reassured by goodness.

Mark Twain, a good hater in any event, despised Bret Harte with special enthusiasm, both as a man and as an artist. To Twain, Harte's stories were as phony as the broken twigs and "scholarly savages" of the Leatherstocking Series. In *Roughing It,* the narrator makes it clear that the Goshoot Indians, "treacherous, filthy, and repulsive," have nothing in common with Uncas and Chingachgook. Nor does he minimize the depravity of white badmen in the manner of Harte. Remembering his fascination with Old World symbols of death, one might even say that Twain's narrator seems eager to talk of these harsh things, that the violence of the frontier has been deliberately sought out by this young man. (Had he not, after all, gone West because he envied his brother's opportunity to get hanged or scalped and then write home and tell about the experience?) Meeting the desperado Slade makes him "the proudest stripling that ever traveled to see strange lands and wonderful people," and the thrill of the encounter consists precisely in the nonredemptive viciousness of the man: "Here, right by my side, was the actual ogre who, in fights and brawls and various ways, *had taken the lives of twenty-six human beings,* or all men lied about him!" To this thrill-seeker, the existence of precious metals under the earth of the Western hills was not the only reason for going underground. Having once descended into the vault of the Capuchin Convent in Rome and stood enthralled ("Here was a spectacle for sensitive nerves!") at the sight of the human skulls and bones that decorated the walls, Twain's wandering sight-seer now steps onto a small platform and goes shooting like a dart down a mineshaft:

> It is like the tumbling down through an empty steeple, feet first. When you reach the bottom, you take a candle and tramp through drifts and tunnels; . . . you admire the world of skeleton timbering; you reflect frequently that you are buried under a mountain, a thousand feet below daylight. . . . when your legs fail you at last, you lie down in a small box-car in a cramped "incline" like a half up-ended sewer and are dragged up to daylight feeling as if you are crawling through a coffin that has no end to it.

Proceeding from the imagery of death (skeleton timbering and coffin-like tunnels) to the actuality, he concludes his account of this underground adventure with the remark, "Of course these mines cave in, in places, occasionally, and then it is worth one's while to take the risk of descending into them and observing the crushing power exerted by the pressing weight of a settling mountain." *Worth one's while.* In some deep and inscrutable place in the personality of this light-hearted innocent, there would seem to be a terrible pessimism which feeds and grows on gruesome sights.

What made Twain's unflinching honesty—one might say compulsive honesty—about the hardness of life on the Western frontier acceptable to a national audience was the fact that his comic spotlight was focused not so much on the violence and the dangers of the West as on his narrator's reactions to these things. In Byrd's *Dividing Line,* and in the humor of Longstreet and his successors, the spotlight had never been fixed on the narrator. In the work of all these men, the hell of being laughed at was reserved for other people: the comic hazards of life left Self-controlled Gentlemen untouched. Viewing violence from a safe distance, the humor of the Southwestern tradition was consequently extremely callous; if Howells's indictment of it as monkeyishly cruel is an overstatement, at least one can say that it was predicated on a suspension of sympathy for the sufferer. In *Roughing It,* on the other hand, the frontier is not a cockpit which is viewed with haughty disdain from a back bench; it is a life into which the narrator is plunged, head over heels. "Mark Twain" is the character who is made to look ridiculous by being gulled into buying a worthless horse, a humiliation that in Longstreet's "The Horse-Swap"

had been reserved for some distantly seen social inferior. By thus focusing
on a scared and gullible young man's comic reactions to the confidence
men, killers, and corpses of the West, rather than on what causes him to
react, Twain drew attention away from the disgusting details of frontier
violence in which the humorists of the Southwestern tradition had reveled,
while at the same time acknowledging their existence. In so doing, he
accommodated his humor to the new national audience without cheating
on the tough realities of his subject.

By substituting a victim's humor for a spectatorial humor, Twain transformed the comic treatment of the American frontier. Not only was his
laughter more compassionate and humane, but the attitude of his narrator
toward the West was psychologically more complex than that of the Self-
controlled Gentleman. The Gentleman's attitude had always remained
the same; the stability of his personality was the whole point about him.
Plunged into the life of Virginia City, Twain's narrator grows up, or at
least changes his mind about lots of things. His experience in Nevada is
an initiation, as Henry Nash Smith has observed, into a new and different
society; and the jokes he tells on himself compose a progression by which
a tenderfoot from the city is slowly transformed into a member of the
Western tribe. A recent critic of Twain's work, Paul Schmidt, has said
that the values of life which the West opens up to Twain's innocent might
be summed up under the heading of color, brotherhood, and freedom:
the vibrant possibilities of a various experience; the democratic com-
panionship of "bright-eyed, quick-moving, strong-handed men"; and
the moral spontaneity of a society uncoerced by the inhibitions and cau-
tious restraints of a more established America. To dramatize the contrast
between the pale life he has left behind with the new vigor that has inspired him in Virginia City, the narrator tells the anecdote of Scotty
Briggs and the parson. Scotty, whose customary suit is "a fire helmet,
flaming red flannel shirt, patent leather belt with a spanner and revolver
attached, coat hung over arm, and pants stuffed into boot tops," speaks
in the vernacular of the Nevada miner—"the richest and most infinitely
varied and copious [slang] that had ever existed anywhere in the world."
The parson, a "fragile, gentle, spirituel new fledgling from an Eastern
theological seminary," speaks in the language of the genteel tradition in
its final stages of desiccation. The conflict between two radically different
styles is the enduring drama of American humor, representing as it does
a conflict between two utterly different concepts of what American life
should be. The ludicrous failure of Scotty Briggs and the parson to com-
municate to one another signifies a more far-reaching incompatibility,
and the anecdote makes it quite clear that as between the two Americas

thus symbolized the narrator prefers Scotty Briggs's. "Virginia City," the narrator says flatly, "afforded me the most vigorous enjoyment of life I had ever experienced."

The tribute is unqualified; ironically, it is also a valedictory. Sounding like the statement of a man who has spiritually come home, the tribute in fact announces his departure from Virginia City. Twain's narrator has been involved in the frontier community; he has learned many things from it, including a new dissatisfaction with his former life; but in the end he rejects it, even as he had rejected Europe. "I began to get tired of staying in one place so long," he says, trying to define the itch that drives him on. "I wanted to see San Francisco. I wanted to go somewhere. I wanted—I did not know *what* I wanted." Trying once more to put his feelings into words, he says simply, "I wanted a change." Restlessness, as Tocqueville noted, is one of the most striking characteristics of the American; certainly the quality shows up repeatedly in American writing—in Melville, in Dreiser, in Sinclair Lewis (himself a man so restless he could not bear to sit still in a room, or even live in the same house on the same continent for very long: the "Minnesota tumbleweed," his first wife called him), among many others. In the second half of *Roughing It,* restlessness emerges as the dominant trait in the narrator's personality. For the move to San Francisco is no solution. Soon Twain's American is running before the wind again: into the mountain country of the California mining camps; back to San Francisco; across the Pacific to Hawaii; to San Francisco again; back to Nevada; back to San Francisco once more—where "I projected a pleasure journey to Japan and thence westward around the world." Changing his mind, he sails for New York, where he signs on for an excursion, that will take him, he says, to Europe and the Holy Land. Uncommitted, unsure of himself, with no secure base anywhere, the narrator sets off at the end, as he had at the beginning of the book, in pursuit of adventures—perhaps seeking in the very process of change itself the solidity he cannot find in permanence.

The Pilot and the Passenger:
Landscape Conventions and the Style
of *Huckleberry Finn*

by Leo Marx

Nowadays it is not necessary to argue the excellence of *The Adventures of Huckleberry Finn*. Everyone seems to agree that it is a great book, or in any event one of the great American books. But we are less certain about what makes it great. Why is it in fact more successful than most of Mark Twain's other work? No one would claim that it is free of his typical faults. It descends here and there to sentimentality, buffoonery, and (particularly in the closing chapters) just plain juvenility. Nonetheless we persist in regarding the novel as a masterpiece. How are we to account for its singular capacity to engage us? One persuasive answer to the question has been to say that the book's excellence in large measure follows from the inspired idea of having the western boy tell his own story in his own idiom.[1] From that seminal idea, it may be said, many of the book's virtues—the convincing sense of life, the fresh lyricism, the wholeness of point of view—follow as the plant from the seed. This approach is persuasive, but it is easier to assert than to demonstrate. My purpose is to establish, on the basis of historical evidence and explicit critical values, certain ways in which the use of the narrator contributed to the novel's greatness.

The point to begin with is that it is Huckleberry Finn's story. And what he imparts to it, in a word, is style. The style is unique. To get a vivid impression of its uniqueness one need only compare the novel with

"The Pilot and the Passenger: Landscape Conventions and the Style of *Huckleberry Finn*" by Leo Marx. From *American Literature*, XXVIII (May 1956), 129-146. Copyright © 1956 by Duke University Press. Reprinted by permission of the author and Duke University Press.

[1] Today this view is something of a commonplace, and there would be no point in attempting to assign priorities. Much of my appreciation of its importance, however, I owe to Henry Nash Smith, and to the illuminating study by Paul Steward Schmidt, "Samuel Clemens's Technique as a Humorist, 1857-1872," unpublished Ph.D. thesis, University of Minnesota, 1951.

Life on the Mississippi and *The Adventures of Tom Sawyer,* the other
books in which Clemens re-creates the world of the Mississippi Valley.
The three are linked in many ways, but above all by geography. In each
the landscape is a primary source of unity and meaning. The same countryside, indeed sometimes the same scene, is described in each. Take, for
example, the lyrical description of the dawn in *Huckleberry Finn,* the
passage beginning, "Two or three days and nights went by; I reckon I
might say they swum by, they slid along so quiet and smooth and lovely."
This celebrated piece of writing, recently cited as exemplifying our national manner in prose,[2] may serve as a measure of stylistic achievement.
As it happens, a similar description of the sunrise is to be found in each
of the other Mississippi books. (All three are reprinted at the end of this
essay, and to follow the argument they should be read at once.) Anyone
who reads them in sequence will, I am confident, be struck by the superiority of the *Huckleberry Finn* version. I mean later to discuss the grounds
for this judgment; here it is only necessary to recognize the difference. It
is an impressive difference, and one which obviously turns upon narrative
method or, if you will, style. The distinguishing mark of style in turn
is language.

But these remarks do not answer the original question. To say that
vernacular narration is a distinctive feature of *Huckleberry Finn* is one
thing; it is quite another to account for Mark Twain's success with that
technique. After all, we know that he used it elsewhere without comparable results. Moreover, it means nothing to contend that the novel is
great because it is written in the native idiom unless, that is, we mean to
impute some intrinsic or absolute value to the vernacular. That would
be ridiculous. What we want to know, then, is why this method worked
best for Clemens at this juncture. I assume that only a strong need can
have called forth so original a style.

One of Clemens' persistent motives, clearly, was to convey a certain
experience of his native landscape. *The Adventures of Huckleberry Finn*
is, among other things, the fulfillment of a powerful pastoral impulse.
Probably no one needs to be told that. But what is perhaps less obvious
is that the vernacular style made possible the expression of emotions
Clemens had long been working to put in words. The three attempts to
depict the sunrise on the Mississippi reveal something of that liberating
process. In each case the "theme" is the same: the observer's sense of
beauty and harmony in nature. But for some reason, in the *Huckleberry
Finn* version Clemens manages to create for us what, in the other two,

---

[2] "The Emergence of a National Style," *Times Literary Supplement,* September 17,
1954, pp. xii-xiv.

he had only been able to describe. When, in reading the three passages consecutively, we come to the last, a sudden release of imaginative energy makes itself felt. The whole experience comes into bright focus. Sentences flow in perfect cadence, without strain or stilted phrase or misplaced word. It is as if the shift to the vernacular had removed some impediment to fullest expression.

I

What the impediment was Clemens reveals in "Old Times on the Mississippi." This series of articles written for the *Atlantic Monthly* in 1875 was his first sustained effort to represent the valley society he had known before the Civil War. In those chapters which now comprise the first volume of *Life on the Mississippi* his theme is "learning the river." Here the narrator recalls his initiation into a unique western mystery: Mississippi piloting. He makes clear that this vocation has to be learned by an apprentice on the spot; no books, no school, no theory can equip him. What he has to learn is a new language—indeed a language of nature. It is not simply the abstract technique of piloting, but a particular piece of western geography which he must possess. He has to "know the river" by day and by night, heading upstream and heading downstream. He must memorize the landscape. It is this knowledge which will forever distinguish him from the uninitiated. When ignorant passengers gaze at the face of the water they see "nothing but . . . pretty pictures." [3] But when the trained pilot looks at the river the river tells its "mind" to him. Nature, he explains, has been made to deliver him "its most cherished secrets." This experience is exhilarating, and in re-creating it Clemens managed to impart the exhilaration to his prose. (Notice that the second volume, which lacks the theme, is dull by comparison.) Yet—and here the problem arises—the narrator confesses that in acquiring the new lore he loses something too: the "grace, the beauty, the poetry" of the majestic river. It is gone. In learning the matters of fact necessary to his western vocation the pilot loses, or so he thinks, the capacity to enjoy the beauty of the landscape.

To illustrate his dilemma he compares two ways of experiencing a sunset on the river. It is a brilliant sunset. First he describes it as, in his innocence, he once might have enjoyed it. At that time he would have observed "soft distances," "dissolving lights," and "graceful curves." The painter's terms are significant. In much of Clemens' work we find landscapes similarly framed, noble pictures seen as through a "Claude glass."

---

[3] (New York, 1906), p. 83. The account of the sunset is on pp. 82-85.

For instance, Venice, in *Innocents Abroad,* is like "a beautiful picture—very soft and dreamy and beautiful." [4] Or of Lake Tahoe, in *Roughing It,* we are told that a "circling border of mountain domes, clothed with forests, scarred with landslides, cloven by cañons and valleys, and helmeted with glittering snow, fitly framed and finished the noble picture." [5] Clemens was working, needless to say, within the convention of the picturesque. Yet it should be added at once that he was not entirely comfortable in that mode. He often betrays his dissatisfaction by making comedy of the elevated style. In *Innocents Abroad* he allows a description of a Mediterranean vista to reach grandiose rhetorical heights. Then he quickly destroys the illusion with a revealing and self-conscious gag: "[Copyright secured according to law.]" [6] A similar impulse, in *Roughing It,* leads him to say, of a "majestic panorama," that "nothing helps scenery like ham and eggs." [7] Clemens was a writer of travel books and he recognized, as these remarks indicate, that the established rhetoric of landscape portrayal could not bear steady exposure to the immediate human fact. But if that style, at least when most elegant, was ludicrous, how was a writer to convey the loveliness of scenery? Clemens manifestly did not know. He resorted again and again to the conventional mode, using it straight as well as for burlesque.

Returning now to the sunset in "Old Times," we find that Clemens uses a language as trite as the paintings he must have had in mind. The pilot, discussing the lost beauty of the scene, says that he once would have enjoyed the sight of boughs that "glowed like flame" and trails upon the water that "shone like silver." This vocabulary is the literary counterpart of the painter's picturesque, an appropriately conventional medium for a conventional idea of beauty. In the presence of nature the pilot stands "like one bewitched" in a "speechless rapture." But this ecstasy, observe, was what he felt before his initiation. Afterwards, ". . . if that sunset scene had been repeated, I should have looked upon it without rapture, and should have commented upon it inwardly after this fashion: 'This sun means that we are going to have wind to-morrow; that floating log means that the river is rising, small thanks to it; that slanting mark on the water refers to a bluff reef which is going to kill somebody's steamboat one of these nights . . . that silver streak in the shadow of the forest is the "break" from a new snag. . . .' " And so on. Beauty, the pilot learns, is for those who see only the surface of nature. Behind every perception of the beautiful there is a fact of another sort. And once he knows the facts "the romance and beauty . . . [are] all gone from the river."

---

[4] (New York, 1906), I, 281.   [5] (New York, 1906), I, 186.   [6] I, 134.   [7] I, 148.

Of course it may be said that this is merely another statement of a familiar modern conflict between two modes of perception, one analytic and instrumental, the other emotive and aesthetic. So it is. But to dispose of the issue thus is to miss the special significance the alternates had for Sam Clemens. In *Life on the Mississippi* each of these ways of apprehending the river characterizes a particular mode of life. One might say a particular culture. One culture is exemplified by the uninitiated spectators and the ignorant novice pilot; the other is reflected in the melancholy wisdom of the older man who tells the story. There are many differences between these two ways of life, but the most important is the relation to nature fostered by each. The passengers are strangers to the river. They lack the intimate knowledge of its physical character a pilot must possess. As spectators, well-trained to appreciate painted landscapes, they know what to look for. They enjoy the play of light on the water. This aesthetic response to nature, given the American geography, Clemens inevitably associates with the cultivated, urban East. But the pilot, on the other hand, is of the West, and his calling such that he can scarcely afford to look upon the river as a soft and beautiful picture. He is responsible for the steamboat. To navigate safely he must keep his mind on the menacing "reality" masked by the trail that shines like silver.

The pilot's dilemma is a recurrent theme of our nineteenth century literature. It was an age which attributed special meanings to the landscape, particularly in America. At the level of popular culture images of the landscape were used to depict a national destiny as glorious and beautiful as the surface of the Mississippi at sunset.[8] The nation's scenic splendor was a sign of divine blessing. At the same time, however, this chosen people was engaged in transforming the landscape it celebrated, and in fact subjecting it to the same instrumental method the pilot had learned. Hence it is understandable, quite apart from the influence of European philosophy or literature, that many of our writers were concerned with the penalties and perils attendant upon piercing Nature's mask. Melville's Ahab, driven by a compulsion to penetrate the ocean of mere appearance, also fears he may find "naught beyond."[9] Like the pilot, however, he cannot turn back. For both men the need arises as an almost inescapable consequence of native callings. In *Walden* we find the identical symbolic

[8] Henry Nash Smith calls my attention to this account of sunset on the river: "When the sun went down it turned all the broad river to a national banner laid in gleaming bars of gold and purple and crimson; and in time these glories faded out in the twilight and left the fairy archipelagoes reflecting their fringing foliage in the steely mirror of the stream" (Clemens and Warner, *The Gilded Age*, New York, 1906, I, 42).

[9] Chap. xxxvi, "The Quarter-Deck."

motif. Again the water's surface is a metaphoric boundary between the beautiful and another possible reality. When Thoreau, submitting faith to a test, fills a glass with the "matchless and indescribable light blue" water of the pond, he finds that it is in fact colorless.[10] Throughout the century the alleged values of nature, including its beauty, disappear when considered too curiously. When the pilot's keen eye penetrates the silvery trail he sees the menacing snag. There are two ways of regarding the Mississippi, just as, in *Moby-Dick* there are "gentle thoughts" above the Pacific's surface, and murderous sharks and leviathans below.[11] Ahab and the pilot are committed to knowing; they can only lament the sacrifice, as Ahab put it, of "low enjoyment" for a "higher perception." [12] The bedeviling question of the age, however, was whether that perception was indeed higher.

This was not, for Clemens, an abstract philosophical issue. It would be wrong to think of him, standing at an artist's proper remove, simply manipulating an interesting theme. For him the dilemma had a more compelling and practical urgency: it was a matter of style. He faced it as a writer of prose, and it was as a writer (he was no theorist) that he finally came to grips with it. His solution, if that is the correct word, was implicit in the choice of Huckleberry Finn as narrator of his own adventures.

II

In 1875, when Clemens began work on the Mississippi material, the problem of landscape description became more acute. Writing about the country he had known as a boy and pilot was not quite the same as writing about Venice or Lake Tahoe. Here, for one thing, the picturesque convention was even less appropriate. We may guess that his feeling for his native landscape was such that he aimed at a greater fidelity to experience than the standard mode allowed. But what was the alternative? As he apparently felt, the choice was between the sentimental views of the passengers and the analytical attitude of the pilot, between a lush picture and mere matters of fact. It was an impossible choice. If *Huckleberry Finn* is any indication, what Clemens wanted was to affirm the land-

---

[10] Chap. ix, "The Ponds."

[11] Chap. cxxxii, "The Symphony."

[12] Chap. xxxvii, "Sunset." The rest of the passage is of some interest in view of Melville's symbolization of the same conflict with the same images: "Oh! time was, when as the sunrise nobly spurred me, so the sunset soothed. No more. This lovely light, it lights not me; all loveliness is anguish to me, since I can ne'er enjoy. Gifted with the high perception, I lack the low enjoying power. . . ."

scape's beauty *in its actuality.* To do so, though he surely did not realize it, he had to do nothing less than fashion a literary style. The three versions of the dawn on the river help us to understand something of that process.

In *Tom Sawyer,* which he wrote soon after "Old Times," we see the new mode taking shape. Here we have certain obvious holdovers from the older landscape tradition in the hackneyed use of personification and the sense of the event as pictorial spectacle. "The marvel of Nature shaking off sleep and going to work unfolded itself to the musing boy." On the other hand, the effort to include sharp detail is a gauge of Clemens' need to break out of the painter's style. The microscopic focus upon the green worm is well outside the picturesque, which dealt with the general, not the particular; with the remote, not the near; and above all, with a genteel notion of the beautiful, not worms. In the older mode man was an onlooker or, in the pilot's language, a passenger. (Human figures are rare, or in any case of little consequence, in picturesque landscapes.) But the worm's journey over Tom blends the boy into the fabric of nature, and points toward the well-nigh baptismal immersion of Huck and Jim in the river. Nevertheless, here in *Tom Sawyer* the older tradition remains dominant and finally reasserts itself. The passage progresses to a coda of gaudy pictorial banality: "All Nature was wide awake and stirring, now; long lances of sunlight pierced down through the dense foliage far and near, and a few butterflies came fluttering upon the scene."

Clemens finished *Tom Sawyer* in 1875. "I perhaps made a mistake," he remarked to Howells, "in not writing it in the first person." [13] The following year he began *The Adventures of Huckleberry Finn.* After completing roughly four hundred manuscript pages (or about the first sixteen of forty-two chapters) his inspiration waned and he abandoned the project for seven years. [14] Then, in 1882, he made a trip back to the river as the basis for the second volume of *Life on the Mississippi.* He

[13] July 5, 1875, *Mark Twain's Letters,* ed. Albert Bigelow Paine (New York, 1917), I, 258. Actually, Bernard DeVoto has demonstrated that an early version of *Tom Sawyer* was written in the first person. It is now called "Boy's Manuscript," and probably dates from the years 1870-1872. See *Mark Twain at Work* (Cambridge, Mass., 1942), pp. 3-9. The MS itself is reprinted on pp. 25-44. This MS seems to support my contention that first-person narration itself is no key to the superiority of *Huckleberry Finn.* DeVoto rightly calls this first attempt at fiction "crude and trivial, false in sentiment, clumsily farcical, an experiment in burlesque with all its standards mixed" (p. 7). The fact is that Clemens here used the technique in a thoroughly mechanical fashion. Though the boy is supposed to be talking, his words do not actually reveal a boy's attitude, as in *Huckleberry Finn,* but rather that of a bemused adult observing childish behavior.

[14] For the chronology I am following DeVoto, *Mark Twain at Work.*

finished it in 1883. It is an uneven, hasty and loosely put-together volume. But it illuminates the complex relationship between history and style: "The majestic bluffs that overlook the river . . . charm one with the grace and variety of their forms, and the soft beauty of their adornment. The steep, verdant slope . . . is topped by a lofty rampart of broken, turreted rocks, . . . exquisitely rich and mellow in color—mainly dark browns and dull greens, but splashed with other tints." [15] Again we have a painting with all the picturesque niceties, not excepting the castle. There are sleepy villages, stealthy rafts, and white steamers too. It is a glimpse of the old river, a scene "as tranquil and reposeful as dreamland." But then, suddenly, the "unholy train comes tearing along . . . with its devil's war-whoop and the roar and thunder of its rushing wheels." The railroad, emblem of industrial power, is the demon of the entire volume. It destroys steamboating and the natural beauty of the valley. And in the same stroke it renders the established landscape convention obsolete. Clemens, in this remarkable passage, admits as much. He describes the train, in a metaphor whose concealed term surely is a picturesque canvas, "ripping the sacred solitude to rags and tatters." The second volume of *Life on the Mississippi* marks the passing of a way of life, a mode of apprehending nature, and by inference, a literary style.

III

The increasing obsolescence of the style becomes apparent when we compare the two accounts of the dawn which Clemens wrote after his return to the river.

The first is in *Life on the Mississippi*. The narrator pretends to be a reporter on the spot. What he gives us, however, is another formal landscape painting, "one of the fairest and softest pictures imaginable." Of course it may be said that the style has a certain appropriateness. Clemens in this case actually was a kind of reporter, an official visitor from the East. Yet the passage scarcely succeeds as reporting; it might pass for a description of the dawn on the Rhine or the Amazon. Nor does it fit another role the narrator intermittently assumes, that of the ex-pilot who knows the score. His command of piloting is carefully avoided in honor of the "picture," as if beauty really requires the suppression of knowledge. There is no danger, no thought of treacherous snags. All is beautiful, "soft and rich and beautiful." As compared with the dawn in *Tom Sawyer* this is writing of a conventional order.

Indeed it represents a regression to a divided universe in which beauty

[15] P. 432.

and reality are hermetically separated. Nothing makes this compartmentalization of life plainer than the paragraph which follows the sunrise passage. There we find that although no snags are permitted to mar the sunrise, they have not ceased to haunt the pilot.

> We had the Kentucky Bend country in the early morning—scene of a strange and tragic accident in the old times. Captain Poe had a small stern-wheel boat, for years the home of himself and his wife. One night the boat struck a snag in the head of Kentucky Bend, and sank with astonishing suddenness; water already well above the cabin floor when the captain got aft. So he cut into his wife's stateroom from above with an ax; she was asleep in the upper berth, the roof a flimsier one than was supposed; the first blow crashed down through the rotten boards and clove her skull.

There is no way, within the convention, to treat the beautiful and the murderous rivers as one. The style imposes a hopeless bifurcation of experience. In the second half of *Life on the Mississippi*, consequently, the past and the present, the beautiful and the actual, the benign and the tragic are discrete compartments of life. The result is not literature but a disorderly patchwork.

What happens next is, for an understanding of the creative process, the most illuminating part of the story. For apparently the disheartening journey, so perfunctorily reported in the one book, inspired Clemens to go back to work on his masterpiece. It had re-invigorated the pastoral impulse. He had described how the older and by now idealized society of the valley was being torn apart by the new industrial power. Now the unfinished manuscript offered him a chance to render it whole.[16] In art he might achieve a unified vision of the world he had seen being destroyed in fact. But this was not simply a matter of turning his attention to the past. Just as important was the technique of vernacular narration he had fashioned. It was a style which at last made possible a genuine celebration of the landscape.

These circumstances help to explain the extraordinary lyrical intensity of *Huckleberry Finn*, of which the sunrise is but one example.

There are countless descriptions in literature of the sun coming up across a body of water, but it is inconceivable that a substitute exists for

[16] According to DeVoto, Clemens stopped work on the manuscript just after describing the steamboat—its "long row of wide-open furnace doors shining like red-hot teeth" —colliding with the raft. Clearly the boat is a monstrous embodiment of the forces menacing freedom in this idyllic valley society. The fact that Clemens stopped work at this point is highly suggestive. One might infer that the dilemma posed by the industrial transformation of the society had been acting upon his imagination from the first, but that he had not yet settled upon the literary form of his response. For a parallel in the genesis of Hawthorne's fiction, see "The Machine in the Garden," *New England Quarterly*, XXIX, 27-42 (March 1956).

this one. It is unique in diction, rhythm, and tone of voice. Certainly when we place it alongside the earlier versions we see at once how vital point of view can be. In *Life on the Mississippi,* the narrator, who is also supposed to be on the scene, self-consciously pictures the dawn for a distant audience. He stands apart and reports; his explicit aim is to tell his readers why they should believe him when he says that the scene is "enchanting." Huck, on the other hand, is a participant, at times literally immersed in the river he is telling about. Hence the immediacy of his account. The scene is described in concrete details, but they come to us as subjective sense impressions. All the narrator's senses are alive, and through them a high light is thrown upon the preciousness of the concrete facts. Furthermore, Huck is not, as in the two earlier versions, committed to any abstract conception of the scene. He sets out merely to tell how he and Jim put in their time. Because he has nothing to "prove" there is room in his account for *all* the facts. Nothing is fixed, absolute, or perfect. The passage gains immensely in verisimilitude from his repeated approximations: "soon as night was *most* gone," "*nearly always* in the dead water," a *kind of* dull line," "*sometimes* you could hear," "*but sometimes* not that way." Nature, too, is in process: "the daylight *come,*" "paleness *spreading* around," "river *softened* up," "mist *curl* up," "east *reddens* up," "breeze *springs* up." Both subject and object are alive; the passage has more in common with a motion picture than a landscape painting.

Huck, moreover, "belongs" to this landscape in that his language is native to it. Perhaps this fact, above all, accounts for the exquisite freshness of these lines. Sunrises have not changed much since Homer sang of the rosy-fingered dawn, but here is the first one ever described in this idiom. What is distinctive about it, in other words, ultimately derives from the historical distinctiveness of the narrator, his speech, and the culture from which both emerge. But particularly his speech, for that is the raw material of this art, and we delight in the incomparable fitness of subject and language. Observe, for example, the three successive efforts to convey the solitude and silence at dawn. (It was the "sacred solitude" that the railroad tore to tatters.) Compare: "deep pervading calm and silence of the woods": "eloquence of silence": "not a sound anywheres—perfectly still—just like the whole world was asleep, only sometimes the bullfrogs a-cluttering, maybe." The first is merely commonplace; "eloquence of silence" is neat and fine, and it has the merit of compression and (to invoke a currently popular critical test) paradox. The phrase is so good, in fact, that it has often been used. Yet relative novelty is not the main point. There is nothing novel about "just like the whole world was asleep" either. On the contrary, both phrases are familiar; the difference is that our familiarity with one comes from the written, indeed the printed, word, and the other from the spoken word. One bears the unmistakable mark of a man bent on making phrases; it is literary; the other sounds like a boy talking. The same may be said of several other parallels, such as "the birds were fairly rioting": "jubilant riot of music": "the songbirds just going it." Much of the superior power of *Huckleberry Finn* must be ascribed to the sound of the voice we hear. It is the voice of the boy experiencing the event. Of course no one ever really spoke such concentrated poetry, but the illusion that we are hearing the spoken word is an important part of the total illusion of reality. The words on the page carry our attention to life, not to art, and that after all is what most readers want.

My purpose, I repeat, is not to exalt vernacular narration as a universally superior technique. Each writer discovers methods best suited to the sense of life he must (if he is to succeed) create. In this case, however, the vernacular method liberated Sam Clemens. When he looked at the river through Huck's eyes he was suddenly free of certain arid notions of what a writer should write. It would have been absurd to have had Huck Finn describe the Mississippi as a sublime landscape painting.

Accordingly Clemens, in spite of his evident effort to convey the beauty of the sunrise, permits Huck to report that "by and by you could see a streak on the water which you know by the look of the streak that there's a snag there in the swift current which breaks on it and makes the streak look that way." He is endowed with the knowledge of precisely those matters of fact which had seemed to impair the pilot's sense of beauty. Huck now accepts that fearful principle of nature responsible for the death of Captain Poe's wife. Now at last, through the consciousness of the boy, the two rivers are one. Mingled with the loveliness of the scene are things not so lovely: murderous snags, wood piled by cheats, and—what could be less poetic?—the rank smell of dead fish. Huck is not the innocent traveler, yet neither is he the initiated pilot. He sees the snags, but they do not spoil his pleasure. In his person Clemens reaches back to a primal mode of perception undisturbed by the tension between art and science. It does not occur to Huck to choose between beauty and utility. His willingness to accept the world as he finds it, without anxiously forcing meanings upon it, lends substance to the magical sense of peace the passage conveys. When the lights of the river form a continuum with the stars, the boy's sense of belonging reaches the intensity of a religious experience; the two on the raft face the mystery of the creation with the equanimity of saints: "It's lovely to live on a raft. We had the sky up there, all speckled with stars, and we used to lay on our backs and look up at them, and discuss about whether they was made or only just happened."

IV

The passion we feel here may only be compared with love. It is not the conventional sentiment of the early landscapes, but the love of an object as it exists, in all its gloriously imperfect actuality. Indeed, this sequence of Clemens' attitudes toward the landscape is comparable, in several respects, to an intricate love relationship. In all three of the Mississippi books his deep feeling for the landscape is evident. But at first, as the pilot in *Life on the Mississippi* reveals, a conflict blocks its full expression. He tells of a violent shift from one extreme conception of nature to another. At first the landscape is sheer perfection—soft, rich, and beautiful; then it suddenly comes to seem a merely indifferent, if not hostile, force. After having been submissive and adoring, he now is wary and aggressive. But in *Huckleberry Finn* there is no trace of either attitude. Here the narrator feels neither adoration nor hostility. The boy gives us a full account of his experience of nature, sensations unpleasant as well as pleasant, matters of fact and matters of feeling, objects attractive and repellent. At dawn, on the river, Huck knows neither anxiety nor guilt, but an intense feeling of solidarity with the physical universe.[17]

[17] How revealing that Clemens, who seldom if ever was able to depict a mature love relation, should have been able to express this passion only in the words of an adolescent! Those interested in a psychological analysis of his work should examine this highly suggestive material. Notice, for example, the unmistakable sexual connotations of the two attitudes toward landscape. On the beautiful surface nature has obvious feminine characteristics (softness, dimples, graceful curves), but the subsurface is represented by objects with strongly masculine overtones (logs, bluff reefs, menacing snags). In Melville the symbolism is explicit. For instance, in the passage from "The Symphony" (see above), the air is "pure and soft" and has a "woman's look," while in the waters beneath the sea rush mighty leviathans and sharks, the "murderous thinkings of a masculine sea." Perhaps these sexual identifications are the key to the alternating submission and aggression noted in Clemens' treatment of the landscape (an object, finally, of love)— as if he were projecting an inner conflict. Henry A. Murray has made the point about Melville ("In Nomine Diaboli," *New England Quarterly*, XXIV, 435-452, Dec., 1951). Of course Melville and Clemens were not alone, among our nineteenth century writers, in presenting an apparent antithesis between (feminine) beauty and (masculine) reality. The subject would seem to warrant close examination, particularly in view of the frequency with which social scientists have noted the conflict between aggressive competitiveness and a desire to yield as peculiarly characteristic of American society. See, e.g., Franz Alexander, *Our Age of Unreason* (Philadelphia, 1942); Arnold W. Green, "The Middle-Class Male Child and Neurosis," *American Sociological Review*, II, 31-41 (February 1946); Karen Horney, *The Neurotic Personality of Our Time* (New York, 1937).

It is obvious that this capacity for realistic affirmation coincides with the disappearance, however temporary, of the earlier conflict. Needless to say, the conflict was no mere fiction. It was vital to Clemens, as it was endemic in a society at once so passionately committed to—and at war with—nature. As a writer, however, he felt the destructive consequences of this tension most acutely in his work. It was impossible to do justice to American experience by treating nature, in the conventional manner, as benign and beautiful. Clemens knew better, and his continuing impulse was to parody the accepted mode. To him the landscape, no matter how lovely, concealed a dangerous antagonist. He knew that nature had to be watched, resisted, and—when possible—subdued. Unfortunately this often meant its obliteration as an object of beauty, hence of love. Nothing impressed this upon Clemens with such force as what he saw happening to the Mississippi Valley in 1882.

In the incomplete manuscript of *Huckleberry Finn,* to which he then returned with renewed imaginative vigor, he found a solution. Here was a tale told by a boy who—granted his age, his education, and the time he lived—could not possibly feel the anxiety Clemens felt. To Huck nature was neither an object of beauty nor the raw material of progress. Or, rather, it was both. He was as tough and practical as the pilot, and as sensitive to color and line as an artist; he kept his eye on dangerous snags, but he did not lose his sense of the river's loveliness. Moreover, he spoke a language completely unlike the stilted vocabulary of the literary cult of nature. His speech, never before used in a sustained work of fiction, was as fresh and supple as his point of view. The interaction of a narrative technique and the heightened emotion to which that technique lent expression helps account for the singular power of the sunrise passage. Behind the mask of Huck Finn, Clemens regained that unity of thought and feeling he felt himself, along with his contemporaries, to be losing.

But this is not to say that Clemens had suddenly thought his way out of the dilemma. We have only to read his later work to see that he had not. What he did was to discover a way around it—a sublimation, as it were, of the conflict. The discovery came to him not conceptually, but spontaneously, in the practice of his art. For all the intricacies of a problem at once psychological, philosophical, and historical, the "solution" was simple and primarily aesthetic. In one sense it consisted merely of placing himself behind the mask of a narrator for whom the problem did not exist. This device, however, was only the first step; it provided a point of view—an ideological, not an aesthetic truth. The more diffi-

cult task was to endow this viewpoint, for which there existed no appropriate literary style, with literary vitality, with life. He accomplished this
by maintaining a fidelity to the experience of his narrator so disciplined
that it cut beneath established conventions. The point of view became
a style. Unfortunately, Clemens did not realize the dimensions of this
achievement. But since his time many of our best writers, responding to
pressures not unlike those he felt, have recognized the usefulness of the
mode he devised.

Nor was the vernacular style useful only to depict landscape. Most of
the book is as fine, in various ways, as the sunrise passage. Clemens not
only fashioned a vital style, he sustained it. Its merit was the product not
so much of technical virtuosity as of the kinds of truth to which it gave
access. *The Adventures of Huckleberry Finn* contains insights neither
a pilot nor a passenger could have had. It is a book, rare in our literature,
which manages to suggest the lovely possibilities of life in America without neglecting its terrors.

Mark Twain: The Three Dawns

I

When Tom awoke in the morning, he wondered where he was. He sat up
and rubbed his eyes and looked around. Then he comprehended. It was the
cool gray dawn, and there was a delicious sense of repose and peace in the
deep pervading calm and silence of the woods. Not a leaf stirred; not a sound
obtruded upon great Nature's meditation. Beaded dewdrops stood upon the
leaves and grasses. A white layer of ashes covered the fire, and a thin blue
breath of smoke rose straight into the air. Joe and Huck still slept.

Now, far away in the woods a bird called; another answered; presently the
hammering of a woodpecker was heard. Gradually the cool dim gray of the
morning whitened, and as gradually sounds multiplied and life manifested
itself. The marvel of Nature shaking off sleep and going to work unfolded
itself to the musing boy. A little green worm came crawling over a dewy
leaf, lifting two-thirds of his body into the air from time to time and "sniffing
around," then proceeding again—for he was measuring, Tom said; and
when the worm approached him, of its own accord, he sat as still as a stone,
with his hopes rising and falling, by turns, as the creature still came toward
him or seemed inclined to go elsewhere; and when at last it considered a
painful moment with its curved body in the air and then came decisively
down upon Tom's leg and began a journey over him, his whole heart was
glad—for that meant that he was going to have a new suit of clothes—without the shadow of a doubt a gaudy piratical uniform. Now a procession of
ants appeared, from nowhere in particular, and went about their labors;
one struggled manfully by with a dead spider five times as big as itself in its

arms, and lugged it straight up a tree-trunk. A brown spotted lady-bug climbed the dizzy height of a grass-blade, and Tom bent down close to it and said, "Lady-bug, lady-bug, fly away home, your house is on fire, your children's alone," and she took wing and went off to see about it—which did not surprise the boy, for he knew of old that this insect was credulous about conflagrations, and he had practised upon its simplicity more than once. A tumblebug came next, heaving sturdily at its ball, and Tom touched the creature, to see it shut its legs against its body and pretend to be dead. The birds were fairly rioting by this time. A catbird, the Northern mocker, lit in a tree over Tom's head, and trilled out her imitations of her neighbors in a rapture of enjoyment; then a shrill jay swept down, a flash of blue flame, and stopped on a twig almost within the boy's reach, cocked his head to one side and eyed the strangers with a consuming curiosity; a gray squirrel and a big fellow of the "fox" kind came scurrying along, sitting up at intervals to inspect and chatter at the boys, for the wild things had probably never seen a human being before and scarcely knew whether to be afraid or not. All Nature was wide awake and stirring, now; long lances of sunlight pierced down through the dense foliage far and near, and a few butterflies came fluttering upon the scene.—*The Adventures of Tom Sawyer,* Chapter XIV.

II

I had myself called with the four-o'clock watch, mornings, for one cannot see too many summer sunrises on the Mississippi. They are enchanting. First, there is the eloquence of silence; for a deep hush broods everywhere. Next, there is the haunting sense of loneliness, isolation, remoteness from the worry and bustle of the world. The dawn creeps in stealthily; the solid walls of black forest soften to gray, and vast stretches of the river open up and reveal themselves; the water is glass-smooth, gives off spectral little wreaths of white mist, there is not the faintest breath of wind, nor stir of leaf; the tranquillity is profound and infinitely satisfying. Then a bird pipes up, another follows, and soon the pipings develop into a jubilant riot of music. You see none of the birds; you simply move through an atmosphere of song which seems to sing itself. When the light has become a little stronger, you have one of the fairest and softest pictures imaginable. You have the intense green of the massed and crowded foliage near by; you see it paling shade by shade in front of you; upon the next projecting cape, a mile off or more, the tint has lightened to the tender young green of spring; the cape beyond that one has almost lost color, and the furthest one, miles away under the horizon, sleeps upon the water a mere dim vapor, and hardly separable from the sky above it and about it. And all this stretch of river is a mirror, and you have the shadowy reflections of the leafage and the curving shores and the receding capes pictured in it. Well, that is all beautiful; soft and rich and beautiful; and when the sun gets well up, and distributes a pink flush here and a powder of gold yonder and a purple haze where it will yield the best effect, you grant that you have seen something that is worth remembering.
—*Life on the Mississippi,* Chapter XXX.

III

Two or three days and nights went by; I reckon I might say they swum
by, they slid along so quiet and smooth and lovely. Here is the way we put
in the time. It was a monstrous big river down there—sometimes a mile and
a half wide; we run nights, and laid up and hid daytimes; soon as night was
most gone we stopped navigating and tied up—nearly always in the dead
water under a towhead; and then cut young cottonwoods and willows, and
hid the raft with them. Then we set out the lines. Next we slid into the
river and had a swim, so as to freshen up and cool off; then we set down on
the sandy bottom where the water was about knee-deep, and watched the
daylight come. Not a sound anywheres—perfectly still—just like the whole
world was asleep, only sometimes the bullfrogs a-cluttering, maybe. The first
thing to see, looking away over the water, was a kind of dull line—that was
the woods on t'other side; you couldn't make nothing else out; then a pale
place in the sky; then more paleness spreading around; then the river
softened up away off, and warn't black any more, but gray; you could see
little dark spots drifting along ever so far away—trading-scows, and such
things; and long black streaks—rafts; sometimes you could hear a sweep
screaking; or jumbled-up voices, it was so still, and sounds come so far; and
by and by you could see a streak on the water which you know by the look
of the streak that there's a snag there in a swift current which breaks on it
and makes that streak look that way; and you see the mist curl up off of the
water, and the east reddens up, and the river, and you make out a log cabin
in the edge of the woods, away on the bank on t'other side of the river, being
a wood-yard, likely, and piled by them cheats so you can throw a dog through
it anywheres; then the nice breeze springs up, and comes fanning you from
over there, so cool and fresh and sweet to smell on account of the woods and
the flowers; but sometimes not that way, because they've left dead fish laying
around, gars and such, and they do get pretty rank; and next you've got the
full day, and everything smiling in the sun, and the song-birds just going it!
  A little smoke couldn't be noticed now, so we would take some fish off of
the lines and cook up a hot breakfast. And afterwards we would watch the
lonesomeness of the river, and kind of lazy along, and by and by lazy off to
sleep. Wake up by and by, and look to see what done it, and maybe see a
steamboat coughing along up-stream, so far off towards the other side you
couldn't tell nothing about her only whether she was a stern-wheel or side-
wheel; then for about an hour there wouldn't be nothing to hear nor nothing to see—just solid lonesomeness. . . .
  Sometimes we'd have that whole river all to ourselves for the longest time.
Yonder was the banks and the islands, across the water; and maybe a spark—
which was a candle in a cabin window; and sometimes on the water you
could see a spark or two—on a raft or a scow, you know; and maybe you
could hear a fiddle or a song coming over from one of them crafts. It's lovely
to live on a raft. We had the sky up there, all speckled with stars, and we
used to lay on our backs and look up at them, and discuss about whether

they was made or only just happened. Jim he allowed they was made, but I allowed they happened; I judged it would have took too long to *make* so many. Jim said the moon could 'a' *laid* them; well, that looked kind of reasonable, so I didn't say nothing against it, because I've seen a frog lay most as many, so of course it could be done. We used to watch the stars that fell, too, and see them streak down. Jim allowed they'd got spoiled and was hove out of the nest.—*Adventures of Huckleberry Finn,* Chapter XIX.

Tom Sawyer

by Walter Blair

> You don't know about me without you have read a book by the
> name of *The Adventures of Tom Sawyer.* . . . That book was made
> by Mr. Mark Twain, and he told the truth, mainly. There was things
> which he stretched, but mainly he told the truth.
> —*Adventures of Huckleberry Finn,* opening paragraph

The Adventures of Tom Sawyer, to which Mark Twain turned, or
rather returned, after "Old Times," carried him into the writing of
Huckleberry Finn. He composed *Tom Sawyer,* as he would *Huck,* in different places at various times. One version of Tom and Becky's love story
he wrote in Buffalo in 1870. His recollection was that he wrote about
Tom's whitewashing trick in London in 1872. He started the "final"
version of the book in Hartford in 1873 or 1874. During the summer
of 1874, in Elmira, he averaged five thousand words a day. September
2, discovering that "that day's chapter was a failure, in conception, moral
truth to nature, and execution," he decided "I had worked myself out,
pumped myself dry." He was to recall that this was at page 400, and
subsequently he made an important discovery:

> When the manuscript had lain in a pigeonhole two years I took it out one
> day and read the last chapter that I had written. It was then that I made the
> great discovery that when the tank runs dry you've only to leave it alone and
> it will fill up again in time while you are asleep—also while you are at work
> at other things and are quite unaware that this unconscious and profitable
> cerebration is going on. There was plenty of material now, and the book
> went and finished itself without any trouble.

In this account the writer perhaps was recalling the pigeonholing of
his partial version of 1870 or of 1872; for, after less than a year, he evidently resumed writing in Hartford about mid-May, 1875. By July 5,
1875, he had "finished the story . . . about 900 pages of MS, and maybe
1000 when I have finished 'working out' vague places."

Clemens once told his friend Brander Matthews that his tank refilled because he remembered boyhood happenings:

> He began the composition of "Tom Sawyer" with certain of his boyish recollections in mind, writing on and on until he utilized them all, whereupon he put his manuscript aside and ceased to think about it, except in so far as he might recall from time to time, and more or less unconsciously, other recollections of those early days. Sooner or later he would return to his work to make use of the memories he had recaptured in the interval. After he had harvested this second crop, he again put his work away, certain that in time he would be able to call back other scenes and other situations. When at last he became convinced that he had made his profit out of every possible reminiscence, he went over what he had written with great care, adjusting the several instalments one to the other, sometimes transposing a chapter or two and sometimes writing into the earlier chapters the necessary preparation for adventures in the later chapters unforseen when he was engaged on the beginnings of the book. Thus he was enabled to bestow on the completed story a more obvious coherence than his haphazard procedure would otherwise have attained.[1]

The many details from memory in *Tom Sawyer* offer some support for this simple account. The St. Petersburg of the novel is the Hannibal, "the white town drowsing in the sunshine," of "Old Times." Tom's house is the old Clemens house, Becky Thatcher's house that of a childhood sweetheart. The schoolhouse and the church where Tom undergoes boredom are modeled after identifiable buildings. Cardiff Hill, where Tom re-enacts Robin Hood's adventures, is Holliday's Hill; the cemetery where Tom and Huck watch the murder is the Baptist Cemetery; Jackson's Island, scene of the Gang's career as pirates, is Glasscock's Island; the stillhouse branch, scene of the treasure hunt, is part of the actual Hannibal; McDougal's cave, where Tom and Becky are lost and Injun Joe dies, is McDowell's cave downstream to the south.

"Huck Finn is drawn from life," says the preface, "Tom Sawyer also, but not from an individual—he is a combination of the characteristics of three boys whom I knew. . . ." Paine holds that Tom's characteristics came from Sam Clemens himself and from Will Bowen and John Briggs, two Hannibal contemporaries, though other members of Sam's gang have been mentioned for the honor.[2] At any rate, Tom was based on actual characters. And real-life prototypes of all the other leading figures in the book have been identified.

---

[1] Brander Matthews, "Memories of Mark Twain," in *The Tocsin of Revolt and Other Essays* (New York, 1922), pp. 265-267. The conversation took place in 1890.

[2] Theodore Hornberger, "An Introduction" to *Mark Twain's Letters to Will Bowen* (Austin, 1941), pp. 3-4. Twain says that he himself played a trick ascribed to Tom and that, like Tom, he was often guilty of truancy. *Autobiography*, II, 91-92.

"Most of the adventures recorded in this book," the preface continues, "really occurred; one or two were experiences of my own, the rest those of boys who were schoolmates of mine." The author's jottings over the years substantiate this to some extent. August 5, 1866, on a trip to the Sandwich Islands he wrote, "Superstitions: Wash hands in rainwater standing in old hollow stump to remove warts. . . . Split a bean, bind it on wart—wait till midnight and bury it at cross-roads in dark of the moon." These recipes, recalled from boyhood, are discussed in chapter vi. A few days before, in the same notebook, Clemens had noted, "Cat and Painkiller," [3] and some years after writing the novel he made a note for his *Autobiography*, "Peter and Davis painkiller" and "Water-cure." [4] In chapter xii Aunt Polly tries a water treatment on Tom ("stood him up in the woodshed and drowned him with a deluge of cold water"). This failing, she hears of a "Pain-Killer . . . simply fire in liquid form." She doses Tom with this, and he feeds some to a cat, Peter, who wrecks the house.

The same notes for the *Autobiography* contain this: "fired cannon to raise drowned bodies of Christ Levering [a boyhood Hannibal contemporary] and me—when I escaped from the ferryboat [and was thought drowned]." [5] In chapter xiii the boys on Jackson's Island watch the ferryboat shooting a cannon over the side:

> "I know now!" exclaimed Tom; "somebody's drowned!"
> "That's it!" said Huck; "they done that last summer, when Bill Turner got drownded; they shoot a cannon over the water, and that makes him come up to the top."

On January 25, 1868, writing to Will Bowen, Clemens said, "I still remember the louse you bought of poor Arch Fuqua"; in chapter vii Tom and Joe Harper torture a tick in school. The details, Clemens has testified, "are strictly true, as I have reason to remember." [6] February 6, 1870, in another letter to Bowen, Clemens recalled how "we used to undress and play Robin Hood in our shirt-tails, with lath swords, in the woods" [7] —a pastime re-created in chapter viii.

Clemens' testimony and his relating of these real scenes to the book led Paine to decide that "the personal details of this story were essentially

---

[3] Notebooks 4-5, Mark Twain Papers (hereafter *MTP*), © copyright 1960 by Mark Twain Co.

[4] DV 131, *MTP*.

[5] *MTP*, © copyright 1960 by Mark Twain Co. See also *Letters to Will Bowen*, p. 19.

[6] *Letters to Will Bowen*, p. 17; Twain's testimony is in a footnote, *Boy's Manuscript*, in Bernard DeVoto, *Mark Twain at Work* (Cambridge, Mass., 1942; hereafter *MTaW*), p. 39.

[7] *Letters to Will Bowen*, p. 19.

nothing more than the various aspects of his own boyhood." DeLancey
Ferguson said in his excellent biography, "The atmosphere and incidents
of . . . Hannibal boyhood came back to his memory as he wrote; he had
only to set them down." [8] In 1954 Jerry Allen, convinced that the novel is
literally true, incorporated many of Tom's adventures in her biography,
The Adventures of Mark Twain, as actual events. It is easy to demonstrate, nevertheless, that here, as in "Old Times," Twain made many
changes when he transformed fact into fiction.

Despite recognizable aspects, St. Petersburg is for the most part far
lovelier than Hannibal. In chapter i, to dramatize the elegance of a new
boy which irritates Tom, Mark calls St. Petersburg a "poor little shabby
village"; that is what the old Hannibal really was. But except in a few
similar phrases St. Petersburg and its environs are realms of quiet delight
bathed in summer air fragrant with the aroma of meadows, woodlands,
and flowers. The idyllic setting was one aspect of the book that led Twain
to call it "simply a hymn, put into prose to give it a worldly air."

He chose characters which suited his purposes. Unpublished memories
of real Hannibal folk prove that the town could have stocked a Spoon
River or a Peyton Place. The Ratcliff boy "had to be locked in a small
house . . . and chained. . . . Would not wear clothes, winter or summer. . . . Believed his left hand had committed a mortal sin . . . and
chopped it off." His brother "became a fine physician in California ven-
tured to marry but went mad. . . ." Dr. Jim Lampton was "captured by
Ella Hunter, a loud vulgar beauty from a neighboring town. Young Dr.
John McDowell boarded with them; followed them from house to house;
an arrant scandal. . . ." Mary Moss, shut in solitude to study so that
she would be a credit to her lawyer husband in society, after two years
"had become wedded to her seclusion and her melancholy brooding. . . .
Saw no company, not even the mates of her childhood." [9] There are no
fictional prototypes of characters such as these.

Characters copied from life are modified. In an interview in the Port-
land *Oregonian,* August 11, 1895, the author indicated that, though he
drew Tom and Huck from actuality, he changed their names, and for
an interesting reason:

> I have always found it difficult to choose just the name that suited my ear.
> "Tom Sawyer" and "Huckleberry Finn" were both real characters, but "Tom

---

[8] DeLancey Ferguson, *Mark Twain: Man and Legend* (Indianapolis, 1943), p. 175.
On p. 29, however, Ferguson stated, more accurately, "*Tom Sawyer* is not autobiographical in its details, but in its personalities, altered or heightened for dramatic purposes, it is essentially lifelike."

[9] DV 47, *MTP,* © copyright 1960 by Mark Twain Co.

Sawyer" was not the real name of the former, nor the name of any person I ever knew, . . . but the name was an ordinary one—just the sort that seemed to fit the boy, some way, by its sound. . . . No, one doesn't name his characters haphazard. Finn was the real name of the other boy, but I tacked on the "Huckleberry." You see, there was something about the name "Finn" that suited, and "Huck Finn" was all that was needed to somehow describe another kind of a boy than "Tom Sawyer," a boy of lower extraction or degree. Now, "Arthur Van de Vanter Montague" would have sounded ridiculous, applied to characters like either "Tom Sawyer" or "Huck Finn."

Except for the fact that either Clemens or the reporter was inaccurate about the name "Finn" the account is believable. (The character Emmeline Grangerford in *Huckleberry Finn* acquired her name similarly.)

Characters usually had much more than their names changed. Jane Clemens, Aunt Polly's prototype, had willful ways, family pride, a sharp tongue, and a clever mind; Aunt Polly has none of these. The writer testified that though his brother Henry "is Sid . . . Sid was not Henry. Henry was a much finer and better boy. . . ." Tom Blankenship, unlike Huck, who is copied after him, had two sisters, a mother, and a father; he, rather than Sam, led the boys' gang; he, rather than Sam, thought of digging for treasure.[10] Muff Potter was (as Twain said of Tom) "of the composite order of architecture," embodying qualities of several Hannibal ne'er-do-wells. The prototype of Injun Joe was not the villain that Injun Joe of the novel is. Tom Sawyer, like the narrator of *Innocents Abroad* and *Roughing It* and the cub pilot of "Old Times," is probably a much better-read and more romantic lad than any of the characters after whom he is modeled.

True, some incidents had counterparts in actuality. But consider these memorable scenes: the grave robbery, the murder of the doctor, the appearance of the boys at their own funeral, Tom's taking Becky's punishment and being praised for it by her father, Tom's testifying at the trial, Injun Joe's plotting to mutilate Widow Douglas, Huck's rescue of her, Becky's and Tom's tribulations in the cave, Tom's rescue of Becky, the discovery of the treasure, Injun Joe's horrible death.

Some of these, as Booth Tarkington suggests, are not based upon actual happenings but upon "adventures that all boys, in their longing dreams, make believe they have." [11] Others, as DeVoto remarks, are "ghastly stuff . . . murder and starvation, grave robbery and revenge, terror and panic, some of the darkest emotions of men, some of the most terrible

[10] J. W. Ayres, "Recollections of Hannibal," *Palmyra Spectator*, August 22, 1917.
[11] "Introduction" to Cyril Clemens, *My Cousin Mark Twain* (Emmaus, Pa., 1939).

fears of children, and the ghosts and demons and death portents of the slaves." [12] These were not as inappropriate to Sam Clemens' Hannibal as modern readers may believe: located on the rough frontier, it had been more violent than most small towns. During his boyhood, Sam three times came close to drowning, and before he was seventeen he witnessed the abortive lynching of an abolitionist, a death by fire, a hanging, an attempted rape, two drownings, two attempted homicides, and four murders. The town's religion stressed hell-fire damnation. Folklore of whites and Negroes featured topics differing from those recommended by authorities on juvenile literature today—witches, ghosts, death, and putrefaction. But however true these episodes were to the atmosphere of Hannibal, careful search has indicated that none was based upon an actual event.

Mark Twain, then, greatly modified settings, characters, and happenings. Three processes brought changes: his shifting memories and moods, the influence of his biography and his reading in the 1870's, and his manipulation of materials.

The author's memory, like most memories, was tricky. One checking his recollections over the years against ascertainable facts finds that, as Dixon Wecter says, sometimes they were surprisingly accurate. But they were at times quite inaccurate. Often, too, moods colored his remembering. Shortly after his marriage he wrote Will Bowen:

> Your letter has stirred me . . . and I have rained reminiscences for four and twenty hours. The old life has swept before me like a panorama; the old days have trooped by in their old glory again. . . . Heavens what eternities have swung their hoary cycles about since . . . Jimmy Finn was town drunkard and . . . slept in the vat . . . since we used to go swimming above the still-house branch . . . since . . .

And there followed a long paragraph of savored reminiscences. [13] A process which he has described in chapter liv of *Innocents Abroad* is at work here:

> Schoolboy days are no happier than the days of after life, but we look back upon them regretfully because we have forgotten our punishments at school, and how we grieved when our marbles were lost and our kites destroyed— because we have forgotten all the sorrows and privations of that canonized epoch and remember only its orchard robberies, its wooden sword pageants, and its fishing holidays.

---

[12] DeVoto, *Portable Mark Twain*, p. 33.   [13] *Letters to Will Bowen*, p. 18.

In the summer of 1876, in another mood, he wrote Bowen a very different sort of letter about old Hannibal days:

> As to the past, there is but one good thing about it, . . . that it *is* the
> past. . . . I can see by your manner of speech, that for more than twenty
> years you have stood dead still in the midst of the dreaminess, the melan-
> choly, the romance, the heroics, of sweet but sappy sixteen. Man, do you
> know that this is simply mental and moral masturbation? It belongs emi-
> nently to the period usually devoted to *physical* masturbation, and should
> be left there and outgrown. . . . You need a dose of salts. . . .[14]

The mood of *Tom Sawyer* is that of the earlier letter. Amateur and
professional psychologists will note with interest that the earlier reminiscences followed close upon the writer's marriage. So did the narrative
which Paine found in the Papers, labelled " 'Boy's Manuscript,' probably
written about 1870," and filed. Long after, Bernard DeVoto saw its significance: it was "the embryo" of *Tom Sawyer*. It develops at length one
line of narrative in the novel—a boyish courtship during which the hero
suffers much distress.[15] Clemens himself had only recently been as ardent,
as despairing—and sometimes almost as gauche—in his courtship of
Olivia Langdon: it is fascinating to see how this humorist, soon after
his own grim battle, treats similar material in a boy's travesty of grown-up
love-making.[16] By the time he rewrote this as part of *Tom Sawyer,* even
more remote from his agonizing experiences, he could write of them in an
even gayer fashion.

There are other parallels between Clemens' recent situation and that
of his boyish characters. "But you," he had written Livy in January, 1869,
"will break up all my irregularities when we are married, and *civilize*
me, and make of me a model husband and an adornment to society—
won't you . . . ?"[17] Billy Rogers, in *Boy's Manuscript,* and Tom, his
later embodiment, are likewise subjected to "civilizing" influences in the
hope that they will become "model boys"; and their creator, already (as
will be shown) able to look back with detachment on his own period of
being housebroken, could exploit some of his recent difficulties humor-

---

[14] *Ibid.,* pp. 23-24. This was the original draft; Clemens took the trouble to "rewrite
[the letter], saying the same harsh things softly."

[15] *MTaW,* p. 6.

[16] Gladys Carmen Bellamy, *Mark Twain as a Literary Artist* (Norman, 1950), p. 333,
guesses that this "may have been begun as a sort of playful, whimsical love letter to
Olivia"; and cites incidents in its early pages which parallel happenings during the
courtship. I tend to doubt this because the style and tone differ from those of most
Clemens' courting letters, and I think that at that time he was too involved to make
fun of his courtship.

[17] *Love Letters,* p. 56.

ously. More: in chapter vi he could introduce a character whom Tom envies because he is even less restrained:

> Huckleberry [Finn] came and went, at his own free will . . . he did not have to go to school or to church, or call any being master or obey anybody . . . he could sit up as late as he pleased . . . he never had to wash, nor put on clean clothes; he could swear wonderfully. In a word, everything that goes to make life precious, that boy had. So thought every harassed, hampered, respectable boy in St. Petersburg.

Interestingly, Huck has the same freedom as quite a different kind of hero whom Twain praised in "Old Times" less than a year later:

> . . . a pilot, in those days, was the only unfettered and entirely independent human being that lived in the earth. Kings are but the hampered servants of parliament and people; parliaments sit in chains forged by their constituency; the editor of a newspaper cannot be independent . . . ; no clergyman is a free man . . . ; writers of all kinds are manacled servants of the public. We write frankly and fearlessly, but then we "modify" before we print. In truth, every man and woman and child has a master, and worries and frets in servitude, but in the day I write of, the Mississippi pilot had *none*.[18]

Thus both memories colored by time and personal attitudes impelled Twain, in the 1870's, to write nostalgically about life in an idyllic Southwestern town in the days before the Civil War.

Literary influences also operated. Dime novels, melodramas, and similar trash are echoed in the sensational courtroom scene, Injun Joe's bloodthirsty schemes for vengeance, his wandering around town unrecognized in a skimpy disguise, and the boys' discovery of Murrel's buried treasure. Respected novels such as those of Dickens, Reade, and Collins encouraged Twain to jam four plots and several unrelated episodes into one book.

And since this was the era of kindly pictures of the past, an idyllic tone was to be expected. Mrs. Stowe's *Oldtown Folks* (1869) and *Sam Lawson's Fireside Stories* (1871), Harte's *The Luck of Roaring Camp and Other Sketches* (1870) about the California of the forty-niners, and Eggleston's *The Hoosier Schoolmaster* (1871) about the Indiana frontier of his youth had started a deluge of fiction about various sections of the country in bygone days. In 1872 Howells remarked that "gradually, but pretty surely, the whole varied field of American life is coming into view in American

[18] Article VI, written and proofread, April, 1875, published in *Atlantic Monthly*, June, 1875.

fiction. . . ." [19] Most writers, like Twain, were trying to be authentic: "I desire," wrote Mrs. Stowe in *Oldtown Folks,* "that you should see the characteristics of those times, and hear them talk. . . . My studies for this object have been . . . taken from real characters, real scenes, and real incidents." But most were nostalgic. Looking back across the chasm which the Civil War had made in American history, writers found the past happier and rosier than the troubled present. There is no evidence that the humorist knew Eggleston at this time; but he knew Harte and his writings well, and annotated a copy of *The Luck of Roaring Camp.* Mrs. Stowe he had recently met as a Nook Farm neighbor. But local-color fiction was everywhere, and any of scores of writers may have acquainted him with it. He, as usual, was apace with literary movements when, happily, he learned that "the boy life out on the Mississippi . . . had a peculiar charm" for him. Reviewing *Tom Sawyer* for the *Atlantic,* in May, 1876, Howells linked it with contemporaneous writings, saying that it "gives incomparably the best picture of life" in the Southwest "as yet known to fiction."

Clemens would have been surprised if other, more specific, literary influences were not operative. In 1869, as he put it, he had "stolen" the dedication of a book by Oliver Wendell Holmes "almost word for word" quite unconsciously, and on apologizing had been reassured by Holmes of the "truth" that "we all unconsciously work over ideas gathered in reading and hearing, imagining they were original with ourselves." [20] Midway in *Tom Sawyer* he again caught himself committing "unconscious plagiarism." [21] In a letter of 1876, the year *Tom Sawyer* appeared, he indicated that he often knowingly transplanted ideas from stories by others into stories of his own. [22]

That same year, after having a bookseller "ransack England"—so his inscription on the flyleaf indicates—he procured a copy of Henry H. Breen's *Modern English Literature: Its Blemishes and Defects* (London, 1857). Clemens showed particular interest in a chapter on plagiarism by marking it up more and making more marginal comments on it than any other part of the book, perhaps while preparing a paper on the topic. [23]

---

[19] Howells, "Recent Literature," *Atlantic Monthly,* XXX (October, 1872) , 487.

[20] "Unconscious Plagiarism" (1879), *Mark Twain's Speeches,* ed. Albert Bigelow Paine (New York, 1910), pp. 57-58.

[21] The statement refers to another manuscript in progress.

[22] The original letter, to Howells, in the Berg Collection, is cited with the permission of the New York Public Library.

[23] Clemens spoke on "Plagiarism" to the Saturday Morning Club in 1880. Katharine Seymore Day, "Mark Twain's First Years in Hartford" (unpublished master's thesis, Trinity College, Hartford, 1936), p. 130.

His comments strike one as pretty sophisticated. On page 218 Breen scornfully quotes a statement of Alexander Dumas, whom he calls, rather sweepingly, "the most audacious plagiarist of any time or country." Says Dumas: "The man of genius does not steal; he conquers; and what he conquers, he annexes to his empire. He makes laws for it, peoples it with subjects, and extends his golden scepter over it. And where is the man who, in surveying his beautiful kingdom, shall dare to assert that this or that piece of land is no part of his property?" Though Breen calls this a barefaced plea for literary thievery, Clemens agrees with Dumas in a marginal comment: "A good deal of truth in it. Shakespeare took other people's quartz and extracted the gold from it—it was a nearly valueless commodity before."

Breen scolds Dumas for "claiming a place" for plagiarism and citing Shakespeare and Moliere as examples: "They, indeed, were men of genius, while Dumas is little better than 'un habile arrangeur de la pensée d'autrui.'" Clemens notices that Breen has unwittingly granted the truth of Dumas' statement and writes: "Now here *you* are 'claiming a place for it' &c." [24]

On page 224, where Breen cites some of Pope's borrowings from other writers, Clemens writes, "The thought is nothing—it has occurred to everybody; so has every thought that is worth fame. The *expression* of it is the thing to applaud, and there Pope is best." Again, on page 236, where Breen parallels a passage by Gray with one by Milton, Clemens comments: "Here it is the thought rather than the language." On page 251 he writes of another passage quoted, "an old thought"; on page 253, "a common thought"; on pages 262 and 266, "An old thought—no details."

These marginal bickerings indicate that Clemens was more discriminating in his thinking about literary indebtedness than one might expect. With Pope, he realized that writers could be admired for expressing old ideas in a new way. He realized, too, that an author might make materials his own by adapting them to the fictional world he was creating. Clemens' attitude did not change over the years: at sixty-eight he endorsed the belief that "all our phrasings are spiritualized shadows cast multitudinously from our readings." [25]

The readings of Clemens that might cast such shadows were extensive. He believed that a turning point in his life had been his finding, at fifteen,

[24] Clemens' copy of the book is in *MTP*. Quotations © copyright 1960 by Mark Twain Co.

[25] Clemens is again rephrasing Holmes's letter of 1869, as he recalls it, but he completely agrees.

a page of a biography of Joan of Arc, since this had led to his learning how fascinating history was. During his *Wanderjahren* he was an avid reader, as a tramp printer in Philadelphia and New York, as a printer in Keokuk (where he read Dickens and Poe), as a river pilot, as a San Francisco reporter. Settled down in Hartford, still a lover of books and eager for culture, he had more chances than ever to enjoy this favorite pastime. "For years past," wrote Charles H. Clark in 1885, "he has been an industrious and extensive student in the broad field of general culture. He has a large library and a real familiarity with it, extending . . . into the literature of Germany and France." [26] Any careful study of Clemens' acquaintance with literature supports this claim.[27] Not surprisingly, literary echoes in *Tom Sawyer* are both varied and fairly numerous.

There is the grave-robbing scene in chapter ix. Wecter's search of Hannibal history has revealed no records of grave-robbing there, and Clemens' reminiscences mention no instances. But in a notebook of his for 1885, considering unusual instances of unfunny humorous characters in Charles Dickens, he mentions "the body-snatcher—Tale of 2 Cities." [28] Dickens had been popular since Clemens' boyhood, and evidence proves that Clemens had read his books from 1855 on. Eventually—the precise date is not known—*A Tale of Two Cities* (1859) became a favorite book.[29] In Book 2, chapter xiv, of that novel, a boy goes to bed, lies awake until the middle of the night, then sneaks from his house and goes to a graveyard. There, with horror, he watches three men rob a grave. Since exactly this sequence is followed by Tom, it is quite possible that the idea for the scene came from Dickens' novel.

In chapter xxv, after Tom and Huck have failed to find the hidden treasure: " 'Oh,' says Tom, '*I* know what the matter is! What a blamed lot of fools we are! You got to find out where the shadow of the tree falls at midnight, and that's where you dig!' " From his reading of Poe in Keokuk days or possibly from a later reading, the author here recalled—and burlesqued—the elaborate procedure used in "The Gold Bug" to find buried treasure.

Back in Clemens' youth, a great school of humorists had flourished in the old Southwest from whom he had learned important skills as a comic

[26] Charles H. Clark, "Mark Twain at Nook Farm (Hartford) and Elmira," *Critic*, VI (January 17, 1885), 26. See also Howells, *My Mark Twain* (New York, 1910), p. 15.

[27] The latest and most extensive is by Harold Aspiz, "Mark Twain's Reading—A Critical Study" (unpublished doctoral dissertation, University of California, Los Angeles, 1949).

[28] Notebook 19, TS p. 36, *MTP*.

[29] Aspiz, "Mark Twain's Reading," pp. 207-209.

writer.[30] A pioneer in the school, Augustus Baldwin Longstreet (1790-1870) was a Georgia lawyer who moved down the scale until he became a humorist and eventually a college president. His *Georgia Scenes* had appeared in Georgia in 1835, then in a more popular edition in New York in 1840, and had gone through eight additional printings by 1860. In 1880, jotting down names of humorous books he recalled, the humorist listed this book twice and Longstreet's pseudonym once; and as an old man he testified that he had known Longstreet's writings for a long time.[31] Longstreet's "Georgia Theatrics" tells at length how an imaginative youngster, with many ferocious cries and blows, felled a completely imaginary opponent. A paragraph in chapter xviii of *Tom Sawyer* tells how, when a fellow student has stolen his sweetheart, Tom has a similar theatrical rehearsal: ". . . he went through the motions of thrashing an imaginary boy—pummeling the air, and kicking and gouging. 'Oh, you do, do you? You holler 'nough, do you? Now, then, let that learn you!' And so the imaginary flogging was finished to his satisfaction." Since the humor and the situation are almost the same as in Longstreet, and since some of the language is close to Longstreet's, this appears to be one of Twain's literary shadows.

Elsewhere, he shows indebtedness to a Yankee humorist, B.P. Shillaber (1814-1890), whose magazine *The Carpet-Bag* the Hannibal *Journal* often quoted when Sam set type for it. Probably Sam contributed to this magazine his first published sketch. By 1870, Shillaber and Clemens had met, and Shillaber had published in the Boston *Post* a poem, "Congratulatory," following Clemens' marriage. *Roughing It* contains a mention of one Ballou's "Partingtonian fashion of loving and using big words for their own sakes, and independent of any bearing they might have upon the thought." The reference is to Shillaber's character in *Life and Sayings of Mrs. Partington* (1854) and *Mrs. Partington's Knitting Work* (1859)— a great user of malapropisms. Mrs. Partington has an uncanny resemblance to Aunt Polly: she looks like her (her portrait turns up as an illustration—presumably picturing Tom's aunt—in the first edition); she has the same enthusiasm for patent medicines; she is a Calvinist restrained from doing her duty by her tender heart. Like Aunt Polly (and unlike Jane Clemens), she is a widow who has taken charge of the rearing of an orphaned nephew, Ike.

[30] Franklin J. Meine, "Introduction," *Tall Tales of the Southwest* (New York, 1930); DeVoto, *Mark Twain's America* (Boston, 1932), pp. 79-98; Blair, *Native American Humor* (New York, 1937), pp. 153-158.
[31] Notebook 15, *MTP*; J. D. Wade, *Augustus Baldwin Longstreet* (New York, 1924), p. 168.

And Ike, like Tom, is full of mischief; but a character says of him, "Where there is no malice, mischief is no sin." Aunt Polly, in chapter xv, says of Tom: "he warn't *bad,* so to say, only mischievous . . . warn't any more responsible than a colt." Ike has many adventures similar to Tom's. While listening to his aunt's pious lectures, he swipes doughnuts. He misbehaves in church. ("You have been acting very bad in meeting," says his aunt, "and I declare I could hardly keep from boxing your ears in the midst of the lethargy.") He feigns sickness to avoid school. He plays tricks on cats. He pretends he is a pirate, drawing his inspiration from exactly the same source Tom uses—*The Black Avenger, or The Pirates of the Spanish Main.*[32]

Another probable influence was an extremely popular book by Thomas Bailey Aldrich, *The Story of a Bad Boy* (1869), with which Howells compared *Tom Sawyer* on reviewing it. After meeting Aldrich (and his wife) in 1871, Clemens saw him often. In 1908 he remembered that Aldrich's novel had a connection with *Tom Sawyer*—probably, Paine guesses, because the book came to his attention when "he began discussing his own boy story." Tom Bailey, Aldrich's hero and narrator, anticipates Tom Sawyer: he has a dull time at Sunday school, sneaks out of his bedroom window for night-time adventures, imitates the heroes of books which he has read, camps with other boys on an island where "we played we were . . . Spanish sailors." [33] Particularly interesting is the fact that shortly before *Boy's Manuscript,* Aldrich's novel recounts a love affair during the course of which Tom Bailey acts out a childish burlesque of sentimental lovesickness:

> I avoided my playmates. . . . I did not eat as much as was good for me. I took lonely walks. I brooded in solitude. . . . I used to lie in the grass and gloat over the amount and variety of mournful expressions I could throw into my features. . . . I no longer joined the boys on the playground at recess. I stayed at my desk reading some lugubrious volume. . . . A translation of The Sorrows of Werther fell into my hands . . . , and if I could have committed suicide without killing myself, I should certainly have done so. . . . In a quiet way I never enjoyed myself better in my life than when I was a Blighted Being.[34]

Clemens, having had childish love affairs of his own, drew upon memories of them when he wrote fiction about boys in love. But it seems likely that he learned some of the possibilities of such comedy and ac-

---

[32] For additional parallels see Blair, *Native American Humor,* pp. 150-152.
[33] *Writings of Thomas Bailey Aldrich* (Boston and New York, 1897), pp. 67-70, 75, 82, 59, 159-170.
[34] *Ibid.,* pp. 240-245.

quired details from Aldrich. Billy Rogers notes in his diary phenomena very similar to those in Aldrich:

> I don't care for apples, I don't care for molasses candy, swinging on the gate don't do me no good, and even sliding on the cellar door. . . . I said the world was a mean, sad place, and had nothing for me to love and care for in it—and life, life was only misery. It was then that it first came into my head to take my life . . . but then she would only be sorry for a little while . . . and I would be dead for always. I did not like that.[35]

Tom Sawyer suffers similarly, and like Aldrich's hero wishes for suicide without death:

> He no longer took an interest in war, nor even in piracy. . . . He put his hoop away, and his bat. . . . [chapter xii] The boy's soul was steeped in melancholy; his feelings were in happy accord with his surroundings. It seemed to him that life was but a trouble, at best, and he more than half envied Jimmy Hodges, so lately released. . . . If he only had a clean Sunday school record, he would be willing to go. . . . Ah, if he could only die *temporarily!* [chapter viii]

If, as I suggest, Twain learned from Aldrich how to picture Boy as Blighted Being, we owe him as well as Twain our thanks for these passages.

A number of writings allied to Shillaber's accounts of Ike and Aldrich's book influenced more than occasional incidents in *Tom Sawyer:* they provided the over-all structure (such as it is) of the novel. These were humorous pieces attacking fashionable serious juvenile fiction of the nineteenth century. In this moralizing fiction, two kinds of children clearly labelled "good" and "bad" appeared. Good children—Little Rollos, Little Evas, Alger boys came to good ends, and their creators urged readers to go and do likewise. Bad children, their foils, came to bad ends—the boy who played hooky, for instance, "grew up to be a very wicked man, and at last committed a murder"[36]—and their creators warned readers not to get into similar messes.

Beginning in the 1840's and well into the 1870's, at least a dozen popular humorists—a group usually antiromantic, antisentimental, and amoral —attacked these misrepresentations of youth by picturing boys in a "more realistic" fashion—as merely mischievous, irresponsible creatures who matured into normal adults. In the 1860's Henry Ward Beecher was at-

[35] *MTaW*, pp. 28, 36.

[36] The story, which appeared in a reader, is quoted by E. D. Branch in *The Sentimental Years* (New York, 1934), pp. 312-313. For other examples and documentation for the discussion in the rest of this section, see Walter Blair, "On the Structure of *Tom Sawyer,*" *Mod. Philol.,* XXXVII (August, 1939), 75-88.

tacking from his pulpit the "impossible boys, with incredible goodness," of fiction. "Boys," he said, "have a period of mischief much as they have measles and small-pox." And by the time of *Tom Sawyer,* many humorists had taken pot shots at the "Model Boy." Four in addition to Shillaber and Aldrich were George W. Harris of Tennessee, James M. Bailey of Connecticut, Robert J. Burdette of Iowa, and Charles B. Lewis of Michigan.

In the *Californian,* December 23, 1865, appeared "The Christmas Fireside. For Good Little Girls and Boys, by Grandfather Twain," the author's first contribution to this type of literature—later retitled "The Story of the Bad Little Boy Who Did Not Come to Grief." In a notebook in 1868 Twain wrote an unpublished sketch, "The Story of Mamie Grant, the Child-Missionary," deriding the stories about pious Sunday-school infants. In 1870 he wrote a companion piece to his first, "The Story of the Good Little Boy Who Did Not Prosper." These were burlesques in the mode—inverted fables. During his early months in Hartford, so his neighbor Charles Dudley Warner records, the humorist said facetiously, "I tried a Sunday-school book once; but I made the good boy end in the poorhouse, and the bad boy go to Congress." [37] A contemporary reviewer of *Tom Sawyer* in the San Francisco *Chronicle* said that it was similarly unorthodox: "Twain has run the traditional Sunday-school boy through his literary mangle . . . the skin of that strumous young pietist is now neatly tacked up to view on the Sunday-school door of today as a warning."

Tom Sawyer then is a humorous—though not burlesque—version of "The Story of a Bad Boy Who Did Not Come to Grief." Opening chapters show Tom stealing, lying, playing hooky, and fighting—proving that he is what juvenile fictionists would call a Bad Boy; but the author clearly admires him. Twain soon indicates his contempt and dislike for "the Model Boy of the village," pious Willie Mufferson, and for Tom's goody-goody half-brother Sid. Twain's preachment is that Tom is what a normal boy should be; his mischief is a harmless part of his maturing; and he will become a well-adjusted adult.

Accordingly, each of several lines of action begins with Tom's behaving in an irresponsible childish fashion and ends with an incident signifying his approach to responsible maturity. The love story begins with his fickle desertion of a former sweetheart and his ungainly attempts to win Becky; it ends with his chivalrously undergoing punishment for her and bravely helping her in the cave. The story of Tom and Muff Potter be-

[37] "Sixth Study," *Backlog Studies,* in *The Complete Writings of Charles Dudley Warner* (Hartford, 1904) , I, 249-250, originally published in May, 1872.

gins with the superstitious trip to the graveyard; it ends with Tom's defiance of boyish superstition and his courageous testimony in court. At
the end, in a conversation with Huck, Tom, though still a boy, is talking
very much like an adult.

The end of each line of action also departs from conventional patterns
in juvenile fiction. Tom and his companions, who have run away to
Jackson's Island, have played hooky, and have smoked (all vile sins in
Sunday-school stories), are greeted with cheers when they return. Tom
becomes a hero because he saves Potter, is compared with George Washington because he takes Becky's punishment, is lionized because he res-
cues Becky. To top it all, Tom and the even more disreputable Huck at
the end acquire a fortune such as traditionally had been reserved only
for the best of Alger's little heroes.

Literary influences thus shaped both incidents and the over-all pattern
of *Tom Sawyer.*

More important, of course, than Twain's literary dependence was his
adaptation of "borrowed" materials into appropriate parts of a narrative
which, regardless of its origins, is all of a piece. More than a little artistic
skill was required to give such diverse materials the color of Twain's personality and the tone of this book, and to intertwine diverse but similar
stories throughout the novel.

Still, Twain's art was probably more noteworthy in individual episodes,
many of which readers remember long after the rest of the book has been
forgotten. His handling of several of these was the result of "literary rehearsals" like those preparatory for the description of Hannibal in "Old
Times."

An instance is the St. Petersburg Sunday-school services in chapter iv.
As far back as 1856, young Sam Clemens had written a comic essay for a
girl friend, Annie Taylor, describing how a swarm of bugs, attracted by
the light overhead, gathered around his printing case one night. By degrees—in accordance with the tall-tale tradition of Southwestern humor—
these insects were "humanized" until they became a religious mass meeting "presided over by a venerable beetle" perched on a lock of Sam's
hair, "while innumerable lesser dignitaries . . . clustered around . . .
keeping order . . . endeavoring to attract attention . . . to their own
importance by industriously grating their teeth." [38] In 1873, in chapter liii
of *The Gilded Age,* telling about Senator Dilworthy's electioneering in
the Cattleville Sunday-school, the author remarked similar phenomena
and added others, including Dilworthy's pious speech to the children.

[38] Letter to Annie Taylor, May 25 [1856], Kansas City *Star Mag.,* March 21, 1926.

The *Tom Sawyer* chapter goes over the same ground for a third time, with its superintendent, librarian, teachers, pupils, and visitor (Judge Thatcher here) all "showing off" before the judge delivers his version of the visiting celebrity's speech. The humorist therefore may be said to have practiced twice for the final—and best—rendition of the scene.

Chapter v, the church services which follow, had been similarly rehearsed in a letter of 1871 which Clemens wrote to Livy from Paris, Illinois, after a service there—a compounding of recent notations with some from the past, since "It was as if twenty-five years had fallen away . . . and I was a lad of eleven again in Missouri village church." [39] The second rendition combines details of the practice run with new ones appropriate to the novel.

Similarly a paragraph in a newspaper letter dated April 16, 1867, on Sam Clemens' boyhood experience as a member of Hannibal's Cadets of Temperance was a rehearsal for a better paragraph in chapter xxii ascribing the same experience to Tom.

Another instance is chapter xxi, Examination Day in Tom's school. On January 14, 1864, the author had written for the *Territorial Enterprise* a story about exercises in Miss Clapp's school in Carson City, Nevada. This contained descriptions of recitations by students and a spelling bee, and it quoted a childish composition which was read and commented upon by others.[40] In August, 1868, he sent *Alta California* an account of a burlesque of such exercises staged aboard the *Montana* on a recent ocean voyage. Dressed in boys' costumes, the men had recited poems, declaimed orations; and the humorist had read a composition, "The Cow." The program was reproduced and performances were described.[41] Before writing the chapter in his novel, therefore, he had twice set down versions of the scene. To see how he retained some details, deleted others, and added still others is to see the scene moving by degrees to its final perfection. It is noteworthy, too, that a visit to a similar exhibition in a young ladies' academy, probably in 1870 or 1871, suggested some of the new matter—the compositions read by several young ladies.[42]

Boy's Manuscript is an earlier handling of incidents in *Tom Sawyer.* In it, as DeVoto has noticed,

[39] *My Father Mark Twain* (New York, 1931), p. 9. The account, somewhat abbreviated and amended, is on pp. 9-12.

[40] *Mark Twain of the Enterprise,* ed. Henry Nash Smith with the assistance of Frederick Anderson (Berkeley and Los Angeles, 1957), pp. 134-138.

[41] Reprinted in *The Twainian,* November-December 1948, p. 5.

[42] Letter to Miss Noyes dated Hartford, February 23, 1882: "The Chapter in *Tom Sawyer* which you refer to was suggested by that mournful experience . . . in your school." *MTP,* © copyright 1960 by Mark Twain Co.

a heroine named Amy . . . inflicts on the hero the same agonies and ec-
stasies that Becky Thatcher was to inflict on Tom. Billy Rogers makes love
to her in almost the same terms Tom uses. . . . Like Tom also he does
battle for her with a boy called Wart Hopkins. . . .

When we first meet Wart Hopkins he is on his way back from a cross-
roads where he has buried a bean that has blood on it: from this seed the
central action of *Tom Sawyer* was to grow. Before this he has been in the
circus business with Billy, and that too was to have its part in the book, together with the sham battle, the tooth, the sore toe, and the posturing and
parading before Amy's house. More striking is the louse which is tormented
on Bill Bowen's desk. It has become a more seemly tick when we see it again
in *Tom Sawyer* and Bill Bowen . . . has become Joe Harper, but the scene
is duplicated almost exactly.[43]

Also, Paine believes—though DeVoto disagrees—that there was another
rehearsal of much of the novel in the form of a play.

Nor were written rehearsals the only kind. In 1872 Clemens says, in
London, "I told Irving and Wills, the playwright, about the whitewashing of the fence by Tom Sawyer, and thereby captured on cheap terms
a chapter; for I wrote it out when I got back to the hotel while it was
fresh in my mind." [44] And on the opening manuscript page of chapter i
Twain wrote: "Put in thing from Boy-lecture." These two bits of evidence
suggest that parts of the book, at least, were orally rehearsed.

Passages rehearsed in those ways were for the most part based upon
memories of actual happenings. Because of such reworkings, these parts
of the book may have been the ones he remembered best. This may explain his frequent claims that most adventures in the novel "really occurred." As a result of their authenticity and the practiced art which
shaped them, these memorable episodes contribute much to the impression the book gives of being realistic.

Clearly, though, the merits of the book did not result from a simple
recording of remembered facts. Even actual happenings—a study of the
rehearsals makes evident—were transmuted into new things. The nostalgic mood, created by the era and by the life the author was living as he
wrote, was an important ingredient. So was the fear, a recollection from
childhood, which was also part of the mood. DeVoto's point is valid:
"Mark is nowhere truer to us, to himself, or to childhood than in the
dread which holds this idyl enclosed." [45] The humorist's reading, past

[43] *MTaW*, pp. 6-7.
[44] Dictation August 19, 1907, *Autobiography, MTP*, © copyright 1960 by Mark Twain
Co. This version apparently was written in the first person and was incorporated with
changes to the third person in the manuscript at Georgetown.
[45] *Portable Mark Twain* (New York, 1946), p. 33.

and present, contributed episodes, an over-all scheme, and a theme which concerned the true nature of boyhood. And parts of the book and the book as a whole benefited greatly from his skill as an artist. During the composition of *Tom Sawyer* the author, still a novice at fiction writing, had found material congenial to him. He had learned the advantage of pigeon-holing a manuscript while "his tank filled up again." He had learned how to utilize his memories to suit his purposes. These discoveries would be important when he embarked shortly upon the writing of a sequel.

A Sound Heart and a Deformed Conscience

by Henry Nash Smith

I

In writing *Huckleberry Finn* Mark Twain found a way to organize into a larger structure the insights that earlier humorists had recorded in their brief anecdotes.[1] This technical accomplishment was of course inseparable from the process of discovering new meanings in his material. His development as a writer was a dialectic interplay in which the reach of his imagination imposed a constant strain on his technical resources, and innovations of method in turn opened up new vistas before his imagination.

The dialectic process is particularly striking in the gestation of *Huckleberry Finn*. The use of Huck as a narrative persona, with the consequent elimination of the author as an intruding presence in the story, resolved the difficulties about point of view and style that had been so conspicuous in the earlier books. But turning the story over to Huck brought into view previously unsuspected literary potentialities in the vernacular perspective, particularly the possibility of using vernacular speech for serious purposes and of transforming the vernacular narrator from a mere persona into a character with human depth. Mark Twain's response to the challenge made *Huckleberry Finn* the greatest of his books and one of the two or three acknowledged masterpieces of American literature. Yet this triumph created a new technical problem to which there was no solution; for what had begun as a comic story developed incipiently tragic implications contradicting the premises of comedy.

Huckleberry Finn thus contains three main elements. The most con-

[1] This essay makes constant use of Walter Blair's impressive *Mark Twain & Huck Finn* (Berkeley, 1960). But my reading of *Huckleberry Finn* has of course been influenced also by other books and articles. I should mention particularly chapter 15 in Daniel G. Hoffman's *Form and Fable in American Fiction* (New York, 1961), which deals expertly with the folklore in the novel.

spicuous is the story of Huck's and Jim's adventures in their flight toward freedom. Jim is running away from actual slavery, Huck from the cruelty of his father, from the well-intentioned "sivilizing" efforts of Miss Watson and the Widow Douglas, from respectability and routine in general. The second element in the novel is social satire of the towns along the river. The satire is often transcendently funny, especially in episodes involving the rascally Duke and King, but it can also deal in appalling violence, as in the Grangerford-Shepherdson feud or Colonel Sherburn's murder of the helpless Boggs. The third major element in the book is the developing characterization of Huck.

All three elements must have been present to Mark Twain's mind in some sense from the beginning, for much of the book's greatness lies in its basic coherence, the complex interrelation of its parts. Nevertheless, the intensive study devoted to it in recent years, particularly Walter Blair's establishment of the chronology of its composition[2], has demonstrated that Mark Twain's search for a structure capable of doing justice to his conceptions of theme and character passed through several stages. He did not see clearly where he was going when he began to write, and we can observe him in the act of making discoveries both in meaning and in method as he goes along.

The narrative tends to increase in depth as it moves from the adventure story of the early chapters into the social satire of the long middle section, and thence to the ultimate psychological penetration of Huck's character in the moral crisis of Chapter 31. Since the crisis is brought on by the shock of the definitive failure of Huck's effort to help Jim, it marks the real end of the quest for freedom. The perplexing final sequence on the Phelps plantation is best regarded as a maneuver by which Mark Twain beats his way back from incipient tragedy to the comic resolution called for by the original conception of the story.

II

Huck's and Jim's flight from St. Petersburg obviously translates into action the theme of vernacular protest. The fact that they have no means of fighting back against the forces that threaten them but can only run away is accounted for in part by the conventions of backwoods humor, in which the inferior social status of the vernacular character placed him in an ostensibly weak position. But it also reflects Mark Twain's awareness of his own lack of firm ground to stand on in challenging the established system of values.

[2] "When Was *Huckleberry Finn* Written?" *American Literature* 30:1-25 (March 1958).

Huck's and Jim's defenselessness foreshadows the outcome of their efforts to escape. They cannot finally succeed. To be sure, in a superficial sense they do succeed; at the end of the book Jim is technically free and Huck still has the power to light out for the Territory. But Jim's freedom has been brought about by such an implausible device that we do not believe in it. Who can imagine the scene in which Miss Watson decides to liberate him? What were her motives? Mark Twain finesses the problem by placing this crucial event far offstage and telling us nothing about it beyond the bare fact he needs to resolve his plot. And the notion that a fourteen-year-old boy could make good his escape beyond the frontier is equally unconvincing. The writer himself did not take it seriously. In an unpublished sequel to *Huckleberry Finn* called "Huck Finn and Tom Sawyer among the Indians," which he began soon after he finished the novel, Aunt Sally takes the boys and Jim back to Hannibal and then to western Missouri for a visit "with some of her relations on a hemp farm out there." Here Tom revives the plan mentioned near the end of *Huckleberry Finn:* he "was dead set on having us run off, some night, and cut for the Injun country and go for adventures." Huck says, however, that he and Jim "kind of hung fire. Plenty to eat and nothing to do. We was very well satisfied." Only after an extended debate can Tom persuade them to set out with him. Their expedition falls into the stereotyped pattern of Wild West stories of travel out the Oregon Trail, makes a few gibes at Cooper's romanticized Indians, and breaks off.[3]

The difficulty of imagining a successful outcome for Huck's and Jim's quest had troubled Mark Twain almost from the beginning of his work on the book. After writing the first section in 1876 he laid aside his manuscript near the end of Chapter 16.[4] The narrative plan with which he had impulsively begun had run into difficulties. When Huck and Jim shove off from Jackson's Island on their section of a lumber raft (at the end of Chapter 11) they do so in haste, to escape the immediate danger of the slave hunters Huck has learned about from Mrs. Loftus. No long-range plan is mentioned until the beginning of Chapter 15, when Huck says that at Cairo they intended to "sell the raft and get on a steamboat and go way up the Ohio amongst the free states, and then be out of trouble." [5] But they drift past Cairo in the fog, and a substitute plan of making their way back up to the mouth of the Ohio in their canoe is frustrated when the canoe disappears while they are sleeping: "we talked

[3] The story is preserved in the form of galley proof of type set by the Paige machine, DV 303, Mark Twain Papers.
[4] *Mark Twain & Huck Finn,* p. 151.
[5] *Writings* (Definitive Edition, New York, 1922-25), XIII, 112.

about what we better do, and found there warn't no way but just to go along down with the raft till we got a chance to buy a canoe to go back in." [6] Drifting downstream with the current, however, could not be reconciled with the plan to free Jim by transporting him up the Ohio; hence the temporary abandonment of the story.

III

When Mark Twain took up his manuscript again in 1879, after an interval of three years, he had decided upon a different plan for the narrative. Instead of concentrating on the story of Huck's and Jim's escape, he now launched into a satiric description of the society of the prewar South. Huck was essential to this purpose, for Mark Twain meant to view his subject ironically through Huck's eyes. But Jim was more or less superfluous. During Chapters 17 and 18, devoted to the Grangerford household and the feud, Jim has disappeared from the story. Mark Twain had apparently not yet found a way to combine social satire with the narrative scheme of Huck's and Jim's journey on the raft.

While he was writing his chapter about the feud, however, he thought of a plausible device to keep Huck and Jim floating southward while he continued his panoramic survey of the towns along the river. The device was the introduction of the Duke and the King. In Chapter 19 they come aboard the raft, take charge at once, and hold Huck and Jim in virtual captivity. In this fashion the narrative can preserve the over-all form of a journey down the river while providing ample opportunity for satire when Huck accompanies the two rascals on their forays ashore. But only the outward form of the journey is retained. Its meaning has changed, for Huck's and Jim's quest for freedom has in effect come to an end. Jim is physically present but he assumes an entirely passive role, and is hidden with the raft for considerable periods. Huck is also essentially passive; his function now is that of an observer. Mark Twain postpones acknowledging that the quest for freedom has failed, but the issue will have to be faced eventually.

The satire of the towns along the banks insists again and again that the dominant culture is decadent and perverted. Traditional values have gone to seed. The inhabitants can hardly be said to live a conscious life of their own; their actions, their thoughts, even their emotions are controlled by an outworn and debased Calvinism, and by a residue of the eighteenth

[6] *Writings*, XIII, 130.

century cult of sensibility. With few exceptions they are mere bundles of tropisms, at the mercy of scoundrels like the Duke and the King who know how to exploit their prejudices and delusions.

The falseness of the prevalent values finds expression in an almost universal tendency of the townspeople to make spurious claims to status through self-dramatization. Mark Twain has been concerned with this topic from the beginning of the book. Chapter 1 deals with Tom Sawyer's plan to start a band of robbers which Huck will be allowed to join only if he will "go back to the widow and be respectable";[7] and we also hear about Miss Watson's mercenary conception of prayer. In Chapter 2 Jim interprets Tom's prank of hanging his hat on the limb of a tree while he is asleep as evidence that he has been bewitched. He "was most ruined for a servant, because he got stuck up on account of having seen the devil and been rode by witches." [8] Presently we witness the ritual by which Pap Finn is to be redeemed from drunkenness. When his benefactor gives him a lecture on temperance,

> the old man cried, and said he'd been a fool, and fooled away his life; but now he was a-going to turn over a new leaf and be a man nobody wouldn't be ashamed of, and he hoped the judge would help him and not look down on him. The judge said he could hug him for them words; so *he* cried, and his wife she cried again; pap said he'd been a man that had always been misunderstood before, and the judge said he believed it. The old man said that what a man wanted that was down was sympathy, and the judge said it was so; so they cried again.[9]

As comic relief for the feud that provides a way of life for the male Grangerfords Mark Twain dwells lovingly on Emmeline Grangerford's pretensions to culture—her paintings with the fetching titles and the ambitious "Ode to Stephen Dowling Bots, Dec'd.," its pathos hopelessly flawed by the crudities showing through like the chalk beneath the enameled surface of the artificial fruit in the parlor: "His spirit was gone for to sport aloft/In the realms of the good and great." [10]

The Duke and the King personify the theme of fraudulent role-taking. These rogues are not even given names apart from the wildly improbable identities they assume in order to dominate Huck and Jim. The Duke's poses have a literary cast, perhaps because of the scraps of bombast he remembers from his experience as an actor. The illiterate King has "done considerable in the doctoring way," but when we see him at work it is mainly at preaching, "workin' camp-meetin's, and missionaryin'

[7] *Writings*, XIII, 2.   [8] *Writings*, XIII, 9.   [9] *Writings*, XIII, 30.   [10] *Writings*, XIII, 143.

around." [11] Pretended or misguided piety and other perversions of Christianity obviously head the list of counts in Mark Twain's indictment of the prewar South. And properly: for it is of course religion that stands at the center of the system of values in the society of this fictive world and by implication in all societies. His revulsion, expressed through Huck, reaches its highest pitch in the scene where the King delivers his masterpiece of "soul-butter and hogwash" for the benefit of the late Peter Wilks's fellow townsmen:

> By and by the king he gets up and comes forward a little, and works himself up and slobbers out a speech, all full of tears and flapdoodle, about its being a sore trial for him and his poor brother to lose the diseased, and to miss seeing diseased alive after the long journey of four thousand mile, but it's a trial that's sweetened and sanctified to us by this dear sympathy and these holy tears, and so he thanks them out of his heart and out of his brother's heart, because out of their mouths they can't, words being too weak and cold, and all that kind of rot and slush, till it was just sickening; and then he blubbers out a pious goody-goody Amen, and turns himself loose and goes to crying fit to bust.[12]

IV

Huck is revolted by the King's hypocrisy: "I never see anything so disgusting." He has had a similar reaction to the brutality of the feud: "It made me so sick I most fell out of the tree." [13] In describing such scenes he speaks as moral man viewing an immoral society, an observer who is himself free of the vices and even the weaknesses he describes. Mark Twain's satiric method requires that Huck be a mask for the writer, not a fully developed character. The method has great ironic force, and is in itself a technical landmark in the history of American fiction, but it prevents Mark Twain from doing full justice to Huck as a person in his own right, capable of mistakes in perception and judgment, troubled by doubts and conflicting impulses.

Even in the chapters written during the original burst of composition in 1876 the character of Huck is shown to have depths and complexities not relevant to the immediate context. Huck's and Jim's journey down the river begins simply as a flight from physical danger; and the first episodes of the voyage have little bearing on the novelistic possibilities in the strange comradeship between outcast boy and escaped slave. But in Chapter 15, when Huck plays a prank on Jim by persuading him that the separation in the fog was only a dream, Jim's dignified and moving rebuke

---

[11] *Writings*, XIII, 169.   [12] *Writings*, XIII, 227-228.   [13] *Writings*, XIII, 160.

suddenly opens up a new dimension in the relation. Huck's humble apology is striking evidence of growth in moral insight. It leads naturally to the next chapter in which Mark Twain causes Huck to face up for the first time to the fact that he is helping a slave to escape. It is as if the writer himself were discovering unsuspected meanings in what he had thought of as a story of picaresque adventure. The incipient contradiction between narrative plan and increasing depth in Huck's character must have been as disconcerting to Mark Twain as the difficulty of finding a way to account for Huck's and Jim's continuing southward past the mouth of the Ohio. It was doubtless the convergence of the two problems that led him to put aside the manuscript near the end of Chapter 16.[14]

The introduction of the Duke and the King not only took care of the awkwardness in the plot but also allowed Mark Twain to postpone the exploration of Huck's moral dilemma. If he is not a free agent he is not responsible for what happens and is spared the agonies of choice. Throughout the long middle section, while he is primarily an observer, he is free of inner conflict because he is endowed by implication with Mark Twain's own unambiguous attitude toward the fraud and folly he witnesses.

In Chapter 31, however, Huck escapes from his captors and faces once again the responsibility for deciding on a course of action. His situation is much more desperate than it had been at the time of his first struggle with his conscience. The raft has borne Jim hundreds of miles downstream from the pathway of escape and the King has turned him over to Silas Phelps as a runaway slave.[15] The quest for freedom has "all come to nothing, everything all busted up and ruined." Huck thinks of notifying Miss Watson where Jim is, since if he must be a slave he would be better off "at home where his family was." But then Huck realizes that Miss Watson would probably sell Jim down the river as a punishment for running away. Furthermore, Huck himself would be denounced by everyone for his part in the affair. In this fashion his mind comes back once again to the unparalleled wickedness of acting as accomplice in a slave's escape.

The account of Huck's mental struggle in the next two or three pages is the emotional climax of the story. It draws together the theme of flight

---

[14] In *Mark Twain and Southwestern Humor* (Boston, 1959, pp. 216-219) Kenneth Lynn points out that Mark Twain's dawning recognition of moral depth in Huck's character created a difficulty for him at this point. Mr. Lynn's analysis has led me to modify my earlier view of the problem of plot construction in the novel.

[15] *Writings*, XIII, 294.

from bondage and the social satire of the middle section, for Huck is
trying to work himself clear of the perverted value system of St. Petersburg. Both adventure story and satire, however, are now subordinate to
an exploration of Huck's psyche which is the ultimate achievement of the
book. The issue is identical with that of the first moral crisis, but the later
passage is much more intense and richer in implication. The differences
appear clearly if the two crises are compared in detail.

In Chapter 16 Huck is startled into a realization of his predicament
when he hears Jim, on the lookout for Cairo at the mouth of the Ohio,
declare that "he'd be a free man the minute he seen it, but if he missed it
he'd be in a slave country again and no more show for freedom." Huck
says: "I begun to get it through my head that he *was* most free—and who
was to blame for it? Why, *me.* I couldn't get that out of my conscience,
no how nor no way." He dramatizes his inner debate by quoting the
words in which his conscience denounces him: "What had poor Miss
Watson done to you that you could see her nigger go off right under your
eyes and never say one single word? What did that poor old woman do
to you that you could treat her so mean? Why, she tried to learn you your
book, she tried to learn you your manners, she tried to be good to you
every way she knowed how. *That's* what she done." The counterargument
is provided by Jim, who seems to guess what is passing through Huck's
mind and does what he can to invoke the force of friendship and gratitude: "Pooty soon I'll be a-shout'n' for joy, en I'll say, it's all on accounts
o' Huck; I's a free man, en I couldn't ever ben free ef it hadn' ben for
Huck; Huck done it. Jim won't ever forgit you, Huck; you's de bes' fren'
Jim's ever had; en you's de *only* fren' ole Jim's got now." Huck nevertheless sets out for the shore in the canoe "all in a sweat to tell on" Jim, but
when he is intercepted by the two slave hunters in a skiff he suddenly
contrives a cunning device to ward them off. We are given no details
about how his inner conflict was resolved.[16]

In the later crisis Huck provides a much more circumstantial account
of what passes through his mind. He is now quite alone; the outcome of
the debate is not affected by any stimulus from the outside. It is the memory of Jim's kindness and goodness rather than Jim's actual voice that
impels Huck to defy his conscience: "I see Jim before me all the time:
in the day and in the night-time, sometimes moonlight, sometimes storms,
and we a-floating along, talking and singing and laughing." [17] The most
striking feature of this later crisis is the fact that Huck's conscience, which

[16] *Writings,* XIII, 122-124.   [17] *Writings,* XIII, 296.

formerly had employed only secular arguments, now deals heavily in religious cant:

> At last, when it hit me all of a sudden that here was the plain hand of Providence slapping me in the face and letting me know my wickedness was being watched all the time from up there in heaven, whilst I was stealing a poor old woman's nigger that hadn't ever done me no harm, and now was showing me there's One that's always on the lookout, and ain't a-going to allow no such miserable doings to go only just so fur and no further, I most dropped in my tracks I was so scared.[18]

In the earlier debate the voice of Huck's conscience is quoted directly, but the bulk of the later exhortation is reported in indirect discourse. This apparently simple change in method has remarkable consequences. According to the conventions of first-person narrative, the narrator functions as a neutral medium in reporting dialogue. He remembers the speeches of other characters but they pass through his mind without affecting him. When Huck's conscience speaks within quotation marks it is in effect a character in the story, and he is not responsible for what it says. But when he paraphrases the admonitions of his conscience they are incorporated into his own discourse. Thus although Huck is obviously remembering the bits of theological jargon from sermons justifying slavery, they have become a part of his vocabulary.

The device of having Huck paraphrase rather than quote the voice of conscience may have been suggested to Mark Twain by a discovery he made in revising Huck's report of the King's address to the mourners in the Wilks parlor (Chapter 25).[19] The manuscript version of the passage shows that the King's remarks were composed as a direct quotation, but in the published text they have been put, with a minimum of verbal change, into indirect discourse. The removal of the barrier of quotation marks brings Huck into much more intimate contact with the King's "rot and slush" despite the fact that the paraphrase quivers with disapproval. The voice of conscience speaks in the precise accents of the King but Huck is now completely uncritical. He does not question its moral authority; it is morality personified. The greater subtlety of the later passage illustrates the difference between the necessarily shallow characterization of Huck while he was being used merely as a narrative persona, and the profound insight which Mark Twain eventually brought to bear on his protagonist.

The recognition of complexity in Huck's character enabled Mark Twain

---

[18] *Writings*, XIII, 294-295.
[19] The revision of this passage was called to my attention by Walter Blair.

to do full justice to the conflict between vernacular values and the dominant culture. By situating in a single consciousness both the perverted moral code of a society built on slavery and the vernacular commitment to freedom and spontaneity, he was able to represent the opposed perspectives as alternative modes of experience for the same character. In this way he gets rid of the confusions surrounding the pronoun "I" in the earlier books, where it sometimes designates the author speaking in his own person, sometimes an entirely distinct fictional character. Furthermore, the insight that enabled him to recognize the conflict between accepted values and vernacular protest as a struggle within a single mind does justice to its moral depth, whereas the device he had used earlier—in *The Innocents Abroad,* for example—of identifying the two perspectives with separate characters had flattened the issue out into melodrama. The satire of a decadent slaveholding society gains immensely in force when Mark Twain demonstrates that even the outcast Huck has been in part perverted by it. Huck's conscience is simply the attitudes he has taken over from his environment. What is still sound in him is an impulse from the deepest level of his personality that struggles against the overlay of prejudice and false valuation imposed on all members of the society in the name of religion, morality, law, and refinement.

Finally, it should be pointed out that the conflict in Huck between generous impulse and false belief is depicted by means of a contrast between colloquial and exalted styles. In moments of crisis his conscience addresses him in the language of the dominant culture, a tawdry and faded effort at a high style that is the rhetorical equivalent of the ornaments in the Grangerford parlor. Yet speaking in dialect does not in itself imply moral authority. By every external criterion the King is as much a vernacular character as Huck. The conflict in which Huck is involved is not that of a lower against an upper class or of an alienated fringe of outcasts against a cultivated elite. It is not the issue of frontier West versus genteel East, or of backwoods versus metropolis, but of fidelity to the uncoerced self versus the blurring of attitudes caused by social conformity, by the effort to achieve status or power through exhibiting the approved forms of sensibility.

The exploration of Huck's personality carried Mark Twain beyond satire and even beyond his statement of a vernacular protest against the dominant culture into essentially novelistic modes of writing. Some of the passages he composed when he got out beyond his polemic framework challenge comparison with the greatest achievements in the world's fiction.

The most obvious of Mark Twain's discoveries on the deeper levels of Huck's psyche is the boy's capacity for love. The quality of the emotion is defined in action by his decision to sacrifice himself for Jim, just as Jim attains an impressive dignity when he refuses to escape at the cost of deserting the wounded Tom. Projected into the natural setting, the love of the protagonists for each other becomes the unforgettable beauty of the river when they are allowed to be alone together. It is always summer, and the forces of nature cherish them. From the refuge of the cave on Jackson's Island the thunderstorm is an exhilarating spectacle; Huck's description of it is only less poetic than his description of the dawn which he and Jim witness as they sit half-submerged on the sandy bottom.[20]

Yet if Mark Twain had allowed these passages to stand without qualification as a symbolic account of Huck's emotions he would have undercut the complexity of characterization implied in his recognition of Huck's inner conflict of loyalties. Instead, he uses the natural setting to render a wide range of feelings and motives. The fog that separates the boy from Jim for a time is an externalization of his impulse to deceive Jim by a Tow Sawyerish practical joke. Similarly Jim's snake bite, the only injury suffered by either of the companions from a natural source, is the result of another prank played by Huck before he has learned what friends owe one another.[21]

Still darker aspects of Huck's inner life are projected into the natural setting in the form of ghosts, omens, portents of disaster—the body of superstition that is so conspicuous in Huck's and Jim's world. At the end of Chapter 1 Huck is sitting alone at night by his open window in the Widow Douglas' house:

> I felt so lonesome I most wished I was dead. The stars were shining, and the leaves rustled in the woods ever so mournful; and I heard an owl, away off, who-whooing about somebody that was dead, and a whippowill and a dog crying about somebody that was going to die; and the wind was trying to whisper something to me, and I couldn't make out what it was, and so it made the cold shivers run over me. Then away out in the woods I heard that kind of a sound that a ghost makes when it wants to tell about something that's on its mind and can't make itself understood, and so can't rest easy in its grave, and has to go about that way every night grieving. I got so downhearted and scared I did wish I had some company.[22]

The whimpering ghost with something incommunicable on its mind and Huck's cold shivers suggest a burden of guilt and anxiety that is

---

[20] The thunderstorm: *Writings*, XIII, 67-68; dawn on the river: XIII, 163-165.
[21] The fog: *Writings*, XIII, 112-116; the snake bite: XIII, 73-74.
[22] *Writings*, XIII, 4.

perhaps the punishment he inflicts on himself for defying the mores of St. Petersburg. Whatever the source of these sinister images, they develop the characterization of Huck beyond the needs of the plot. The narrator whose stream of consciousness is recorded here is much more than the innocent protagonist of the pastoral idyl of the raft, more than an ignorant boy who resists being civilized. The vernacular persona is an essentially comic figure; the character we glimpse in Huck's meditation is potentially tragic. Mark Twain's discoveries in the buried strata of Huck's mind point in the same direction as does his intuitive recognition that Huck's and Jim's quest for freedom must end in failure.

A melancholy if not exactly tragic strain in Huck is revealed also by the fictitious autobiographies with which he so often gets himself out of tight places. Like the protocols of a thematic apperception test, they are improvisations on the basis of minimal clues. Huck's inventions are necessary to account for his anomalous situation as a fourteen-year-old boy alone on the river with a Negro man, but they are often carried beyond the demands of utility for sheer love of fable-making. Their luxuriant detail, and the fact that Huck's hearers are usually (although not always) taken in, lend a comic coloring to these inventions, which are authentically in the tradition of the tall tale. But their total effect is somber. When Huck plans his escape from Pap in Chapter 7, he does so by imagining his own death and planting clues which convince everyone in St. Petersburg, including Tom Sawyer, that he has been murdered. In the crisis of Chapter 16 his heightened emotion leads him to produce for the benefit of the slave hunters a harrowing tale to the effect that his father and mother and sister are suffering from smallpox on a raft adrift in mid-river, and he is unable to tow the raft ashore. The slave hunters are so touched by the story that they give him forty dollars and careful instructions about how to seek help—farther downstream. Huck tells the Grangerfords "how pap and me and all the family was living on a little farm down at the bottom of Arkansaw, and my sister Mary Ann run off and got married and never was heard of no more, and Bill went to hunt them and he warn't heard of no more, and Tom and Mort died, and then there warn't nobody but just me and pap left, and he was just trimmed down to nothing, on account of his troubles; so when he died I took what there was left, because the farm didn't belong to us, and started up the river, deck passage, and fell overboard." [23]

[23] Huck's planting of false clues: *Writings*, XIII, 45-47; deception of the slave hunters: XIII, 125-126; deception of the Grangerfords: XIII, 137-138.

V

It has become a commonplace of criticism that the drastic shift in tone in the last section of *Huckleberry Finn,* from Chapter 31 to the end, poses a problem of interpretation. The drifting raft has reached Arkansas, and the King and the Duke have delivered Jim back into captivity. They make their exit early in the sequence, tarred and feathered as punishment for one more effort to work the "Royal Nonesuch" trick. . . .

At this point in the story Mark Twain was obliged to admit finally to himself that Huck's and Jim's journey down the river could not be imagined as leading to freedom for either of them. Because of the symbolic meaning the journey had taken on for him, the recognition was more than a perception of difficulty in contriving a plausible ending for the book. He had found a solution to the technical problem that satisfied him, if one is to judge from his evident zest in the complicated pranks of Tom Sawyer that occupy the last ten chapters. But in order to write these chapters he had to abandon the compelling image of the happiness of Huck and Jim on the raft and thus to acknowledge that the vernacular values embodied in his story were mere figments of the imagination, not capable of being reconciled with social reality. To be sure, he had been half-aware from the beginning that the quest of his protagonists was doomed. Huck had repeatedly appeared in the role of a Teiresias powerless to prevent the deceptions and brutalities he was compelled to witness. Yet Providence had always put the right words in his mouth when the time came, and by innocent guile he had extricated himself and Jim from danger after danger. Now the drifting had come to an end.

At an earlier impasse in the plot Mark Twain had shattered the raft under the paddle wheel of a steamboat.[24] He now destroys it again, symbolically, by revealing that Huck's and Jim's journey, with all its anxieties, has been pointless. Tom Sawyer is bearer of the news that Jim has been freed in Miss Watson's will. Tom withholds the information, however, in order to trick Huck and Jim into the meaningless game of an Evasion that makes the word (borrowed from Dumas) into a devastating pun. Tom takes control and Huck becomes once again a subordinate carrying out orders. As if to signal the change of perspective and the shift in his own identification, Mark Twain gives Huck Tom's name through an improbable mistake on the part of Aunt Sally Phelps. We can hardly fail to perceive the weight of the author's feeling in Huck's statement on

---

[24] *Mark Twain & Huck Finn,* p. 151.

this occasion: "it was like being born again, I was so glad to find out who I was." [25] Mark Twain has found out who he must be in order to end his book: he must be Tom.

In more abstract terms, he must withdraw from his imaginative participation in Huck's and Jim's quest for freedom. If the story was to be stripped of its tragic implications, Tom's perspective was the logical one to adopt because his intensely conventional sense of values made him impervious to the moral significance of the journey on the raft. Huck can hardly believe that Tom would collaborate in the crime of helping a runaway slave, and Huck is right. Tom merely devises charades involving a man who is already in a technical sense free. The consequences of the shift in point of view are strikingly evident in the treatment of Jim, who is subjected to farcical indignities. This is disturbing to the reader who has seen Jim take on moral and emotional stature, but it is necessary if everything is to be forced back into the framework of comedy. Mark Twain's portrayal of Huck and Jim as complex characters has carried him beyond the limits of his original plan: we must not forget that the literary ancestry of the book is to be found in backwoods humor. As Huck approaches the Phelps plantation the writer has on his hands a hybrid—a comic story in which the protagonists have acquired something like tragic depth.

In deciding to end the book with the description of Tom's unnecessary contrivances for rescuing Jim, Mark Twain was certain to produce an anticlimax. But he was a great comic writer, able to score local triumphs in the most unlikely circumstances. The last chapters have a number of brilliant touches—the slave who carries the witch pie to Jim, Aunt Sally's trouble in counting her spoons, Uncle Silas and the ratholes, the unforgettable Sister Hotchkiss.[26] Even Tom's horseplay would be amusing if it were not spun out to such length and if we were not asked to accept it as the conclusion of *Huckleberry Finn*. Although Jim is reduced to the level of farce, Tom is a comic figure in the classical sense of being a victim of delusion. He is not aware of being cruel to Jim because he does not perceive him as a human being. For Tom, Jim is the hero of a historical romance, a peer of the Man in the Iron Mask or the Count of Monte Cristo. Mark Twain is consciously imitating *Don Quixote,* and there are moments not unworthy of the model, as when Tom admits that "we got to dig him out with the picks, and *let on* it's case-knives." [27]

---

[25] *Writings*, XIII, 310.
[26] Nat, the Phelps's slave: *Writings*, XIII, 346-347; counting the spoons: XIII, 353-354; the ratholes: XIII, 352-353; Sister Hotchkiss: XIII, 386-389.
[27] Case-knives: *Writings*, XIII, 341.

But Tom has no tragic dimension whatever. There is not even any force of common sense in him to struggle against his perverted imagination as Huck's innate loyalty and generosity struggle against his deformed conscience. Mark Twain maintains a satiric distance from Tom, even adding him to the list of characters who employ the soul-butter style of false pathos. The inscriptions Tom composes for Jim to "scrabble onto the wall" of the cabin might have been composed by the Duke:

1. Here a captive heart busted.
2. Here a poor prisoner, forsook by the world and friends, fretted his sorrowful life.
3. Here a lonely heart broke, and a worn spirit went to its rest, after thirty-seven years of solitary captivity.
4. Here, homeless and friendless, after thirty-seven years of bitter captivity, perished a noble stranger, natural son of Louis XIV.

While he was reading these noble sentiments aloud, "Tom's voice trembled . . . and he most broke down." [28]

VI

Mark Twain's partial shift of identification from Huck to Tom in the final sequence was one response to his recognition that Huck's and Jim's quest for freedom was only a dream: he attempted to cover with a veil of parody and farce the harsh facts that condemned it to failure. The brief episode involving Colonel Sherburn embodies yet another response to his disillusionment. The extraordinary vividness of the scenes in which Sherburn figures only a half-dozen pages all told—is emphasized by their air of being an intrusion into the story.[29] Of course, in the episodic structure of *Huckleberry Finn* many characters appear for a moment and disappear. Even so, the Sherburn episode seems unusually isolated. None of the principal characters is involved in or affected by it: Jim, the Duke, and the King are offstage, and Huck is a spectator whom even the author hardly notices. We are told nothing about his reaction except that he did not want to stay around. He goes abruptly off to the circus and does not refer to Sherburn again.

Like Huck's depression as he nears the Phelps plantation, the Sherburn episode is linked with Mark Twain's own experience. The shooting of Boggs follows closely the murder of "Uncle Sam" Smarr by a merchant named Owsley in Hannibal in 1845, when Sam Clemens was nine years

[28] *Writings*, XIII, 359.
[29] The Sherburn episode: *Writings*, XIII, 195-204.

old.[30] Although it is not clear that he actually witnessed it, he mentioned the incident at least four times at intervals during his later life, including one retelling as late as 1898, when he said he had often dreamed about it.[31] Mark Twain prepares for the shooting in *Huckleberry Finn* by careful attention to the brutality of the loafers in front of the stores in Bricksville. "There couldn't anything wake them up all over, and make them happy all over, like a dog-fight—unless it might be putting turpentine on a stray dog and setting fire to him, or tying a tin pan to his tail and see him run himself to death." [32] The prurient curiosity of the townspeople who shove and pull to catch a glimpse of Boggs as he lies dying in the drugstore with a heavy Bible on his chest, and their pleasure in the reenactment of the shooting by the man in the big white fur stovepipe hat, also help to make Bricksville an appropriate setting for Sherburn's crime.

The shooting is in Chapter 21, and the scene in which Sherburn scatters the mob by his contemptuous speech is in the following chapter. There is evidence that Mark Twain put aside the manuscript for a time near the end of Chapter 21.[33] If there was such an interruption in his work on the novel, it might account for a marked change in tone. In Chapter 21 Sherburn is an unsympathetic character. His killing of Boggs is motivated solely by arrogance, and the introduction of Boggs's daughter is an invitation to the reader to consider Sherburn an inhuman monster. In Chapter 22, on the other hand, the Colonel appears in an oddly favorable light. The townspeople have now become a mob; there are several touches that suggest Mark Twain was recalling the descriptions of mobs in Carlyle's *French Revolution* and other works of history and fiction.[34] He considered mobs to be subhuman aggregates generating psychological pressures that destroyed individual freedom of choice. In a passage written for *Life*

[30] The shooting of Smarr is described by Dixon Wecter in *Sam Clemens of Hannibal* (Boston, 1952), pp. 106-109.

[31] In addition to the version of the shooting and attempted lynching in *Huckleberry Finn*, Mark Twain described the episode in his *Autobiography* in 1898 (I, 131) and in the unpublished manuscript "Villagers of 1840-3" (DV 47, Mark Twain Papers). In "The United States of Lyncherdom" (1901), he mentions seeing "a brave gentleman deride and insult a mob and drive away" (*Writings*, XXIX, 245). Walter Blair suggests that the description of a shooting in a footnote to Chapter 40 of *Life on the Mississippi* also draws on Mark Twain's memory of the shooting of Smarr (*Mark Twain & Huck Finn*, p. 306).

[32] *Writings*, XIII, 195.

[33] Walter Blair fixes the date of composition of Chapter 21 as "probably . . . before March 19, 1883," and says that the rest of the novel was written after June 15, 1883 (*American Literature*, XXX, 20). Except for a sequence corresponding to part of Chapter 12 and all of Chapters 13 and 14, the manuscript preserved in the Buffalo Public Library begins with Chapter 22. The manuscript of Chapters 15-16 has not survived.

[34] *Mark Twain & Huck Finn*, pp. 310-311.

on the Mississippi but omitted from the book Mark Twain makes scathing generalizations about the cowardice of mobs, especially in the South but also in other regions, that closely parallel Sherburn's speech.[35]

In other words, however hostile may the depiction of Sherburn in Chapter 21, in Chapter 22 we have yet another instance of Mark Twain's identifying himself, at least partially, with a character in the novel other than Huck. The image of Sherburn standing on the roof of the porch in front of his house with the shotgun that is the only weapon in sight has an emblematic quality. He is a solitary figure, not identified with the townspeople, and because they are violently hostile to him, an outcast. But he is not weaker than they, he is stronger. He stands above the mob, looking down on it. He is "a heap the best dressed man in that town," and he is more intelligent than his neighbors. The scornful courage with which he defies the mob redeems him from the taint of cowardice implied in his shooting of an unarmed man who was trying to escape. Many members of the mob he faces are presumably armed; the shotgun he holds is not the source of his power but merely a symbol of the personal force with which he dominates the community.

The Colonel's repeated references to one Buck Harkness, the leader of the mob, whom he acknowledges to be "half-a-man," suggest that the scene represents a contest between two potential leaders in Bricksville. Harkness is the strongest man with whom the townspeople can identify themselves. In his pride Sherburn chooses isolation, but he demonstrates that he is stronger than Harkness, for the mob, including Harkness, obeys his command to *"leave*—and take your half-a-man with you."

Sherburn belongs to the series of characters in Mark Twain's later work that have been called "transcendent figures." [36] Other examples are Hank Morgan in *A Connecticut Yankee;* Pudd'nhead Wilson; and Satan in *The Mysterious Stranger.* They exhibit certain common traits, more fully developed with the passage of time. They are isolated by their intellectual superiority to the community; they are contemptuous of mankind in general; and they have more than ordinary power. Satan, the culmination of the series, is omnipotent. Significantly, he is without a moral sense— that is, a conscience, a sense of guilt. He is not torn by the kind of inner struggle that Huck experiences. But he is also without Huck's sound heart. The price of power is the surrender of all human warmth.

Colonel Sherburn's cold-blooded murder of Boggs, his failure to experience remorse after the act, and his withering scorn of the townspeople

---

[35] *Mark Twain & Huck Finn,* pp. 292-294.
[36] Paul Baender, "Mark Twain's Transcendent Figure," unpublished dissertation, University of California (Berkeley), 1956.

are disquieting portents for the future. Mark Twain, like Huck, was sickened by the brutality he had witnessed in the society along the river. But he had an adult aggressiveness foreign to Huck's character. At a certain point he could no longer endure the anguish of being a passive observer. His imagination sought refuge in the image of an alternative persona who was protected against suffering by being devoid of pity or guilt, yet could denounce the human race for its cowardice and cruelty, and perhaps even take action against it. The appearance of Sherburn in *Huckleberry Finn* is ominous because a writer who shares his attitude toward human beings is in danger of abandoning imaginative insight for moralistic invective. The slogan of "the damned human race" that later became Mark Twain's proverb spelled the sacrifice of art to ideology. Colonel Sherburn would prove to be Mark Twain's dark angel. His part in the novel, and that of Tom Sawyer, are flaws in a work that otherwise approaches perfection as an embodiment of American experience in a radically new and appropriate literary mode.

From "Black Magic—and White—in *Huckleberry Finn*"

by Daniel G. Hoffman

I

Tom Sawyer's imagination is crowded with romantic illusions; the village subsists on conventional piety. But Huck moves in a world of superstition. As DeVoto observes, "On page 64 of *Tom Sawyer*, Huckleberry Finn wanders into immortality swinging a dead cat." Huck and his cat symbolize freedom to Tom, who meets them on a Monday morning between his bondage at church the day before and his approaching incarceration in the district school. That dead cat also represents the lure of an unknown and forbidden world of spirits, omens, and dark powers, a world which attracts Tom not only by its Gothicism and horror but because, unlike his romantic escapades, this imaginary realm succeeds in transcending reality by rendering life itself in mythic terms. The boys exchange cures for warts; yet try as he will, Tom can never really enter Huck's world. When he tries to recover by incantation all the marbles he ever lost, Tom's charm is bound to fail, for the first allegiance of his imagination—as we have seen—lies elsewhere. Besides, he is after all a village boy, nephew of the respectable Aunt Polly, brother of the model prig Sid Sawyer; Tom shares their status, and to him Huck is a "romantic outcast." Therefore Tom will never share Huck's secret wisdom—or his freedom.

The association of these superstitions in Mark Twain's mind with freedom from restraint is reiterated in the first chapter of *Huckleberry Finn*. This time it is Huck who sweats through the lessons, about Moses and the "Bulrushers." At last the widow "let it out that Moses had been dead a considerable long time; so then I didn't care no more about him, because I don't take no stock in dead people." Huck is then lectured on going to Heaven by Miss Watson; this is so depressing that by nighttime "I felt so lonesome I most wished I was dead."

> The stars were shining, and the leaves rustled in the woods ever so mournful; and I heard an owl, away off, who-whooing about somebody that was dead, and a whippowill and a dog crying about somebody that was going to die; and the wind was trying to whisper something to me, and I couldn't make out what it was, and so it made the cold shivers run over me. Then away out in the woods I heard that kind of a sound that a ghost makes when it wants to tell about something that's on its mind and can't make itself understood, and so can't rest easy in its grave, and has to go about that way every night grieving. I got so downhearted and scared I did wish I had some company. Pretty soon a spider went crawling up my shoulder, and I flipped it off and it lit in the candle; and before I could budge it was all shriveled up. I didn't need anybody to tell me that that was an awful bad sign and would fetch me some bad luck, so I was scared and most shook the clothes off of me. I got up and turned around in my tracks three times and crossed my breast every time; and then I tied up a little lock of my hair with a thread to keep witches away. But I hadn't no confidence.

Freedom from the restraints of civilization, yes; but such freedom has its dangers too. For Huck, the omens are an acknowledgment of the fact of death. "I didn't take no stock in dead people" applies to the dead lessons in Bible or school, not to these immanent realities. These portents are an admission of evil as a positive force in the natural world. His exorcisms attempt to control the operation of malevolent powers. But while he knows far more about such things than Tom does, Huck is still a mere disciple. The magus is Nigger Jim.

But when we first meet him, Jim is a slave. His superstitions, like the hagiolatry of the ignorant peasants in *The Innocents Abroad,* are the manacles upon his soul. Mark Twain dramatizes his bondage by the quality of his beliefs. Far from controlling nature, Jim in slavery is helpless before the dark powers, a gullible prey to every chance or accident which befalls him. This is made humorously manifest in chapter 2, when Tom and Huck find Jim snoozing on the widow's kitchen steps. Tom hangs his hat on a branch and leaves a five-cent piece on the table. "Afterward Jim said the witches bewitched him and put him in a trance, and rode him all over the state, and then set him down under the trees again, and hung his hat on a limb to show who done it." Other slaves come from miles around to hear Jim's expanding account of this marvel. It gives him status! But he is more than ever enslaved to his fears; and a week later Miss Watson decides to sell him down the river to a more arduous bondage. That is a fear he cannot transform into personal distinction through the artistic control of a tall tale. Jim runs away to Jackson's Island.

On the island he lives in terror of capture. Huck, having escaped from Pap, is there before him. Still the fearful, haunt-ridden man-child, Jim takes Huck for a ghost and drops to his knees, imploring, "Doan' hurt me —don't! I hain't ever done no harm to a ghos'. I alwuz liked dead people, en done all I could for 'em. You go en git in de river ag'in, wah you b'longs." But once he learns in earnest that Huck is alive, Jim realizes that he himself is free. The mighty river rises and the two move camp to a womb-like cavern. Animals take refuge in the trees, and "they got so tame, on account of being hungry, that you could paddle right up and put your hand on them if you wanted to; but not the snakes and turtles." This is an uneasy Eden, menaced by the implacable flooding river.

Now that he is free in this ambiguous paradise the nature of Jim's superstitious beliefs undergoes a change. We hear no more of ghosts and witches. Instead, Jim instructs Huck in the lore of weather, in the omens of luck, in the talismans of death. "Jim knowed all kinds of signs." Seeing young birds skip along means rain; catching one brings death. You must tell the bees when their owner dies or they will weaken and perish. Death is never far from the superstitious imagination. Jim goes on—don't shake the tablecloth after sundown, or count the things you cook for dinner, or look at the moon over your left shoulder—these bring bad luck. "It looked to me like all the signs was about bad luck, and so I asked him if there warn't any good-luck signs. He says: 'Mighty few—an' *dey* ain't no use to a body. What you want to know when good luck's a-comin' for? Want to keep it off?' " Luck is the folk concept of what the Greeks called Fate, the Anglo Saxons, Wyrd. There is a stoical wisdom in Jim's resignation before it which makes a manly contrast to the psalm-singing optimism of Miss Watson and the revivalists, and to Tom's romantic evasions of reality.

Soon after they see the young birds flying, sure enough, it rains: a huge, frightening storm that reasserts the dominance of nature over man. The river rises, and as was foretold in so many of their omens, the House of Death floats by. When Jim's omens come true he is no more a gullible supplicant to witches. He is a magus now, a magician in sympathetic converse with the spirits that govern—often by malice or caprice—the world of things and men.

As soon as Jim begins to feel his freedom, his attitude toward Huck develops. One of the grand ironies of this book is that while it seems to show Huck protecting Jim, Jim is also taking care of Huck all along.

Jim's folk wisdom saved Huck from the storm; Jim builds the wigwam
on the raft. "I'd see him standing my watch on top of his'n, 'stead of calling me, so I could go on sleeping." Just after the storm, when the House
of Death floats by, it is Jim who goes aboard first, sees the corpse, and
won't let Huck behold it. Huck boyishly salvages an old straw hat, a
Barlow knife, "a ratty old bedquilt. . . . And so, take it all around, we
made a good haul." These squalid remnants, we discover much later, constitute Huck's patrimony from Pap, the father whose savagery he fled. So
terrible was the self-destructive anarchic energy of Pap that Huck had to
simulate self-destruction to escape him. But now it is Jim who compre-
hends the degradation of Pap's death and protects Huck from that cruel
knowledge. Jim is now free to take the place that Pap was never worthy
to hold as Huck's spiritual father. When Jim and Huck shove off from
the House of Death their odyssey begins. Jim can now act as Huck's
father, and Huck's first act is to protect him, as a son might do.

Because of this filial relationship, Huck cannot play tricks on Jim as he
could on Tom or Ben Rogers. This he discovers when he kills a rattler
and coils it in Jim's bed. Jim had warned him, "it was the worst bad luck
in the world to touch a snake-skin." The dead snake's mate coils round it
and bites poor Jim. But Jim has a folk cure—eating the snake's head
roasted, tying the rattles around his wrist, and drinking whiskey. Just as
his omens come true, his cures cure. Again we see Jim as medicine man,
free to control—within mortal limits—his universe.

Another aspect of Jim's shamanistic role is his power to interpret
oracles and dreams. Here, too, when in slavery this attribute parodies
itself because Jim then held pretensions without power. He had a hairball from the fourth stomach of an ox with which he "used to do magic."
Huck consults him after seeing Pap's footprints in the snow, to learn
what Pap would do. Accepting Huck's counterfeit quarter, Jim reels off
a counterfeit prophecy, concluding, "You wants to keep 'way fum de
water as much as you kin." But when Huck returns to his room, "there
sat Pap—his own self!" and the only escape from Pap is to flee by water.
Jim's next oracular occasion comes when he and Huck find each other
after being separated by the fog. Huck, as a joke, convinces Jim that they
had been together on the raft all the time; Jim must have dreamed their
separation. So Jim "said he must start in and 'terpret it, for it was sent
for a warning." Towheads and currents stand for men who will aid or
hinder them; their cries were warnings of trouble ahead, but all would
work out well in the end. Then Huck points to the leaves, the rubbish,
the smashed oar. Jim ponders:

What do they stan' for? I's gwyne tell you. When I got all wore out wid work, en wid de callin' for you, en went to sleep, my heart wuz mos' broke bekase you wuz los', en I didn' k'yer no mo' what become er me en de raf'. En when I wake up en find you back ag'in, all safe en soun', de tears come, en I could 'a' got down on my knees en kiss yo' foot, I's so thankful. En all you wuz thinkin' 'bout wuz how you could make a fool uv ole Jim wid a lie. Dat truck dah is *trash;* en trash is what people is dat puts dirt on de head er dey fren's en makes 'em ashamed.

This speech, so moving in its avowal of dignity, combines Jim's attempt at magical interpretation (which is in fact accurate) with the realism that underlies it, and with his staunch adherence to the code of simple decencies by which good men must live. It is indeed the first major turning-point of the romance. It reinforces the lesson of the snakeskin: Huck now realizes that he is bound to Jim by ties too strong for mischievous trifling, ties so strong that he must break the strongest mores of the society he was raised in to acknowledge them. "It was fifteen minutes before I could work myself up to go and humble myself to a nigger; but I done it, and I warn't ever sorry for it afterward, neither."

Now that Huck has learned how he and Jim are inseparable, circumstances at once thrust them apart. In the next chapter their raft is run over by a paddlewheeler; when Huck gets ashore and sings out for Jim he finds himself alone. This, he thinks, is what comes of handling that snakeskin. He is taken in by the Grangerfords and does not find Jim again until after the shooting. Then the Duke and Dauphin come aboard. From this point on Jim and Huck are never again alone together, and Jim does not act as magus again. His powers have their mysterious source in the river, partaking of its inscrutable might. For if the river is a god, Jim is its priest. The river god is indifferent to humanity; he runs on, uncontaminated by the evils along his shores, asserting now and then in dominance and power over "the damned human race." Only when Jim is alone with Huck on the river island or drifting on the current is he so free from the corruption of civilization that he can partake of the river god's dark power. Jim responds on a primitive level to that power, through which he can interpret the signs that are older than Christianity.

But now he is on the sidelines while Huck observes the Duke and King play out their grasping roles. After their failure to filch Mary Jane Wilks' patrimony, the King sells Jim to Tom Sawyer's Uncle Silas. Huck sets out to find him. Suddenly aware of his guilt in having aided a runaway slave, Huck wrestles again with his conscience. In a memorable climax to his discovery of his own natural goodness, Huck dares to defy

the codes of Miss Watson's church and of Tom Sawyer's village by stealing Jim out of slavery again: "All right, then, I'll go to hell."

There are witches again on Uncle Silas' farm, for this is slave territory.
Silas' slave, Nat, wears wool in his hair to ward them away, thinks he is
bewitched when Tom tells him he is, knows this is true when a pack of
hounds leap into Jim's cell through the escape hole the boys had Jim dig
beneath the bed. But Jim knows better. Although manacled while Nat
has the run of the place, Jim is spiritually free. Now that he has experienced the freedom of life on the raft, life in accord with the rhythms of
nature, mere chains will not reduce him to subjection again. As Tom
knows, he is legally free anyway. But Jim does not know this; his fortitude
during his imprisonment is one of the signs of his moral stature.

Jim's stature is made manifest at the end of the book when, having
suffered such needless discomfitures at Tom's hands, he voluntarily gives
himself up in the swamp to help the doctor nurse back to health the boy
who had plagued him. Then, brought back to the farm as he knew he
would be—in chains, suffering the abuse of an angry mob, in momentary
danger of lynching—Jim refuses to recognize Huck in the crowd lest he
involve this other, truer friend in his own misfortunes. Jim's loyalty is so
great that he is willing to sacrifice his freedom for his young friends' sakes.
His selflessness is truly noble, a far cry from the chuckle-headedness of the
slave who was ridden all over the country by witches when Tom Sawyer
lifted his hat.

II

During the decade when critical opinion at last recognized the inherent
dignity of Jim, *Adventures of Huckleberry Finn,* in response to strong
pressure from the N.A.A.C.P., was removed from the high-school curricu-
lum in our largest city.[1] The most eloquent statement of the objections
of a Negro reader to Mark Twain's characterization of Jim is that of the
novelist Ralph Ellison:

> Writing at a time when the blackfaced minstrel was still popular, and shortly
> after a war which left even the abolitionists weary of those problems asso-
> ciated with the Negro, Twain fitted Jim into the outlines of the minstrel
> tradition, and it is from behind this stereotype mask that we see Jim's dignity
> and human capacity—and Twain's complexity—emerge. Yet it is his source
> in this same tradition which creates that ambivalence between his identifica-
> tion as an adult and parent and his "boyish" naïveté, and which by contrast

---

[1] New York *Times,* September 12, 1957, pp. 1-2.

makes Huck, with his street-sparrow sophistication, seem more adult. . . . Jim's friendship for Huck comes across as that of a boy for another boy rather than as the friendship of an adult for a junior; thus there is implicit in it not only a violation of the manners sanctioned by society for relations between Negroes and whites, there is a violation of our conception of adult maleness.[2]

Speaking of the blackfaced minstrel, the "smart-man-playing-dumb," Mr. Ellison remarks that his role grows "out of the white American's manichean fascination with the symbolism of blackness and whiteness." This color symbolism is openly appropriated in *Huckleberry Finn;* it is used in full awareness of its ironies. We remember Pap's first appearance in the book—his face "was white . . . a white to make a body's flesh crawl —a tree-toad white, a fishbelly white"; he it is who out of pride of color would secede from the government because it permits "a free nigger from Ohio—a mulatter, most as white as a white man," to vote. This early in the book the falsity of the manichean color symbolism is dramatized.

But there is no gainsaying Mr. Ellison that when Jim analyzes the stock market, or asks "Was Sollerman Wise?" or kowtows to the bogus royalty or endures his torturous liberation for Tom's amusement he is indeed akin to the Mr. Bones of minstrel fame. I hope to have shown, however, that this is what he begins as, what he emerges from. Jim plays his comic role in slavery, when he bears the status society or Tom imposes upon him; not when he lives in his intrinsic human dignity, alone on the raft with Huck.

If Jim emerges from the degradation of slavery to become as much a man as Mark Twain could make him be, we must remember that Jim's growth marks a progress in Twain's spiritual maturity too. "In my school days I had no aversion to slavery. I was not aware that there was anything wrong with it. No one arraigned it in my hearing . . . the local pulpit taught us that God approved it, that it was a holy thing." [3] In 1855 Sam Clemens wrote home to his mother that a nigger had a better chance than a white man of getting ahead in New York. Mark Twain began with all the stereotypes of racial character in his mind, the stereotypes that he as well as Jim outgrows.

It is clear that supernatural folklore plays an important part in Twain's handling of Jim. Since this lore is used to differentiate Jim from the white characters, there remains the question of Mark Twain's accuracy in assign-

[2] "The Negro Writer in America: An Exchange," *Partisan Review,* XXV (Spring 1958), pp. 215-16.
[3] *Mark Twain's Autobiography,* ed. Alfred Biglow Paine (New York, 1924), p. 101.

ing folk belief to the black man.[4] In the preface to *Tom Sawyer,* Mark Twain makes explicit his assumption about the provenience of folk beliefs: "The odd superstitions touched upon were all prevalent among children and slaves in the West at the period of this story—that is to say, thirty or forty years ago" (1835-45). In both books the only whites who are superstitious are either young boys or riffraff like Pap—the two categories of white folks who might have picked up the lore of the slave quarters. The only "white" superstition in *Huckleberry Finn,* attributed to the villagers in general, is belief in the power of bread and quicksilver to discover a drowned corpse.[5] More typical of the attitude of white characters toward superstition is the derision of the raftsmen when their companion tells the ghost story of the murderer pursued by the corpse of his slain child floating in a barrel beside the raft.[6] Twain's usual assumption is that white persons of any status higher than trash like Pap have little knowledge of, and no belief in, superstition.[7]

Mark Twain's memory played him wrong. Every one of the beliefs in witch-lore and in omens he used in *Huckleberry Finn* proves to be of European rather than African origin and to have been held widely among the whites as well as among the Negroes of the region. The witch who is warded off by tying one's hair with threads and who rides her victims by night is an old familiar European folk figure:

> This is that very Mab
> That plaits the manes of horses in the night

whom Mercutio described in *Romeo and Juliet* (I, iv, 88-9). Jim's fear of snakeskins, his belief that one must tell the bees of their keeper's death, his conviction that counting the things you cook for supper, or shaking the tablecloth after sundown, or speaking of the dead, or seeing the moon over your left shoulder all bring bad luck, and that a hairy chest means he's "gwine be rich"—all these were known among the white folk of the

---

[4] "Regarding the feelings, emotions, and the spiritual life of the Negro the average white man knows little," writes Newbell Niles Puckett in his magisterial *Folk Beliefs of the Southern Negro* (Chapel Hill, 1926), vii. "Should some weird, archaic, Negro doctrine be brought to his attention he almost invariably considers it a 'relic of African heathenism,' though in four cases out of five it is a European dogma from which only centuries of patient education could wean even his own ancestors."

[5] The identical belief is reported by Harry Middleton Hyatt in *Folklore from Adams County Illinois* (New York, 1935), a region on the opposite shore of river above Hannibal; item no. 10283.

[6] I follow Bernard DeVoto (*The Portable Mark Twain*) in considering this episode, usually printed as chapter 3 of *Life on the Mississippi,* an integral part of the book for which it was originally written.

[7] Pap wears a cross of nails in the heel of his boot as a charm against the devil.

Mississippi valley.[8] Only his divination with a hairball from the stomach of an ox is a Negro belief of voodoo origin.

Why, then, does Mark Twain make such a point of having only Negroes, children, and riffraff as the bearers of folk superstitions in the recreated world of his childhood? *Huckleberry Finn* was written while Twain lived among the insurance magnates, the manufacturing millionaires, and the wealthy literati of the Nook Farm colony in Hartford, Connecticut. It had been many years since he had lived in a superstitious frontier community, and in his own not-too-reliable memory this folklore became associated with the slaves he had known in his boyhood. The original of Jim, he writes in his *Autobiography,* was " 'Uncle Dan'l,' a middle-aged slave" on the farm of Mrs. Clemens' brother John Quarles. "I can see the white and black children grouped around the hearth" of the slave's kitchen, "and I can hear Uncle Dan'l telling the immortal tales which Uncle Remus Harris was to gather into his book and charm the world with." [9] On such nights Dan'l's favorite encore was no animal fable but—as Twain wrote it down years later, in 1881, for Joel Chandler Harris' benefit—"De Woman wid de Gold'n Arm," [10] a ghost story widely collected by folklorists since. In those days, "every old woman" was an herb doctor; in Hannibal and Florida the young Sam Clemens knew also old Aunt Hannah, so old she had talked with Moses, who tied threads in her hair against witches. A subtle emotional complex binds together *superstition : slaves : boyhood freedom* in Mark Twain's mind. These three aspects of his experience had occurred most vividly together, and he seems, in his greatest book, not to have thought of any one of them without invoking both of the others. There is, then, no invidious intention behind his characterizing Jim by the superstitions common to both races.

I hope in the foregoing pages to have cleared Mark Twain of the imputation that "the humor of those scenes of superstition . . . illustrates the ridiculous inadequacy and picturesque inventiveness of the fearful human responses to the powers of evil," for such an interpretation—it is that of Francis Brownell [11]—would put all of Jim's folk beliefs in the service of the degrading ministrel characterization to which Mr. Ellison

[8] I have traced in detail the European origins and white provenience of these beliefs in "Jim's Magic: Black or White?" *American Literature,* XXXII (March 1960), 47-54.

[9] *Autobiography,* pp. 100, 112.

[10] *Mark Twain to Uncle Remus,* ed. Thomas H. English (Atlanta, 1953), pp. 11-13. Mark Twain gives another version of the tale in "How to Tell a Story."

[11] "The Role of Jim in *Huckleberry Finn,*" *Boston University Studies in English,* I (1955), 81.

objects. The minstrel stereotype, as we have seen, was the only possible starting-point for a white author attempting to deal with Negro character a century ago. How else could young Sam Clemens have known a Negro in the Missouri of the 1840's except as the little white boy on familiar terms with his uncle's household retainer? The measure of Mark Twain's human understanding—Mr. Ellison calls it his complexity—is evident when we compare Jim to the famous Negro character in the writings of Mark Twain's friend, Joel Chandler Harris, remembering that Sam Clemens was in real life to "Uncle" Dan'l as the little boy in Harris' books is to Uncle Remus. The Georgia author's Negro fabulist never ceases to be the minstrel in blackface. The poetic irony in the Uncle Remus books is one of which Harris was probably unaware: the Negro's human dignity survives the minstrel mask not in Uncle Remus' character but in the satirical stories he tells the white boy. That many of these were thinly veiled avowals of the Negro's pride and dignity and refusal to submit his spirit to the unjust yoke of custom would not seem to have occurred to Joel Chandler Harris, whose conscious literary strategy was to palliate Northern antagonism of the South by idealizing ante-bellum plantation life.[12] But Mark Twain tries to make Jim stride out of his scapegoat minstrel's role to stand before us in the dignity of his own manhood. It is true that Mark Twain's triumph here is incomplete: despite the skillful gradation of folk belief and other indications of Jim's emergent stature, what does come through for many readers is, as Mr. Ellison remarks, Jim's boy-to-boy relationship with Huck, "a violation of our conception of adult maleness." We remember that Mark Twain himself admired Uncle Remus extravagantly, and much as he means for us to admire Jim—much as he admires Jim himself—the portrait, though drawn in deepest sympathy, is yet seen from the outside. The closest that Mark Twain gets to Jim's soul, and the furthest from the stereotyped minstrel mask, is the ethical coherence with which the author's manipulation of folk superstitions allows him to endow the slave. In both his emergence toward manhood through the exercise of his freedom and in his supernatural power as interpreter of the oracles of nature, Jim comes to be the hero of his own magic. The test and proof of natural goodness, which raises Jim and Huck above religious hypocrisy and selfish romanticism, is its transforming power upon him. The fear-ridden slave becomes in the end a source of moral energy. The shifting of Jim's shape

---

[12] This is a point I have discussed in some detail in a review of *Joel Chandler Harris —Folklorist* by Stella Brewer Brookes, in *Midwest Folklore* I (Summer 1951), pp. 133-8. See also John Stafford, "Patterns of Meaning in *Nights with Uncle Remus*," *American Literature,* XVIII (May 1946), pp. 89-108.

is reversed at the end, as he sinks back from his heroism to become the bewildered freed darky of reconstruction days, grateful to the young white boss for that guilt-payment of forty dollars. (It did bring true his only good luck omen: a hairy breast and arms meant that he's "gwineter be rich . . . signs is signs!") For Jim has status now, a status imposed by society, not, as was his moral eminence, determined by his inner nature. And it is status of which Huck is now afraid; for at the end he is preparing to flee again, this time to "light out for the territory ahead of the rest. . . . Aunt Sally she's going to adopt and sivilize me, and I can't stand it. I been there before." For Huck, *"there"* means the stasis of being a part of society. His voyage, like Jim's, was a quest for freedom too; after their idyl and their ordeals, both find only the equivocal freedom of status at the end of their odyssey.

Huck and Oliver

by W. H. Auden

About six months ago I re-read *Huckleberry Finn,* by Mark Twain, for the first time since I was a boy, and I was trying when I read it to put myself back in the position of what it would seem like to re-read the book without knowing the United States very well. Because *Huckleberry Finn* is one of those books which is a key book for understanding the United States; just as I think one could take other books, English books—shall I say *Oliver Twist?*—as corresponding pictures of a British attitude.

When you read *Huckleberry Finn,* the first thing maybe that strikes somebody who comes from England about it is the difference in nature and in the attitude towards nature. You will find the Mississippi, and nature generally, very big, very formidable, very inhuman. When Oliver goes to stay in the country with Mrs. Maylie, Dickens writes:

> Who can describe the pleasure and delight and peace of mind and tranquillity the sickly boy felt in the balmy air, and among the green hills and rich woods of an inland village.

All very human, very comforting. Huck describes how he gets lost in a fog on the Mississippi, and he writes as follows:

> I was floating along, of course, four or five miles an hour; but you don't ever think of that. No, you *feel* like you are laying dead still on the water; and if a little glimpse of a snag slips by, you don't think to yourself how fast *you're* going, but you catch your breath and think, my! how that snag's tearing along. If you think it ain't dismal and lonesome out in a fog that way, by yourself, in the night, you try it once—you'll see.

One of the great differences between Europe in general and America is in the attitude towards nature. To us over here, perhaps, nature is always, in a sense, the mother or the wife: something with which you enter into a semi-personal relation. In the United States, nature is some-

"Huck and Oliver" by W. H. Auden. From *The Listener,* L, No. 1283 (October 1, 1953), pp. 540-541. Copyright 1953 by W. H. Auden. Reprinted by permission of the author. This essay was transcribed from a radio broadcast over the BBC.

thing much more savage; it is much more like—shall we say?—St. George and the dragon. Nature is the dragon, against which St. George proves his manhood. The trouble about that, of course, is that if you succeed in conquering the dragon, there is nothing you can do with the dragon except enslave it, so that there is always the danger with a wild and difficult climate of alternating, if you like, between respecting it as an enemy and exploiting it as a slave.

The second thing that will strike any European reader in reading *Huckleberry Finn* is the amazing stoicism of this little boy. Here he is, with a father who is a greater and more horrible monster than almost any I can think of in fiction, who very properly gets murdered later. He runs into every kind of danger; he observes a blood feud in which there is a terrible massacre, and he cannot even bear, as he writes afterwards, to think exactly what happened. Yet, in spite of all these things, which one would expect to reduce a small child either into becoming a criminal or a trembling nervous wreck, Huck takes them as Acts of God which pass away, and yet one side of this stoicism is an attitude towards time in which the immediate present is accepted as the immediate present; there is no reason to suppose that the future will be the same, and therefore it does not, perhaps, have to affect the future in the same kind of way as it does here.

Then, more interestingly, the European reader is puzzled by the nature of the moral decision that Huck takes. Here Huck is with his runaway slave, Jim, and he decides that he is not going to give Jim up, he is going to try to get him into safety. When I first read *Huckleberry Finn* as a boy, I took Huck's decision as being a sudden realization, although he had grown up in a slave-owning community, that slavery was wrong. Therefore I completely failed to understand one of the most wonderful passages in the book, where Huck wrestles with his conscience. Here are two phrases. He says:

> I was trying to make my mouth *say* I would do the right thing and the clean thing, and go and write to that nigger's owner and tell where he was; but deep down inside I knowed it was a lie, and He knowed it. You can't pray a lie—I found that out.

He decides that he will save Jim. He says:

> I will go to work and steal Jim out of slavery again; and if I could think up anything worse, I would do that, too; because as long as I was in, and in for good, I might as well go the whole hog.

When I first read the book I took this to be abolitionist satire on Mark Twain's part. It is not that at all. What Huck does is a pure act of moral improvisation. What he decides tells him nothing about what he should do on other occasions, or what other people should do on other occasions; and here we come to a very profound difference between American and European culture. I believe that all Europeans, whatever their political opinions, whatever their religious creed, do believe in a doctrine of natural law of some kind. That is to say there are certain things about human nature, and about man as a historical creature, not only as a natural creature, which are eternally true. If a man is a conservative, he thinks that law has already been discovered. If he is a revolutionary he thinks he has just discovered it; nobody knew anything in the past, but now it is known. If he is a liberal, he thinks we know something about it and we shall gradually know more. But neither the conservative, nor the revolutionary, nor the liberal has really any doubt that a natural law exists.

It is very hard for an American to believe that there is anything in human nature that will not change. Americans are often called, and sometimes even believe themselves to be, liberal optimists who think that the world is gradually getting better and better. I do not really believe that is true, and I think the evidence of their literature is against it. One should say, rather, that deep down inside they think that all things pass: the evils we know will disappear, but so will the goods.

For that very reason you might say that America is a country of amateurs. Here is Huck who makes an essentially amateur moral decision. The distinction between an amateur and a professional, of course is not necessarily a matter of learning; an amateur might be a very learned person, but his knowledge would be, so to speak, the result of his own choice of reading and chance. *Vice versa,* a professional is not necessarily unoriginal, but he will always tend to check his results against the past and with his colleagues. The word "intellectual" in Europe has always meant, basically, the person who knew what the law was, in whatever sphere, whether it was religion, medicine, or what have you. There has always been a distrust in the States of the person who claimed in advance to know what the law was. Naturally, in any country where people are faced with situations which are really new, the amateur often is right where the professional is wrong; we sometimes use the phrase "professional caution," and that sometimes applies when situations are quite different. On the other hand, the amateur tends, necessarily, to think in terms of immediate problems and to demand immediate solutions, because if you believe that everything is going to be completely different the day after tomorrow, it is no good trying to think about that.

A third thing, coupled with that, is that on reading *Huckleberry Finn* most Europeans will find the book emotionally very sad. Oliver Twist has been through all kinds of adventures; he has met people who have become his friends, and you feel they are going to be his friends for life. Huck has had a relationship with Jim much more intense than any that Oliver has known, and yet, at the end of the book, you know that they are going to part and never see each other again. There hangs over the book a kind of sadness, as if freedom and love were incompatible. At the end of the book Oliver the orphan is adopted by Mr. Brownlow, and that is really the summit of his daydream—to be accepted into a loving home. Almost the last paragraph of *Oliver Twist* runs:

> Mr. Brownlow went on, from day to day, filling the mind of his adopted child with stores of knowledge . . . becoming attached to him, more and more, as his nature developed itself, and showed the thriving seeds of all he wished him to become. . . .

How does Huck end:

> I reckon I got to light out for the Territory ahead of the rest, because Aunt Sally she's going to adopt me and sivilise me, and I can't stand it. I been there before.

In that way, of course, he is like a character in *Oliver Twist*—the Artful Dodger. But in the case of the Artful Dodger, Dickens shows us this charming young man as nevertheless corrupt, and over him hangs always the shadow of the gallows; he is not the natural hero, as Huck is in *Huckleberry Finn*.

In addition to the attitude towards nature, the attitude towards natural law, there are two more things one might take up briefly; the attitude towards time, and the attitude towards money. Imagine two events in history, (a) followed by (b), which in some way are analogous. The danger to the European will be to think of them as identical, so that if I know what to do over (a), I shall know exactly what to do with (b). The danger in America will be to see no relation between these things at all, so that any knowledge I have about (a) will not help me to understand (b). The European fails to see the element of novelty; the American fails to see the element of repetition. You may remember that both Oliver and Huck come into some money. In Oliver's case it is money that is his by right of legal inheritance. In Huck's case, it is pure luck. He and Tom Sawyer found a robber's cache. The money came to them only because it could not be restored to its rightful owners. The money, therefore, is not something that you ever think of inheriting by right.

One might put it this way: in Europe, money represents power—that is to say, freedom from having to do what other people want you to do, and freedom to do what you yourself want to do; so that in a sense all Europeans feel they would like to have as much money themselves as possible, and other people to have as little as possible.

In the States, money, which is thought of as something you extract in your battle with the dragon of nature, represents a proof of your manhood. The important thing is not to have money, but to have made it. Once you have made it you can perfectly well give it all away. There are advantages and disadvantages on both sides. The disadvantage in Europe is a tendency towards avarice and meanness; the danger in America is anxiety because, since this quantitative thing of money is regarded as a proof of your manhood, and to make a little more of it would make you even more manly, it becomes difficult to know where to stop. This ties up with something that always annoys me: when I see Europeans accusing Americans of being materialists. The real truth about Americans is they do not care about matter enough. What is shocking is waste; just as what shocks Americans in Europe is avarice.

I have mentioned a few of these things because we live in a time when it has never been so important that America and Great Britain should understand each other. Many misunderstandings arise, not over concrete points, but over a failure to recognize certain presuppositions or attitudes which we all make, according to our upbringing, in such a way that we cannot imagine anybody taking any other one. When those are understood, it is much more possible to help each other's strong points and weaknesses by exchanging them to our mutual profit.

In so far as that can be done, and I am sufficiently much of a liberal optimist to believe it can, the alliance between the States and Great Britain can become a real and genuine and mutually self-critical thing, instead of the rather precarious relationship forced by circumstances which it seems to be at present.

A Connecticut Yankee in King Arthur's Court:
The Machinery of Self-Preservation

by James M. Cox

A Connecticut Yankee in King Arthur's Court holds much the same position in Mark Twain's work that *Pierre* occupies in Melville's. Before both books stand single masterpieces; after them come books of genuine merit, books even greater than they themselves are, but books more quietly desperate, as if the creative force behind them had suffered a crippling blow and had trimmed itself to the storm of time. And both books reach resolutions involving self-destruction. Melville's hero is a writer so caught in the ambivalences of love and creativity that suicide becomes his last refuge. Twain's Hank Morgan, a robust superintendent of a machine shop who has been plunged into a sixth century feudal world, discovers himself in the role of a superman inventor who can remake the world. And he does remake it—only to blow up his technological marvels and defeat himself. Despite a certain audacity of conception, however, both works disintegrate into extravagant failures; indeed, their desperate resolutions suggest a desperation behind the fiction, as if the writer were involved in destroying a part of himself, thereby breaking an identification with a threatening aspect of his psychic life. In these works reality and fiction coalesce in such a way that the writer is drawn more and more into his creation until he can end it all only by fighting his way out.

Such a struggle is particularly evident in *A Connecticut Yankee*. Indeed, there is probably no better description of the quality of the book than Twain's famous reply to Howells' praise of the novel: "Well, my book is written—let it go. But if it were only to write over again there wouldn't be so many things left out. They burn in me; and they keep multiplying and multiplying; but now they can't ever be said. And besides, they would require a library—and a pen warmed up in hell." Two main assumptions animate Twain's hyperbole: (1) that the book is an incomplete expression of repressed attitudes; (2) that the remaining attitudes are self-generatively threatening the writer's personality. Both these assumptions point to the final incompleteness of *A Connecticut Yankee;* indeed, Twain's remark to Howells is in its way a remarkably accurate summary of the novel. It is not my purpose to go beyond that summary but to determine what is being summarized. For Twain's remark will not define the novel, but the novel will define—or better, *realize*—the remark. By beginning with the novel, I hope to go on to show the forces which burned in Twain, the terms he attempted to make with them in *A Connecticut Yankee,* and the terms his genius finally made with him.

The form of *A Connecticut Yankee* is what we may call an inverted Utopian fantasy, and a graphic way to see that inversion is to compare Twain's novel with Edward Bellamy's *Looking Backward,* which appeared in 1887 and was a best seller by the time the *Yankee* was ready for publication. Bellamy's fantasy involves a dream in which Julian West is precipitated into the future, where, faced with the material and ideological evolution evident in the year 2000 A.D., he sees his own nineteenth century in a perspective at once meager and startling. Through all this experience, West is the observer, the listener, the interrogator who assimilates the persuasive criticism which the imaginary age affords.

Twain, however, instead of going into an imaginary land outside history where the terms of criticism could operate abstractly and logically, plunged into history, and his novel became a going backward in order to look forward. Hank Morgan, the superintendent of a Colt Arms machine shop, thus emerges into the sixth century Arthurian world and is able to see this feudal pastoral from the presumable advantage of democratic industrialism. But unlike Julian West, Morgan is not the amazed, yet credulous listener. Unable to resist the lure of potential power residing in his technological advantage, he "invents" labor-saving devices, instigates reforms, and organizes the people until he is finally able to proclaim a republic in England. For a brief moment his regime prevails, but the Church, never quite defeated, plays upon the superstition of the populace, declares an interdict, and revolts against the Yankee's authority. He in turn blows up his world along with the assaulting forces of the past, until, surrounded by electrocuted knights he is condemned to a thirteen century sleep by Merlin. Morgan is the chief actor of his chronicle; just as his nineteenth century machine-shop colloquial vernacular collides with the Maloryese which Twain ascribes to the Arthurian subjects, his political philosophy comes to grips with the aristocratic assumptions of the King's realm.

In saying that *A Connecticut Yankee* is an extravagant failure, I do not mean to imply that the book lacks amusing incidents, for there are happy moments when Twain exploits the incongruities inherent in his conception of a Yankee mechanic clattering through the world of chivalry. Thus, Hank's burlesque of knighthood retains a certain pungency. His mounting the knights on bicycles or forcing them to wear placards advertising such items as Persimmons Soap or Peters Prophylactic Toothbrushes are memorable examples of Twain's rowdy humor; and Morgan's harnessing the incidental power of a praying ascetic in order to operate a shirt factory shows a recklessness of taste which still has power to shock a safe gentility. Taken as a whole, however, the book is a grim reading experience, for as Morgan assumes power in the Arthurian world the fantasy begins to rout the criticism and progression degenerates into mere sequence. The waste of energy which results is perhaps most manifest in the startling disproportion between Hank Morgan's emotion and his reason. His consuming indignation so outstrips his critical intelligence that his ideas are reduced to clamorous fulminations and noisy prejudices causing him to become an object of curiosity instead of an agent of ideas.

Nor is curiosity an inappropriate response, since one of Morgan's most characterizing compulsions is his urge to draw attention to himself. His indignation, his prejudices, his achievements, his incessant boasting, and finally his style—which is overstatement from the moment he greets us until he finally collapses under Merlin's spell—are all manifestations of his desire to show off. Wherever he appears, the Yankee must shine, and more than food or woman or even life itself he loves the effect. He himself in a rare moment of insight observes that the crying defect of his character is his desire to perform picturesquely. Thus he plans his actions with an eye for their stage value, usually specializing in technicolor explosions and other noisy demonstrations which electrify his audiences. Even the sad-faced Mark Twain ruefully observes of the Yankee's dying call to arms, "He was getting up his last 'effect'; but he never finished it."

Constantly advertising his ideas, his mechanical aptitude, and his stagey jokes, Morgan becomes a grotesque caricature of the enlightenment he advocates. He prances and struts through every conceivable burlesque, flaunting himself before the stunned Arthurian world into which he bursts until he becomes the real buffoon of his own performance. More mechanical than any of the gadgets in which he specializes, he grinds laboriously through his "acts," his only means of attracting attention being to run faster and faster, to do bigger and bigger things, until the mechanism of his character flies apart. And fly apart it finally does. There is an ironic appropriateness in the ending of the novel when Morgan, trapped in his cave by the stench from the rotting bodies of his victims and condemned to a thirteen century sleep by Merlin, emerges deranged before us—adrift in space, unmoored from time.

Mark Twain was aware of the Yankee's limitations, going so far as to confide to Dan Beard, who was to illustrate the book, "This Yankee of mine . . . is a perfect ignoramus; he is boss of a machine shop, he can build a locomotive or a Colt's revolver, he can put up and run a telegraph line, but he's an ignoramus nevertheless." And he insisted in a letter to Mrs. Fairbanks that he did not intend the book as a satire but as a *contrast* between two radically different ages. In view of Morgan's career and Twain's own statements, it is small wonder that certain critics have maintained that Twain was satirizing not the sixth century but the nineteenth. Thus Parrington insisted that Twain was "trimming his sails to the chill winds blowing from the outer spaces of a mechanistic cosmos," and Miss Gladys Carmine Bellamy has more recently observed that the book is a "fictional working out of the idea that a too-quick civilization breeds disaster."

Plausible though such arguments are in the light of the Yankee's ultimate failure, the tone of the novel often goes in precisely the opposite direction; for although the Yankee finally destroys himself, Twain's major investment in the novel is in the Yankee's attitudes. After all, most of those attitudes were the same ones Mark Twain swore by at one time or another during his public life, and the usual response to the novel has been that Twain was lampooning monarchy and chivalry. Furthermore, there is abundant evidence that Twain intended just such criticism. As early as 1866, Twain was attacking feudalism in the Sandwich Islands; and his belief in the superiority of democracy to monarchy goes back to the very beginning of his career; his hatred of an established church stretches equally far back—and further forward. Thus, ten years after the Yankee's diatribes against the ancient authority of the church, Twain still retained enough of his old animus against organized religion to mount a sustained, logical attack against Mary Baker Eddy, whose Christian Science he feared would become the official religion of the Republic. Finally, Matthew Arnold's strictures upon American culture particularly exasperated Twain, and there is clear evidence that some of the Yankee's attitudes are a direct response to Arnold's criticisms.

But in turning his narrative over to Morgan, Twain sacrificed whatever satiric intent he may have had in mind, for instead of converting the indignation which stands behind satire into the ironic observation, apparent indifference, and mock innocence which constitute it, Twain paraded his indignation in front of the world to be criticized. Moreover, the person of the Yankee stood between the idea and its dramatization shortcircuiting logic in such a welter of emotion that he became the problem with which Twain had to deal.

The nature of Twain's struggle is implicit in the slender frame around the story. Chronically incapable of erecting the complex plots which he thought characterized the novel, Twain often resorted to stock devices for getting into his narratives. But, as Walter Blair has pointed out in his hands those devices become significant form charged with his own motives. In this frame, Twain employed the author-meets-narrator stratagem, managing to gain an excuse for telling his tale at the same time he introduced his hero. Following a guided tour through Warwick Castle, itself a representative of the stock past of the tourist's imagination, Twain encountered a stranger "who wove such a spell about me that I seemed to move among the shadows and dust and mold of a gray antiquity, holding speech with a relic of it." The very rhetoric which Twain ascribes to himself is filled with the clichés of travelogue nostalgia. Throughout this brief introduction, Twain portrays himself as a dewy-eyed tourist bent on caressing images of the past. In this moment of sentimental retrospection while the guide attempts to explain the presence of a bullet hole in an ancient piece of armor, the stranger appears, like a fabulous genie come from a bottle, and into Twain's ear alone proclaims himself the author of the bullet hole. The "electric surprise of this remark" momentarily shatters the tourist Mark Twain's retrospective dream, and by the time he recovers, the stranger has disappeared. That evening, however, sitting by the fire at the Warwick Arms "steeped in a dream of the olden time," Twain is again abruptly confronted by the stranger, who, knocking upon the door to interrupt the dream, takes final charge of the narrative.

What the artist Mark Twain makes apparent in this brief frame is that Morgan is a projection, or, more accurately, an anti-mask of the tourist Mark Twain's stock nostalgia. For just as Morgan has put a bullet hole through the antique armor, so does he puncture the sentimental dream of the past. Moreover, he comes unbidden to menace at the same time he accompanies the dreamer on the journey back into time. Speaking with a casual and confident authority, he even announces that he is the antithesis of sentimentality: "I am a Yankee of Yankees—and practical; yes, and nearly barren of sentiment, I suppose—or poetry, in other words." His narrative is appropriately preserved on a palimpsest, since the Yankee's personal history is the record of an effort to overwrite the past.

The Yankee's role, as it is defined in the frame, is one of burlesquing

"Mark Twain's" tourist version of the past. The one emotion which is anathema to Morgan is reverence, and wherever he encounters the posture—whether in sentimental nostalgia or in a feudal aristocracy—his reaction is one of aggressive ridicule. This unqualified irreverence was by no means new in Twain's work. It was a necessary adjunct to a writer whose own creative impulse was essentially nostalgic. When we look upon Twain's work we realize that the past—his personal past—was his own armor. His great work is staged within his and America's remembered Southern geography of boyhood which the indignation and mechanization of the Civil War had reduced to the status of an island in the remote past. Although Twain shared the indignation enough to transplant himself morally and literally into the Hartford neighborhood of Harriet Beecher Stowe, his creative imagination discovered itself in the primal world before the War. Sentimental as his longing for the past could be— he speaks in his Autobiography of "the pathetic past, the beautiful past, the dear and lamented past"—it nevertheless inspired at the same time it drove him back upon his memory. The rich cargo he brought back from these "voyages into the uncharted sea of recollection," as he once called them, redeemed the meagerness of his wish to go.

One of Twain's chief protections against this intense longing for the past was his capacity for burlesque. Burlesque was the reality principle which could both mock and check the nostalgic impulse, and as early as *The Innocents Abroad* Twain had mastered the technique of shifting from platform nostalgia to burlesque. One of his favorite stances in all of his writing is along that borderland where pathos dissolves into broad ridicule, and it is often difficult to tell whether Twain is trapped in clichés or simply exploiting them. This complexity of vision characterizes much of *The Innocents Abroad* and even manifests itself in the very pun in the title of *A Tramp Abroad*. Indeed, Twain's success in writing travel books comes largely from his pervasive concern with attitudes toward history.

But Hank Morgan is more than merely an agent of ridicule; he goes beyond burlesque to threaten the whole existence of the past—any past. The image of Camelot into which he erupts is a "soft, reposeful summer landscape, as lovely as a dream and as lonesome as Sunday. The air was full of the smell of flowers and the buzzing of insects, and the twittering of birds, and there were no people, no wagons, there was no stir of life, nothing going on." Here is one of those ambivalent descriptions so recurrent in Twain's work. It is almost sentimental, almost, indeed, a cliché, and yet it could be Jackson's Island or Holliday's Hill, or the vision from a raft on the Mississippi. It is that summer idyl around which Twain perpetually revolved and in which his memory forever renewed itself.

Even Morgan feels the spell of its beauty, but his indignation at the slavery he discovers within its borders arouses him to destroy the sanctuary. He is finally a Connecticut *Yankee,* and slavery in Arthur's kingdom outrages him as much as slavery in Missouri. It is the archetypal evil justifying his determination to overthrow the past. What enables him to accomplish his task is his ability as an inventor and a businessman. What we have, in effect, is a Tom Sawyer fantasy being played out by an adult who, in an increasingly menacing way, means business. At the end of the fantasy, Morgan is electrocuting knights so rapidly and so thoroughly that there is no way of identifying the dead. They are merely an alloy of brass and buttons. Just as Twain drives the Yankee as clown through act after act of burlesque, he also drives the republican gadgeteer through a long line of inventions to destruction. And yet just as burlesque had been a valuable component of Twain's earlier humor, the prefigurations of Hank Morgan businessman are among his most celebrated character creations.

There is, for example, Twain himself in *Roughing It,* the restless and passionate victim of gold fever; there is Colonel Sellers, the extravagant speculator whose thoughts, fairly humming with infinite inventions and projects, are invested in a golden tomorrow at the same time they are busy preparing for it; there is Samuel Clemens in *Old Times on the Mississippi,* the adventurer on steamboats, his adventure itself a kind of Arabian Night's tale of youthful ambition realized; and finally there is Tom Sawyer, that shrewd boyhood businessman always so caught in a vision of his future glory that he cannot resist showing himself off at every opportunity. These dreaming characters often fail in their prophecies, but their presence in Twain's world is prophetic, just as their power for Twain, and for us, is compelling. They are, all of them, great characters, and without them Twain's literary achievement would have been vastly less significant than it was. Proof of their almost independent being within Twain's mind is the fact that Colonel Sellers and Tom Sawyer have assumed a mythic life outside the fiction in which they appeared. Twain himself must have sensed the alarming potential of such characters when he refused to carry Tom Sawyer into manhood on the grounds that he would "just lie like all other one-horse men in literature and the reader would conceive a hearty contempt for him." By keeping Tom trapped in the idyl of the past—or as DeVoto aptly phrased it, "the phantasy of boyhood"—Twain could transform the dream work which produced Tom into dream play.

Although Twain usually managed to control these characters *in* literature, he could not confine the creative forces behind them to literature
alone. By the time he wrote *Huckleberry Finn,* they were not only operating inside the novel in the person of Tom Sawyer, who, interestingly
enough, threatened to turn the novel upside down with his burlesque;
they were encroaching from the outside as well, having led Twain from
investments in a steam generator, a steam pulley, a new method of
marine telegraphy, a watch company, an insurance house, a new process
of engraving (the kaolatype) into two huge projects: the Webster Publishing Company, in which Twain was chief investor and senior partner; and
the Paige typesetting machine. Even while Twain was feverishly working
on *Huckleberry Finn,* he revealed the tension of his divided life in a
bluntly urgent letter to Charles L. Webster: "I cannot answer letters; I
can ill spare the time to read them; my time is brief. I cannot be interrupted by vineyard business or any *other* . . . You are my businessman; &
business I myself will *not transact.* . . . I won't talk business—I will
perish first. I hate the very idea of business in all its forms." The speculative urges, which had once been both source and subject of his literary
capital, had become a threat to his life as a writer, and he was forced to
feed his literary productions into his business holdings: *Huckleberry Finn*
was the first book published by the Webster Publishing Company.

Twain's publishing interests did not, however, demand nearly so much
of his attention, energy, and capital as the Paige typesetting machine.
From 1881, when he first became interested in it, until 1894, when the
bankruptcy to which it brought him forced him to abandon it, the machine devoured $300,000 of his money. At the height of his obsession, in
1888, the same year in which he wrote most of *A Connecticut Yankee,*
he was spending three thousand dollars per month on the invention.
Even these figures fail to reflect the awe with which he regarded the machine. To his brother Orion he described the reverent silence which
gripped those who watched it in operation for the first time. "All the
witnesses," he wrote, "made written record of the immense historical
birth—the first justification of a line of movable type by machinery—
and also set down the hour and the minute."

He spoke of it as a cunning devil at one time; at another, he contended
that it was next to man in intricacy at the same time it surpassed him
in perfection; at still another, he wrote that he loved to sit by the machine by the hour and merely contemplate it. Never was Twain more
enamored of an object, unless it was Olivia Langdon; if she was the
goddess he revered, it was the demon who possessed him and on whom
he wasted his fortune and almost sacrificed his sanity. In his obsessed

vision, the machine was both an intricate world and a mechanical brain whose infinitely interrelated parts he could half comprehend. It became for him, as Tom Burnham has wisely suggested, the concrete embodiment, the diagram, from which his mechanistic philosophy and psychology took their inspiration. More than that, the machine was uniquely wedded to the printed word; it was, after all, a kind of automatic writer capable of working tirelessly with speed and precision.

This then was the mechanical miracle whose advent Twain anxiously awaited as he proceeded with his work on the *Yankee*. On October 5, 1888, he was able to write to Theodore Crane, his wife's brother-in-law:

> I am here in Twichell's house at work, with the noise of the children and an army of carpenters to help. Of course they don't help, but neither do they hinder. It's like a boiler factory for racket . . . but I never am conscious of the racket at all, and I move my feet into position of relief without knowing when I do it . . . I was so tired last night that I thought I would lie abed and rest, today; but I couldn't resist . . . I want to finish the day the machine finishes, and a week ago the closest calculations for that indicated October 22—but experience teaches me that their calculations will miss fire as usual.

The letter might well stand as a foreword to *A Connecticut Yankee*. The process of composition as Twain describes it—a dully driven effort which goes on almost outside himself—is perfectly explained by his wish to finish the book on the day the machine was to be completed. Twain was saying, in effect, that he was a machine-driven writer; more important, he revealed that the novel had come to have a strange identification with the machine. There is, however, the hint of fatal doubt about the Paige contraption. To accommodate one's writing to its schedule was to be involved in a frustrating regimen of uncertainty. We know that the machine was not perfected on October 22; neither was the novel completed on that date. Not until the summer of 1889, after seasons of supreme hope punctuated by periods of depression or anxious alarm about the mechanical marvel, did Twain succeed in bringing the novel to its conclusion.

That Twain could bring the book to an end at all and break the vicious identification between it and the machine signifies a victory for the writer. For Hank Morgan is to a large extent the concrete embodiment of Twain's obsession with Paige's invention. At least, available evidence argues the plausibility of such a conclusion. Intruding into Twain's reverie, he assumes the power in the book that he held in the Hartford world outside the novel. In the cosmos of the novel, however, Twain is the Yankee's master; although the Yankee is Boss of the machine world he imposes upon the face of the Arthurian landscape, Twain operates the machinery of the novel and compels the Yankee to jump through act after act with ever increasing velocity until all his improvisations are exhausted. In bringing Morgan to death Twain was symbolically killing the machine madness which possessed him. If the devices Twain employs in the narrative do not always succeed as art—even if they are mere parts of the machinery of this mechanical novel—the novel nevertheless remains an act of personal salvation, its machinery the machinery of self-preservation.

For instead of being the "Divine Amateur" which he has been called, Twain was finally a professional writer; writing was his last protection. Just as he relied upon his art to protect himself from the financial embarrassments into which his amateur business ventures were leading him, so did he turn to it, as we have seen, to reestablish psychic control over those unleashed creative forces which were wreaking havoc in his private life. In endeavoring to regain control of those forces, Twain was preparing himself against the inevitable fall which awaited him in time. When, in 1894, Henry Rogers, the Standard Oil tycoon whose experience and advice had come to Twain's rescue during his financial failure, wrote that the typesetter had to be relinquished as a total loss, Twain replied from Europe:

> I seemed to be entirely expecting your letter, and also prepared and resigned; but Lord, it shows how little we know ourselves and how easily we can deceive ourselves. It hit me like a thunder-clap. It knocked every rag of sense out of my head, and I went flying here and there and yonder not knowing what I was doing, and only one clearly defined thought standing up visible and substantial out of the crazy storm-drift—that my dream of ten years was in desperate peril and out of the 60,000 or 70,000 projects for its rescue that came flocking through my skull not one would hold still long enough for me to examine it and size it up.

The entire action of Twain's book, published five years earlier, was more than a mere prophecy of the disaster toward which the machine obsession was tending; it was an acting out beforehand of the experience itself and hence a preparation for the end it prophesied. Indeed, the last scene of the novel in which "Mark Twain" hears the Yankee's confused and futile attempt to keep hold of a reality which is dissolving into dream is a rehearsal of Twain's own dilemma as the crisis of his fortunes approached. Writing to Mrs. Theodore Crane in 1893, Twain could only say:

> I dreamed I was born and grew up and was a pilot on the Mississippi and a miner and a journalist in Nevada and a pilgrim in the Quaker City, and had a wife and children and went to live in a villa at Florence—and this dream

goes on and on and sometimes seems so real that I almost believe it is real. I wonder if it is? But there is no way to tell, for if one applies tests they would be part of the dream, too, and so would simply aid the deceit. I wish I knew whether it is a dream or real.

The book could not prevent the disasters; it could only prepare for them, but in its way it represented a victory of the writer over the businessman. In viewing that victory one is almost led to believe that Merlin, who has been crossed, belittled, and ridiculed by the Yankee throughout the book, is—as he was for so many writers during the nineteenth century—the prototype of the artist who emerges from humiliation and shame to exercise his magic power at the last.

Such an interpretation would grossly oversimplify the matter, however, for neither is Twain's victory so dramatic nor the division between writer and businessman so precipitous. As he himself revealed in his letter to Howells, the book failed to express completely the attitudes which burned in him. They were left to burn themselves out in his experience. And I have already suggested that Twain's interest in business was a result of his creative imagination overflowing into his life. To deplore his commercial ventures is to forget that both publishing companies and typesetters are not wholly unrelated to literary creation. After all, the fact that *Huckleberry Finn* was the first product of Twain's publishing house is as gratifying as the knowledge that Thoreau was at one time a manufacturer of pencils.

The figure of the Yankee reveals how closely knit the activities of writing and business were in Twain's mind. The Yankee was not simply a businessman, but an *inventor,* and his power, which was as benign inside the creative imagination as it was malign outside it, was indissolubly linked with Twain's artistic life. To kill the Yankee even symbolically was a serious undertaking, representing a crippling of the inventive imagination, as if Twain were driven to maim himself in order to protect himself. It is not surprising that Twain considered this radical redefinition of himself as a logical end of his writing life. He went so far as to notify Howells that his career was over and that he wished "to pass to the cemetery unclodded." Of course, Twain's career was not over. He wrote again and again because there were financial necessities which required it and because there were personal disasters to come of even greater magnitude than those he was facing.

And *A Connectitcut Yankee* is a rehearsal for that writing as much as it was a preparation for the experience which was to come. I do not have the space to examine in detail the last phase of Twain's career, but I do want to stress a single, salient aspect in which the Yankee anticipated the work to come. A look at the important fiction which Twain wrote after 1889 reveals that a particular figure tends to dominate them—a stranger, who ultimately becomes the Mysterious Stranger. Just as the burlesquer and the incipient businessman had appeared early in Twain's work, so had this stranger. In "The Celebrated Jumping Frog" he had come into the decayed mining camp of Angels and, in order to win a bet from Jim Smiley, had poured enough shot into the jumping frog Dan'l Webster to paralyze him. But even in this story, the stranger is simply required by the terms of the story. His character is never defined and he remains no more than a shadowy personage necessary to the plot.

A Connecticut Yankee marks his full emergence into the foreground of Twain's comic world, for Hank Morgan is the stranger who intrudes into "Mark Twain's" reverie and into the charmed Arthurian paradise. As Twain describes him in the frame, he is strangely detached in countenance and manner, possessed of an all-knowing air as if he were present at the creation of the universe. The role this stranger comes to assume in Twain's fiction—his *act* we might say—is one of disturbing the peace. Into quiet, complacent communities he comes disrupting the society by unmasking and turning it upon itself. Thus Pudd'nhead Wilson, another Yankee stranger, enters Dawson's Landing, drolly observes the community, taking its fingerprints until he alone can disclose the crime which lies hidden at the heart of the society. And the man that corrupted Hadleyburg is a stranger who, somehow wronged by the community in the veiled past, takes elaborate revenge on it by means of a diabolically conceived joke which reveals the moral sham of the society. The stranger is last incarnated in the role of Philip Traum, the Mysterious Stranger, who pronounces the universe a dream.

The stranger's different avatars do not obscure certain distinguishing aspects of his character. He is first of all gaining a curious revenge on the world, a revenge usually taking the form of a practical joke. Second, he has a penchant for philosophy, his thought generally following a pattern of cracker barrel mechanistic determinism. Thus the Yankee, Pudd'nhead, and Philip Traum all insist that man is a machine who must obey the laws of his "make," that he cannot fully create anything. Third, the stranger invents the plots which expose the community. In this last sense, the stranger's plots become the form of Twain's work after *A Connecticut Yankee*. Both *Huckleberry Finn* and *A Connecticut Yankee* are primarily episodic novels, but the plot device which provides the frame of the *Yankee* becomes the essential form of the later work. The whole plot of *Pudd'nhead Wilson*, for example, pivots on mistaken identity devices.

We cannot certainly define the stranger's full significance in Mark

Twain's work, but *A Connecticut Yankee* shows that he is in large part the mechanics of Twain's comedy—the showman who, prior to the Yankee's appearance, was contained behind the dead-pan mask of innocence or within the world of boyhood play. In the figure of the Yankee he emerges into the world of manhood to speak for himself and run the show. Though Mark Twain killed the Yankee he could never quite contain the stranger again.

Thus, in much the same way that its motive turns within it from creation toward destruction, the book stands as a turning point in Twain's career. The work is not a destructive act however; rather it is an incomplete creative gesture, leaving an opening—a ligature—between the form and creative personality of the artist. As such a gesture, *A Connecticut Yankee* is what we may call Mark Twain's treaty with his Genius, for Hank Morgan in the last analysis is the unmasked demon—the practical joker and compulsive showman—so much a part of Mark Twain's humor. Seen in such a way the book is a great comedian's nightmare vision of himself, grotesquely exposing the secret manipulator behind the mechanism of the comic performance. The terms of the treaty may not be as favorable as we would wish, but they were the best that Twain could make with the fatalities of his art. Revealing as it does the inexorable logic of a creative life, the book stands as a channel marker which Mark Twain left behind him in his precarious voyage downstream.

"As Free as Any Cretur . . ."

by Leslie A. Fiedler

The most extraordinary book in American literature unfortunately has not survived as a whole; but its scraps and fragments are to be found scattered through the work of Mark Twain: a cynical comment ascribed to a small-town lawyer and never printed, the wreck of a comic tale framed by apologies and bad jokes, and finally the *Pudd'nhead Wilson* that has come down to us, half melodramatic detective story, half bleak tragedy. What a book the original might have been, before *Those Extraordinary Twins* was detached and Pudd'nhead's *Calendar* expurgated —a rollicking atrocious melange of bad taste and half understood intentions and nearly intolerable insights into evil, translated into a nightmare worthy of America.

All that the surrealists were later to yearn for and in their learned way simulate, Twain had stumbled on without quite knowing it. And as always (except in *Huckleberry Finn*) he paid the price for his lack of self-awareness; he fumbled the really great and monstrous poem on duplicity that was within his grasp. The principle of analogy which suggested to him linking the story of the Siamese Twins, one a teetotaler, the other a drunk, Jekyll and Hyde inside a single burlesque skin—to a tale of a Negro and white baby switched in the cradle finally seemed to him insufficient. He began to worry about broken plot lines and abandoned characters, about the too steep contrast between farce and horror; and he lost his nerve—that colossal gall which was his essential strength as well as his curse. Down the well went the burlesque supernumeraries and finally out of the story; and the poor separated twins remain to haunt a novel which is no longer theirs.

But something in Twain must have resisted the excisions; certainly they were made with a striking lack of conviction, and the resulting book is marred by incomprehensible motivations and gags that have lost their point with the unjoining of the once Siamese twins. The two stories were, after all, one, and the old book a living unity that could not be split without irreparable harm.

Yet *Pudd'nhead Wilson* is, after all, a fantastically good book, better than Mark Twain knew or his critics have deserved. Morally, it is one of the most honest books in our literature, superior in this one respect to *Huckleberry Finn;* for here Twain permits himself no sentimental relenting, but accepts for once the logic of his own premises. The immoral device of Tom's revelation, the fake "happy ending" of *Huck* are avoided in *Pudd'nhead.* It is a book which deals not only with the public issue of slavery, after all, long resolved—but with the still risky private matter of miscegenation, which most of our writers have chosen to avoid; and it creates in Roxy, the scared mulatto mother sold down the river by the son she has smuggled into white respectability, a creature of passion and despair rare among the wooden images of virtue or bitchery that pass for females in American literature. It is a portrait so complex and unforeseen that the baffled illustrator for the authorized standard edition chose to ignore it completely, drawing in the place of a "majestic . . . rosy . . . comely" Roxana—a gross and comic Aunt Jemima.

The scenes between this mother and her unregenerate son, who passes from insolence and cowardice to robbery and murder, and who ends slobbering at the feet of the woman he despises and plots to sell, have the cruelty and magnificence attained only by a great writer telling us a truth we cannot afford to face in a language we cannot afford to forget. It is a book which will be, I am sure, more and more read; certainly it is hard to believe that so rare a combination of wit and the metaphysical shudder will be considered forever of the second rank. Beside this book, *The Mysterious Stranger,* for the last several years a favorite of the writers on Twain, is revealed as the callow and contrived piece of cynicism it is: the best a cultureless man can do when he chooses to "philosophize" rather than dream.

Perhaps the best way to understand *Pudd'nhead* is to read it as a complement to *Huckleberry Finn,* a dark mirror image of the world evoked in the earlier work. Nearly ten years come between the two books, ten years in which guilt and terror had passed from the periphery of Twain's life and imagination to their center. *Huckleberry Finn* also is steeped in horror, to be sure; but it is easier to know this than to feel it. Though the main fable of the earlier book begins with a boy standing off with a rifle, his father gone berserk with the D.T.'s and ends with the revelation of that father's death in a seedy and flooded room scrawled with obscenities, it has so poetic a texture, so genuine though unmotivated a tone of joy— that one finds himself eternally doubting his own sense of its terrible import. In *Pudd'nhead,* however, the lyricism and the euphoria are gone; we have fallen to a world of prose, and there are no triumphs of Twain's rhetoric to preserve us from the revealed failures of our own humanity.

True enough, there is humor in the later book, but on a level of grotesquerie that is more violent and appalling than anything avowedly serious. It is the humor of Dickens' Quilp and Faulkner's idiot Snopes, the humor of the freak. In the chamber of horrors of our recent fiction, the deformed and dwarfed and dumb have come to stand as symbols of our common plight, the failure of everyone to attain a purely fictional norm. Toward this insight, Twain was fumbling almost without awareness, believing all along that he was merely trying to take the curse off of a bitterness he could not utterly repress by being what he liked to think was "funny."

Just as the grotesque in *Puddn'head* tends to break free from the humorous, so the tragic struggles to shed the nostalgic which swathes it still in *Huckleberry Finn.* In the earlier book, it is possible to believe that the flight toward freedom and childhood is more than a flight toward isolation and death. There is always waiting in a bend of the river Aunt Sally's homestead: a utopia of childhood visits and Southern homecooking. But Huck rejected this nostalgic Southland at the end of his own book, and in *Tom Sawyer, Detective,* Twain had introduced death and the threat of madness into that Eden itself.

By the time he was attempting to detach *Pudd'nhead* from the wreck of his larger book, Twain had decided that the only unthreatened utopia is death itself; and amid the animal jokes and easy cynicism of the Calendar quotations set at the head of each chapter, rings the sybil's cry: *Let me die:* "Whoever has lived long enough to know what life is knows how deep a debt of gratitude we owe to Adam, the first great benefactor of our race. He brought death into the world." When he writes this, Twain no longer finds in freedom the pat happy ending waiting to extricate his characters from their moral dilemmas and himself from the difficulties of plotting. He does not abandon the theme of liberty, but renders now the full treacherous paradox, only half of which he had acknowledged earlier.

Everyone remembers the climax of *Huckleberry Finn,* at which Tom, "his eye hot, and his nostrils opening and shutting like gills," cries out of Jim: "They hain't no *right* to shut him up. . . . Turn him loose! He ain't no slave; he's as free as any cretur that walks this earth!" As free as any cretur . . . the wry joke is there already, but Twain can no more see it than can Tom; and we are not permitted to see it as readers as long as we remain within the spell of the book. But in *Pudd'nhead Wilson,* the protagonist, who is obviously Tom himself grown older and an outcast but about to be reinstated into the community, rises to answer his own earlier cry, in such a situation as he has always dreamed: "Valet de Chambre, Negro and slave . . . make upon the window the finger-prints that will hang you!" The double truth is complete: the seeming slave is free, but the free man is really a slave.

The resolution of *Pudd'nhead* is, of course, double; and the revelation which brands the presumed Thomas à Becket Driscoll a slave, declares the presumed Valet de Chambre free. We are intended, however, to feel the "curious fate" of the latter as anything but fortunate; neither black nor white, he is excluded by long conditioning from the world of the free, and barred from the "solacing refuge" of the slave kitchens by the fact of his legal whiteness. Really, his is, as Twain himself remarks, quite another story; what is symbolically important is the deposition of Thomas à Becket—and the meaning of this Twain makes explicit in one of the final jottings in his journal, "The skin of every human being contains a slave." We know at last in what bitter sense Tom's earlier boast is true: "As free as any cretur . . ." *Pudd'nhead Wilson* begins and ends in the village where *Huckleberry Finn* began and *Tom Sawyer* was played out, on the banks of the same river and in the same pre-Civil War years. But between "St. Petersburg" and "Dawson's Landing" there is a terrible difference. In the latest book, we see Twain's mythicized Hannibal for the first time from the *outside;* in the two earlier books, we are already inside of it when the action begins, and there is no opportunity to step back and survey it. But Pudd'nhead comes as a stranger to the place of Twain's belonging; and the author himself takes advantage of this occasion to pan slowly into it, giving us an at first misleadingly idyllic description of its rose-clad houses, its cats, its sleepiness, and its fragrance— all preparing for the offhand give-away of the sentence beginning, "Dawson's Landing was a slaveholding town . . ."

The Civil War is the watershed in Twain's life between innocence and experience, childhood and manhood, joy and pain; but it is politically, of course, the dividing line between slavery and freedom. And Twain, who cannot deny either aspect, endures the contradiction of searching for a lost happiness he knows was sustained by an institution he is forced to recognize as his country's greatest shame. It was the best he could dream: to be free as a boy in a world of slavery!

In *Tom Sawyer,* this contradiction is hushed up for the sake of nostalgia and in the name of writing a child's book; in *Huck* it is preserved with all the power of its tensions; in the last book it falls apart into horror. In

Pudd'nhead Wilson, Hannibal is felt from the beginning not as a Western but as a *Southern* town. The river is no longer presented as the defining edge of the natural world, what America touches and crosses on its way West; but as a passageway into the darkness of the deep South. "Down the river" is the phrase which gives a kind of musical unity to the work—a motif repeated with variations from Roxana's first jesting taunt to a fellow Negro, "If you b'longed to me I'd sell you down the river 'fo' you git too fur gone . . ." to the bleak irony of the novel's final sentence, "the Governor . . . pardoned Tom at once, and the creditors sold him down the river."

A comparison inevitably suggests itself with *Huckleberry Finn* in which the southward motion had served to symbolize (in contempt of fact) a motion toward deliverance. But here the direction of the river that Twain loved is felt only as the way into the ultimate south, the final horror— the absolute pole of slavery. The movement of the plot and the shape of the book are determined by this symbolic motion toward the sea, now transposed from a dream of flight to a nightmare of captivity. It is after she herself has been threatened with such a fate and in order to preserve her son from it, that Roxy switches the children in the cradle. But there is no way to escape that drift downward toward darkness to which the accident of birth has doomed her and her son; by virtue of her very act of evasion she sets in motion the events that bring both of them to the end she had dreaded.

It is not only as a slave-holding town that Dawson's Landing belongs to the South, but also in terms of the code of honor to which everyone in the book subscribes. Patrician and Negro, American and foreigner, freethinker and churchgoer, all accept the notion that an insult can only be wiped out in blood, and that the ultimate proof of manhood is the willingness to risk death in such an attempt. The real demonstration of the unworthiness of the false Tom is his running to the courts for redress in preference to facing a duel. Ironically enough, this very duel was to have been in the book as originally planned a howling travesty of the values of the gentleman; for one of the parties was to have been half of a Siamese twin—and one can see what mad complications would have ensued. The "serious" Twain was, however, as incapable of doubting the code as Tom Sawyer; he could mock it only in pure farce, when he felt it perfectly clear to everyone that he was just kidding. There is in this book no Huck to challenge the many Colonel Sherburnes by rejecting courage as just another temptation—no absolute outcast, armed only with lies, to make it clear that honor is a luxury item for a leisure class. Even Pudd'nhead, for all his skepticism, longs not for bare survival but for style and success—and so he must pay his Tom Sawyerish respects to chivalry.

In *Huckleberry Finn*, the society which Huck finally rejects, his "sivilization," is essentially a world of the mothers, that is to say, of what Christianity has become among the females who sustain it just behind the advancing frontier. It is a sufficiently simple-minded world in which one does not cuss or steal or smoke but keeps clean, wears shoes, and prays for spiritual gifts. Above all, it is a world of those who cannot lie—and the truth, too, Huck finds a virtue beyond his budget. In this world, the fathers appear generally as outcasts and scoundrels, like the Duke and Dauphin and like Pap himself. At best, the paternal is represented by the runaway nigger, the outcast who was never even offered the bait of belonging.

In *Pudd'nhead Wilson*, however, society is defined by the fathers, last defenders of the chivalric code and descendants of the cavaliers. Four in especial represent the world to which Pudd'nhead aspires: York Leicester Driscoll, Percy Northumberland Driscoll, Pembroke Howard and Col. Cecil Burleigh Essex—the names make the point with an insistence that is a little annoying. This is a world continuous with that of Renaissance gallantry, connected with the Court of Elizabeth, which represents for Twain on the one hand a romantic legend, and on the other a kind of lost sexual Eden (celebrated in his privately circulated *1601*), whose potency puts to shame a fallen America where the natives "do it onlie once every seven yeares." The religion of such a society is, of course, not Christian at all; of Driscoll, the noble character murdered by the boy to whom he was a benefactor and almost a father, we are told "to be a gentleman was his only religion."

One half of the story of Thomas à Becket Driscoll (really the slave Valet de Chambre) is the account of his failing this world of the fathers, first in gambling and thieving, then in preferring the courts to the field of honor, finally in becoming out of greed and abject rage, a quasi-parricide. Twain spares us, perhaps from some reluctance to surrender to utter melodrama, more probably from lack of nerve, the final horror. The logic of the plot and its symbolic import both demand really that Tom be revealed at last as the bastard of the man he killed; but we are provided instead with a specially invented double of the dead Driscoll as the boy's begetter, a lay figure called Cecil Burleigh Essex.

In all of the book, only a single mother is allowed the center of the stage—the true mother of the false Tom, the slave girl Roxana. Just as in *Huckleberry Finn*, Nigger Jim is played off against the world of Aunt

Polly-Aunt Sally-Miss Watson, so in this reversed version a Negress is set against the society defined by Driscoll, Howard, and Essex. This is, of course, a just enough stroke, which satisfies our sense of the historical as well as our desire for the typical. If the fathers of the South are Virginia gentlemen, the mothers are the Negro girls, casually or callously taken in the parody of love, which is all that is possible when one partner to a sexual union is not even given the status of a person.

The second and infinitely worse crime of Tom is the sin against the mother, the black mammy who threatens him with exposure; and the most moving, the most realized sections of the book deal with this relationship. Throughout his career, Twain returned over and over to this theme of the rejection of the mother, the denial by the boy of the woman who has loved him with the purest love Twain could imagine. Of this Tom Sawyer is falsely accused by his Aunt Polly; of this Tom Canty is actually guilty at the tearful climax of *The Prince and the Pauper,* so extravagantly admired by its author. It is as if Mark Twain were trying to exorcise the possibility of himself failing the plea he could never forget, the cry of his own mother, clasping him to her over the death-bed of his father: "Only promise me to be a better boy. Promise me not to break my heart."

In *Pudd'nhead,* this tearful romance of the boy as a heartless jilt, becomes involved with the ambiguous relations of black and white in the United States, with the problems of miscegenation and of "passing," and is lifted out of the sentimental toward the tragic. Twain's own judgment of sexual relations between the races is not explicitly stated; but there seems no doubt that he thought of the union between Roxy and Essex as a kind of fall—evil in itself and the source of a doom on all involved. Paired together, *Huck* and *Pudd'nhead* express both sides of a deep, unthought-out American belief, reflected on the one side of Twain by James Fenimore Cooper and on the other by William Faulkner: that there are two relations, two kinds of love between colored and white, one of which is innocent, one guilty, one of which saves, one damns. The innocent relation can only exist between men, or a man and a boy (Natty Bumppo and Chingachgook, Huck and Jim)—a love unphysical and pure; the other, suspect and impure, tries to join the disjoined in passion, and must end either in frustration and death (Cora and Uncas) or in unhappiness for all (Roxana and Essex).

A further reach of complexity is added to the theme by the symbolic meanings inevitably associated with the colors white and black, meanings which go back through literature (Shakespeare's "Dark Lady," for example) and popular religion (the New England habit of calling the Devil "The Black Man") to the last depths of the folk mind. No matter how enlightened our conscious and rational convictions may be in these matters, we are beset by a buried ambivalence based on this archetypal symbolism of light and dark. Twain himself in this very novel speaks unguardedly of the rain trying vainly to wash soot-blackened St. Louis white; and the implication is clear: black is the outward sign of inward evil. In this sense, the Negro puzzlingly wears the livery of the guilt we had thought the white man's. But *why?* It is a question which rings through the white man's literature in America; and the answer returns in an ambiguity endlessly compounded.

Who, having read it once, can ever forget the terrible exclamation in Melville's "Benito Cereno"—the cry which seems intended to dissolve in irony the problem we had hoped would be resolved in certainty, "It is the Black!" But there are even more terrible lines in *Pudd'nhead*: the lonely and baffled query of Tom (how hard it is to believe that it is not a quotation from Faulkner), "What crime did the uncreated first nigger commit that the curse of birth was decreed for him . . ." and the still more appalling response of Roxy to the news that her son has failed the white man's code, "It's de nigger in you dat's what it is!" The name of their own lot turned insult in the mouth of the offended—beyond this it is impossible to go; and we cannot even doubt that this is precisely what Roxy would have said!

Perhaps the supreme achievement of this book is to have rendered such indignities not in terms of melodrama or as a parochial "social problem" but as a local instance of some universal guilt and doom. The false Tom, who is the fruit of all the betrayal and terror and profaned love which lies between white man and black, embodies also its "dark necessity"— and must lie, steal, kill, and boast until in his hybris he reveals himself as the slave we all secretly are. This tragic inevitability is, however, blurred by the demands of the detective story with which it is crossed. The tragedy of Tom requires that he expose and destroy himself; the melodrama of Pudd'nhead Wilson requires that he reveal and bring to justice the Negro who has passed as white; and Twain decided finally that it was Pudd'nhead's book—a success story. Yet there remains beneath the assertion that a man is master of his fate, the melancholy conviction that to be born is to be doomed, a kind of secularized Calvinism.

We have already noticed that Pudd'nhead is Tom Sawyer grown up, the man who has not surrendered with maturity the dream of being a hero; but it must be added that he wants to be a hero on his own terms, to force himself upon a hostile community without knuckling under to its values; that is to say, he would like still to be as an adult the "good bad boy" who put the finger on Indian Joe. Translated out of the vocabulary of boyhood, this means that he has to become first a rebel and then a detective.

He begins as a pariah, the sage whose wisdom is taken for folly: an outsider in a closed society, a free thinker in a world of conformism, a gadgeteer and crank, playing with palmistry and fingerprints. But he is also, like his creator, a jokester; and, indeed, it is his first quip which earns him a reputation for stupidity and twenty years of exclusion. "I wish I owned half of that dog," he says of a viciously howling beast, "because I would kill my half"—and that is almost the end of him. Yet like his creator he wants to succeed in the world he despises; and he yields to it half-unwittingly even before it accepts him, adjusting to its code of honor, its definition of a Negro—while writing down in private or reading before a two man Free Thinkers' Society his dangerous thoughts.

Typically enough, it is as a detective that he makes his comeback. In three earlier books his prototype, Tom Sawyer, had achieved similar triumphs: exposing Injun Joe, revealing Jim's true status, clearing his half-crazed uncle of the charge of murder; but more is involved than this. Ever since Poe's Dupin, the sleuth has been a favorite guise of the writer in fiction—non-conformist and exposer of evil, the poor man's intellectual. He is the one who, revealing in the moment of crisis "who done it," restores the community (as W. H. Auden has suggested in an acute study of the detective story) to a state of grace.

But Twain has the faith neither of a Chesterton nor a Conan Doyle; and the revelations of David Wilson (the name "Pudd'nhead" is sloughed off with his victory) restore civil peace only between him and the community which rejected him: for the rest, they expose only bankruptcy and horror and shame, and stupidity of our definition of a Negro, and the hopelessness of our relations with him. Wilson's disclosure of Roxy's hoax coalesces with Twain's exposure to America of its own secret self; and the double discovery is aptly framed by Wilson's Calendar entries for two of our favorite holidays.

The chapter which contains the courtroom revelation is preceded by the text, "*April 1*. This is the day upon which we are reminded of what we are on the other three hundred and sixty-four." The implication is clear, whether conscious or not, not fools only but slaves! And it is followed by another, even grimmer, "*October 12, the Discovery*. It was wonderful to find America, but it would have been more wonderful to miss it." The Discovery! It is a disconcerting ending for a detective story, which should have faith in all disclosures; but it is the aptest of endings for an American book, the only last word possible to a member of the Free Thinkers' Society. Beyond such bleak wisdom, there is only the cry of Roxy at the moment of revelation, "De Lord have mercy on me, po' miserable sinner dat I is!" But this is forbidden to Mark Twain.

The Symbols of Despair

by Bernard DeVoto

This essay is a chapter, hitherto unwritten, in the biography of Mark Twain. Mr. Paine's *Mark Twain: a Biography* lists some of the manuscripts dealt with here and even devotes a few sentences of description to a few of them. But it is clear that Mr. Paine did not understand their significance and, if he had understood them, I think he would have regarded it as his duty to say nothing about them. Certainly as one reads his *Biography* one gets no proper sense of the effect on Mark Twain of the disasters which these manuscripts deal with.

Those disasters are agonizing as personal history. Our interest, however, is in the manuscripts which came out of them—we are concerned with them as a series of literary episodes. Those episodes occur in the life of a literary genius and by chance, a fortunate chance for criticism, they partly open up an area of literature which is usually closed. They make it possible to document, and so in some small degree to analyze, certain processes of creation. Criticism is usually altogether unable to say how a writer's experience is transformed into works of art. In these manuscripts we can actually see that transformation while it is occurring. We are able to watch Mark Twain while he repeatedly tries and repeatedly fails to make something of experiences that were vitally important to him—and finally we are able to see him fuse and transform them in a work of art. We are able to see the yeasts and ferments actually at work. In the end they do not justify us in saying much about how creative processes may work in other writers. But I think that even a single exposition of how they once worked in one writer is worth making.

One caution. Both psychology and literary criticism are highly speculative fields. This inquiry is more speculative still, in that it is carried on in the no man's land between them. The findings I bring in here are essentially speculative: I cannot prove them. That being said, I may also say that throughout the essay my reference is to demonstrable fact wherever possible. The facts that support my findings are far more numerous, and my argument has a much more solid base, and much stronger links, than there is room even to suggest in the course of a single essay.

A Connecticut Yankee in King Arthur's Court was published in December, 1889. It is the last of Mark Twain's books which we can call certainly of the first rank, and its publication furnishes a convenient date. He was then the most widely known and admired writer in America, and very likely in the world. He was at the summit of his personal happiness. His books had won him not only world-wide fame but a fortune as well. He was the husband of a greatly loved wife, the father of three delightful children, the master of a house famous for the warmth of its hospitality, the center of a small cosmos of beloved friends, an intimate of the famous men and women of his time, courted, praised, sought after, universally loved. His life had a splendor that marked him as the darling of the gods, and that and the splendor of his imagination made more than one person think of him as a mysterious sojourner from somewhere outside the orbit of this earth. The backwoods boy, the tramp printer, the Mississippi pilot, the silver miner, the San Francisco bohemian had become one of the great men of the earth, the hero of a story more romantic than any of Tom Sawyer's dreams.

Our first concern is the series of catastrophes that came in the 1890's. Some years before, he had established his own publishing firm, to publish his books. He had expanded it in order to publish the memoirs of General Grant, and the over-extended business required better management than Mark could give it, better management than anyone could give it whom he hired. The firm faltered, the going got worse, and finally, as a result of the freezing of credit in the panic of 1893, it had to go into receivership. It could have been saved—except that a greater loss had drained Mark's fortune and his wife's as well. Always a speculator, a Colonel Sellers who dreamed of millions but was a predestinate sucker for all salesmen of gold bricks, he had poured nearly a quarter of a million dollars into the development of an invention that was going to make him many times a millionaire. This was the Paige typesetting machine, and his grandiose dream was not absurd, considering the millions which the Mergenthaler Linotype has made. But the Mergenthaler machine succeeded, whereas the Paige machine failed altogether and carried Mark Twain down with it, just at the time when his publishing firm went bankrupt. Furthermore, these same years saw a mysterious alteration in the personality of his youngest daughter, Jean, and finally the terrible mystery was cleared up by the discovery of the still more terrible truth, that she was an epileptic. During these years also his capricious but usually exuberant health failed. He was racked by the bronchitis which he was never again to lose, by the rheumatism which was the inheritance of his frontier youth, and by other ailments which were the result of the enormous strain he was under.

So, in 1895, a bankrupt, little better than an invalid, four months short of sixty years old, Mark Twain started on a lecturing tour which was to take him round the world and pay off his creditors dollar for dollar. His wife and one of his daughters went with him, but they left behind them in America their youngest daughter and their oldest one, Susy, the one who Mark felt was nearest him in mind and spirit. Just a year later, the exhausting trip ended in London, and the children were to join them there. They did not. Across the Atlantic from her parents, Susy died of meningitis. And in the months following, Mark's wife began to decline into the invalidism that was to last through the remaining eight years of her life.

The gods had turned against their darling. Such a sequence of calamities might well drive a man mad; there would be little to wonder at if Mark Twain had broken under them. And the truth is that for a time he lived perilously close to the indefinable line between sanity and madness. Passages of his private anguish in the unpublished papers show to what a tautness the membrane of the mind was stretched, and come near breaking the reader's heart. But we are concerned, not with the man's grief but rather with the use the artist made of it.

For, of course, it is obvious that such events as these cannot occur to the man without happening to the artist as well. The rich man had been bankrupted, and the threatened poverty had imperilled his wife and children. The man of great fame had, or so to the tortured ego it must seem, been somehow toppled from his high place, and always thereafter Mark Twain must carry in his heart some remnant feeling of disgrace. Necessarily, his image of himself had been impaired. These blows which had fallen on him, which had been struck at him, had made him something other than he had been—or at least something other than he had believed and seemed. A man's position in the world, his various successes, his public reputation are interstitial with his ego; an injury to any one injures all and so injures his secret image of himself. But also interstitial with that image is a writer's talent. In the deepest psychological sense, even in a biological sense, a man's work is his life. That is to say, the sources of his talent are inseparably a part of his feeling of wholeness, of his identity, and even, quite nakedly, of his power. An injury to the man must necessarily be an injury on this deep level of personal power—a blow at his virility. And equally, an injury to the inner picture of the man by which life is sustained, must be an injury working outward to impair his work as well. In the dark areas where the roots of life go down, the threatened soul cannot easily distinguish among the parts and organs of personality, and if one of them is endangered then the dim mind knows that all have come in peril.

All this is the merest commonplace of experience. Remembering it, we should expect the series of disasters to have a powerful effect on Mark Twain's writing. And also, remembering that it is the nature of writers to forge their art out of the materials of their lives, we should expect to find in his writing some effort to grapple with the disasters. Art is the terms of an armistice signed with fate. Or, if you like the words better, art is experience appraised, completed, neutralized, or overcome. . . . So let us see.

It was July, 1896, when the lecture tour ended in London. The lectures had made almost enough money to clear Mark's debts but not quite, and there remained to write the book about his trip, *Following the Equator*, which was to complete his task. It was in August, 1896, that Susy died. He began the book in October. And he wrote to his friend Twichell:

> I am working, but it is for the sake of the work—the "surcease of sorrow" that is found there. I work all the days, and trouble vanishes away when I use that magic. This book will not long stand between it and me, now; but that is no matter, I have many unwritten books to fly to for my preservation; the interval between the finishing of this one and the beginning of the next will not be more than an hour.[1]

Observe that he was relying on work, on writing, to hold his grief at arm's length, the grief of Susy's death. But, besides that pitiful purpose, are we not already entitled to see something else? There seems to me already a hint of what was soon to be plainer, that part of his necessity to write was to vindicate himself as a writer, to restore the image that had been impaired. He had to write: he was compelled to.

Following the Equator is the dullest of his books, and writing it was a laborious and sometimes agonizing task. He rebelled at writing it for money. He rebelled at the meaninglessness of the pursuit, which was part of the meaninglessness of life. For, with Susy dead, life seemed to have no meaning except loss and cruelty. But he kept at work and on April 13, 1897, a notebook entry says, "I finished my book today." But it needed revising and on May 18, the notebook says, "Finished the book again." Several pages of notes follow, some of them for a story I shall be describing in a moment, and then on May 23, five days after the end of the book, the notebook says, "Wrote first chapter of above story today." The in-

[1] Letter of Jan. 19, 1897.

terval had been a little longer than the hour he predicted to Twichell, but not much.

With that first chapter, Mark had begun the series of experiments and failures that are our central interest. And also he began other experiments and other failures not closely related to them. What the next months show is a man writing in the grip of a compulsion, driven to write, flogged and scourged to write by the fierce drive within him—a man under compulsion to write for "surcease of sorrow," but still more to reintegrate a blasted talent, and most of all to restore his image of himself after the intolerable impairment it had suffered. But also this compulsive need to write is constantly blocked, displaced, and distorted. It is so frenzied that it seems aimless—and also it is perpetually frustrated. "I couldn't get along without work now," he wrote to Howells. "I bury myself in it up to the ears. Long hours—8 and 9 at a stretch, sometimes." [2] That shows the compulsiveness, and we get a glimpse of the frustration when he writes to Howells in August, 1898, fifteen months after that confident notebook entry, "Last summer I started 16 things wrong—3 books and 13 mag. articles—and could only make 2 little wee things, 1,500 words altogether, succeed—only that out of piles and stacks of diligently-wrought MS., the labor of 6 weeks' unremitting effort." But the truth was more startling and more serious than this glimpse shows, for the inability to make more than on an average two little wee things come out of sixteen starts was to last longer than he thought. It was to last through 1898 and on to 1899, to 1900, to 1904—and in fact the jobs that he completed from 1897 on through the rest of his life represent only a small fraction of the jobs he began. From 1897 on there are scores of manuscripts in the Mark Twain Papers which begin bravely enough and then peter out, some of them after only a few pages, some of them only after many hundred pages of stubborn and obviously heart-wrenching work. Now it is certain that, as Mark grew older, he did not intend to finish some of them—that he began them merely to amuse himself or to jot down a passing observation or perception, or to find release from some mood in the only remedy he was able to depend on. But other manuscripts, especially those we are to deal with, he meant and desperately wanted to complete. He was impelled to come back to them time after time, take them up again, try some other beginning or some other set of characters, impose some other form on them or some new outcome or some other meaning or some other moral—but get on with them, sweat them through, mould them to an end. So time after time he came back to them. And time after time he failed. He could not finish them.

[2] Letter of Jan. 22, 1898.

Such a frustration is a striking thing. There must be a significant reason for the repeated failure of a practiced literary artist, a man who had been writing all his life with marked success. True, Mark Twain had always been subject to enthusiasms and his enthusiasms were short-lived, so that normally he began a good many manuscripts which he never bothered to finish after the going got hard. But this is something else, a repeated and habitual failure, and he did try to finish them—he tried repeatedly, under the compulsion that had enslaved him. He kept coming back to them—and always he failed. This is no casual or meaningless failure; it is obviously closely interwrought with the fundamental energies of his personality.

The end of our search will come in 1905, but we are most concerned with the two and a half years following that notebook entry of May 18, 1897. During that period he wrote so much that, turning the manuscripts over in my hands and trying to make out their relationships, I have frequently told myself that some of them could not possibly belong to these years, that no man could write so much. But there they are, manuscript after manuscript, a staggering number of them, a still more staggering grand total of words. He actually wrote them during these years. During the same years of course, he also wrote other essays, sketches, reminiscences, newspaper articles, which he succeeded in completing and which were published. But here is a many times greater number of manuscripts which he could not finish.

The force that was impelling him to write was, clearly, both desperate and remorseless. Only a man who was hellridden could write so much. Think of the inner desperation this indicates—and think how that desperation must have grown and spread when time after time he was forced to realize that he could not finish what he had begun. His invention ran out, he could not solve the ordinary problems of structure and technique, he could not overcome the ordinary difficulties of his own intentions, he could not push the thing through to an end. Apart from the manuscripts themselves there is little record of his distress, but surely it was a long agony. Secretly, in the hours of black brooding which had become habitual since Susy died, he must have been forever grappling with the most terrible fear that any artist can feel: the fear that his talent has been drained away, that his spark has been quenched, that his achievement is over forever. It is a poison which acts two ways, spreading back to reinforce the poison that begot it. For the failure of the artist must strike close to the deepest identity and potency of the man—and that identity and potency had already been challenged and grievously impaired by the catastrophes we have glanced at. Of course, it must have proceeded out of those catastrophes, or at least been set in motion by them, and few would doubt that his new impotence was related to the impairment he had suffered or that these literary failures issued from the complex sense of failure that had been created in him.

Much of this heap of manuscript is at random. I disregard that part and consider now only what seems significant in the end. And the first support of what I have just said about impairment comes from Mark's attempts to make use once more of the immortal boys who had conferred immortality on his two finest books—and whom he had called upon again, during the anxieties of the early '90's, for those two lesser stories, *Tom Sawyer Abroad* and *Tom Sawyer Detective*. So now he put them to work again, involving them in a long conspiracy of Tom's invention more preposterous and much drearier than the one that turns the last part of *Huckleberry Finn* into burlesque. It is a maze of romance and rank improvisation that is trivial to begin with and speedily becomes disheartening. It is wholly without structure and moves without plan by dint of a feverish extemporization which gets more mechanical and improbable as it goes on. It is dull, humorless, without the enchantment of the great originals. Mark's touch is altogether gone from it and, what points most vividly to the truth, even the prose is dead.

It is pitiful to see a great writer turning back, in such a desperate mood, to the works of his greatness. And this effort to repeat what he had done at the height of his power, summoning ghosts from his earlier books, shows the strength of his fear that power had departed from him. It is the more pitiful that the effort to save himself does not save him: the book is a merciless parody of the great books it turns back to. He must have realized the true nature of the effort he was making, and certainly its failure could not be hidden from him. Few more bitter experiences can happen to an artist. Nor is this manuscript the only one in which he tried to use the two boys, as we shall see, nor are *Huckleberry Finn* and *Tom Sawyer* the only earlier books he called on in his need. Through much of the unfinished work of this period runs a diluted strain of other books, *Pudd'nhead Wilson* in particular, and of ideas, devices, stock themes and treatments which he had found effective in his great days but which were not effective now when he needed them most.

It was at this time, also, that Mark began to think seriously about his autobiography. He had written fragments of it before, notably the account of his publication of Grant's memoirs contained in the first volume of the published portions. But now he wrote a number of more or less systematic sketches and planned to buckle down and write the book. He made many pages of notes for it—lists of people, character sketches, memoranda of exciting or important or amusing events. These jottings run through all the notebooks he kept during this period, a long sequence of them in one book shows a comprehensive plan for the book, and there is a forty-page catalogue of Hannibal people which is well along toward actual biography.[3]

Of all this autobiographical material, by far the largest part concerns two periods of his life. Scattering memoranda cover many years, but most of them deal either with the dead child Susy or with the Hannibal of his boyhood. One long section of a notebook describes the agonizing details of Susy's illness and death, and yearns over the little, trivial, pitiful incidents of her childhood, the promise of her life, the loss and stunning cruelty of her death. These notes he actually worked up into a biographical sketch of Susy; but he could not finish it. He was to come back to it some years later, and to work much of it into the *Autobiography*. But there is even more about Hannibal, and the friends and neighbors of the Clemenses, than there is about Susy.

What is the importance of these facts for our inquiry? Well, it is significant that, in this time of impotence and failure, his mind was constantly turning over not only his memories of his dead daughter, but also his memories of his boyhood. For we know from his books that boyhood was his golden time and that Hannibal was his lost, immortal idyl, not of boyhood only but of home as well. It meant whatever home means of peace, happiness, fulfillment, and especially of security. In the time of desolation whose symbol he was not yet able to forge, he turned back to the years and the place that meant safety. Presently we shall understand why.

Finally, it was at this time that he began to write what he called his Gospel. Twenty years ago or more he had read a paper on philosophical determinism to a club in Hartford, and from time to time thereafter he had shown that the idea was working in him. Now suddenly it began to demand expression—and it was to go on demanding it until he died. A large part of the Mark Twain Papers consists of argumentative or analytical chapters, dialogues, letters, some of them finished, more abandoned, which develop and embroider the twinned themes: man's complete helplessness in the grip of the inexorable forces of the universe, and man's essential cowardice, pettiness, and evil. He went on writing them until within a few months of his death, but actually he began to write them, and wrote the most consecutive of them, in the period we are dealing with. Probably the greater part of those which he privately printed in 1904 as *What Is Man?* were written during these years.

[3] "Villagers of 1840-43."

The importance of *What Is Man?* to our inquiry is that it provides the first dependable indication, very possibly the earliest one, of what was going on in the ferments that were at work. We have asked what was the result on the artist of the calamities that had all but broken the man, and with this book we may make a start toward an answer. For *What Is Man?* is not only a treatise on man's instability, weakness, cowardice, cruelty, and degradation. It is not only an assault on the illusions of free will, integrity, decency, and virtue with which mankind makes tolerable its estate. It is not only an assertion of the familiar logic of determinism, the fixed universe, the infrangible sequence of cause and effect from the beginning of time, holding man helpless, and unalterable by will or wish or effort. If that were all there were to it, surely there would be significance in its getting itself written at this particular period. But it is much more than that. For clearly *What Is Man?* is also a plea for pardon. In describing man's helplessness, it pleads that man cannot be blamed. In asserting man's cowardice, it asserts also that man is not responsible. In painting man as enslaved and dominated by inexorable circumstance, it argues that the omnipotence of circumstance must answer for what Mark is inwardly afraid he is being held to answer for. If man is weak, cowardly, and sentenced to defeat, then one who feels himself weak, cowardly, and defeated cannot be to blame. If man is not responsible, then no man can be held responsible. No one, I think, can read this wearisomely repeated argument without feeling the terrible force of an inner cry: Do not blame me, for it was not my fault.

That theme, which is to be repeated in many forms, is struck clearly in *What Is Man?* So we may now move on to the three groups of manuscripts from whose chaos was to be resolved the answer to that troubled cry. I cannot be sure that my arrangement is chronological—I cannot date all of them in relation to one another. But that does not matter much, for they are variations on themes common to them all, the themes come together in the end, and I can date most of the significant steps in the evolution that is really a debate.

We will follow them rather by idea than by manuscript. A number of ideas are repeated over and over in the various manuscripts, modulated, changed, adapted, blended, and in the end, harmonized.

One of these ideas, and probably the earliest, is that of the great stretch of time which may seem to elapse in a dream whose actual duration, in waking time, is only a few minutes or perhaps a few seconds. And mingled with this idea is another one, which holds the germ of the eventual conclusion, the idea of confusing dream with reality. The notebook entry I have quoted, which says that Mark began the "above story" on a certain day, proposes a story in which a man is to nod for a moment over a cigarette, dream a sequence of events which he thinks has lasted for seventeen years, and on waking from his momentary sleep, so have confused the dream with the reality that he cannot recognize his wife. Accompanying this entry is a list of characters for the story which identifies many of them as actual persons from Mark Twain's past. The significance of this is made greater by the fact that, as I have said, Mark was making plans for his autobiography at exactly the same time.

But the story which he actually began to write, though it preserves the framework of the dream, mostly disregards it in favor of another idea, a different theme, whose significance is apparent at sight and which was to arouse, following this story, his most persistent effort. It is the story of a world-famous personage who is cast down from his high estate. The time is shortly after the Mexican War of 1846, and the hero is the youngest major-general in the American army, whose heroism and gallantry have made him a world figure and destined him for the Presidency as soon as he shall be old enough to hold that office. He is not only world famous but very rich as well, fortunate and happy, married to a beautiful woman whom he worships, the father of two small girls whom he adores, one of whom is talented and promising. He falls asleep over his cigarette and in his dream the family's magnificent house is burned down and, following that, a greater catastrophe swiftly engulfs them. A trusted relative of the general's wife, who has been trusted with the management of their fortune, proves not only to have dissipated the fortune but to have become involved in widespread chicanery and fraud as well. The general's reputation is blackened, he and his beloved family are plunged not only into abject poverty but into overwhelming disgrace as well, and in all ways he and they are ruined. He sinks into unconsciousness, wakes from that a year and a half later, finds himself and his family living in a squalid log cabin in California, learns the bitter struggle his wife has made to support them—and here the manuscript breaks off. It had broken off before this and been resumed, but this time the break was final. Mark Twain could go no farther.

Already my point must be clear; it hardly needs my assurance that the story is crowded with undisguised autobiographical material—lifelong friends of Mark Twain, members of his family, enemies, incidents that had happened to him, scenes and speeches straight from his life. Notice the starkness of the theme: a great and fine personage of unimpeachable integrity is struck down by catastrophe and disgraced in the eyes of all the world. Notice also how it is made clear that the personage was innocently betrayed, that the catastrophe was not his fault.

Following this story, Mark separated out the dream idea and confined it to a sequence which I will describe in a moment, while proceeding to carry the theme of the virtuous man cast down from his high estate into a series of manuscripts which together represent the strongest and most persistent effort in our whole cycle. He kept coming back to this story not only during 1898 and 1899 but as late as 1904. How many different essays he made I cannot say, I can only say that he made them repeatedly. The thing obsessed him and he must get it out. But time after time he found himself blocked and had to quit.

It is much too long a story and, as his efforts crisscrossed and failed, much too complex a story for me to tell here. It concerns the leading citizen of a town which hardly differs from the St. Petersburg of *Tom Sawyer* and the Hannibal of the *Autobiography,* and not only the squire but another citizen, formerly wealthy, who had suffered the loss of his fortune and is now reduced to poverty but everywhere respected for his virtue and integrity. Through an intricate series of circumstances the virtuous man is led by his own weakness to commit murder, and other intricately wrought circumstances throw suspicion on the squire. The theme is frequently lost sight of in the melodramatic incidents that Mark frantically invented to get it told somehow, or anyhow, and in a flood of other themes from all the other ventures of this period. But the theme is the moral cowardice and hypocrisy of mankind, the liability of everyone, even the most virtuous, to yield to his secret weakness, provided only he is tempted, or there is some seeming necessity, or mere chance comes his way. Back and forth across this theme play related themes from *What Is Man?*

Now see what has happened. The theme of catastrophe has been modulated. The protagonist has been split in two. The victim of catastrophe is no longer innocent, as in the major-general's story, he is guilty and knows he is guilty, and a large part of the story is his effort to appease and justify himself. But, though he is guilty, the plea is made for him that he cannot be blamed. In different attempts different reasons are given but they all come to the same thing in the end—that circumstance is omnipotent and what happens must happen, alike to all men. If all men would sin in the given circumstance, then none can be blamed for sinning—the responsibility must be turned back to impersonal fate or to the malevolent God who designed it. But notice that there is here a psychic admission, or an accusation, which the earlier story did not contain. The major-general was betrayed by one he had trusted, but the virtuous man of this cycle, though the plea is made that he was not responsible, is cast down by his own act.

This cycle too is crowded with unmistakable portraits and events from the actual world of Mark's own experience. A greater effort is made to transform and adapt them, but they are there. And it should be clear that they are there by the same compulsion that put the admission or accusation there.

Bear in mind that none of the expedients, new starts, or changed devices had worked: Mark had proved unable to bring any version of his story to fruition. Not even when he went back and borrowed from its predecessor. He tried, that is, telling the same story of the virtuous man made murderer and coward and hypocrite by calamity, as something that happened in a dream—in a dream, furthermore, that was to last for a few minutes only, though it seemed to consume many years. So what began as an independent story became essentially the same story, though with the modulation I have pointed out. And that modulation, I think, discloses the secret self-accusation as it is met by a counter assertion that all men are guilty as circumstances compel them to be.

We have now got far along in our period and must go back, to where the idea of the dream began a different evolution. A number of apparently aimless sketches which have no surface relationship to our inquiry had dealt with sailors or other people marooned in the vast Antarctic waste of ice and darkness. In one of these there had been introduced a legend of an enchanted sea wilderness in the midst of this eternal winter where ships were caught in a central place of calm, circumscribed by the ice and snow, and held drifting forever there with the dead bodies of their crews and passengers preserved by the unearthly cold. Various components of this idea run back farther in Mark's thinking than I can trace them here, but now they have come together in a striking and terrible symbol of desolation.

Mark had not been able to complete any of these casual sketches, but, whether consciously or not, they led to a re-entry and flashed across his mind the bright hope that he had found a variation of the story that tormented him which, this time, he would be able to complete. Again we have the happily married man who is the father of two delightful daughters and again he falls asleep and is to waken after a few minutes, believing that years have passed. But this time, before he falls asleep he looks through a microscope at a drop of water—and that item changes and immensely deepens the story. For in his dream, he and his family are on a mysterious ship sailing they know not where in a perpetual darkness filled with storms of snow and ice. This proves to be an Antarctic waste in the drop of water which he had looked at in the microscope, and in that tortured dream the voyage progresses in mystery and terror—

and also in what I feel to be significance. No one knows where they are, no one knows where they are going or for what purpose or under whose command, but they are in the Great Dark at the edge of the microscope's field, a place of unimaginable desolation, and somewhere far off is the horror of the Great White Glare, which is really the beam cast through the microscope's field by the reflector.

Moreover, on this ship there is some recollection of waking life—the world of reality outside both the microscope and the dream. But this fades, and one comes to doubt it, one comes in the end to believe that the reality one remembers was a dream after all, and that the dream one lives in is the reality. Furthermore, there is a supernatural being on board the ship, the Superintendent of Dreams, who has power over both the ship and the minds of its passengers, who steadily, vindictively, cultivates in their minds the doubt of reality which becomes the belief in dream.[4] And in the terrible darkness, monsters roam the freezing ocean, threatening to snatch victims from the ship and devour them. And finally, there is mutiny and betrayal on this ship, trusted officers who will be untrue and produce catastrophe.

This story also Mark could not finish. He came back to it several times, trying to find an effective outcome for it, trying to give it this slant or that, trying to crystallize round these symbols a coherent expression of the dread they had for him. The frustration still held and he could not do it, but what he did write is markedly superior to anything I have previously mentioned. It is a strange, powerful, and moving story, this uncompleted fragment, which holds you fascinated despite some crudities of construction. There is significance for us in the fact that he was able to make it better literature. And there is more significance in the notes that show how he wanted to finish it. For as the voyage went on, still greater afflictions were to visit the ship. It was to meet other ships caught in the same terrible enchantment. One of them was to contain a fabulous treasure in gold, and this was to madden certain of the already mutinous crew. The baby who had been born to our married couple was to be carried off on another ship, the search for the child was to mingle with the crew's mad lust for the treasure, the wife's heart was to break, her hair was to turn white, and she was finally to go mad with grief, during the ten fruitless years while they tried to find the child. They were to catch up with the other ship at last—but in the Great White Glare, where the child and all the crew and passengers of the second ship were to be killed by the merciless heat. And the Glare was to further madden the gold-maddened

---

[4] I need not point out that the Superintendent of Dreams exactly corresponds to God in *What Is Man?* Watch him become Satan.

mutineers and to dry up the sea, the monsters were to gather, and in a final, apocalyptic phantasy of destruction, the two beloved daughters were to be killed, the grief-crazed wife was to die, all remaining survivors of the first ship were to die also, leaving only the helpless narrator and the loyal Negro who was his servant.

Once more, a great part of the detail of this story was from Mark's experience. Most of the characters are identifiable from his life, or correspond to characters elsewhere in our material who are identifiable. The children's parties, the servants, the arguments can be annotated. The girl who is so loved and who is killed with such cruelty dies in exactly the delirium that the faithful notebooks record of Susy Clemens' fatal illness. And so on.

The pattern had now been repeated many times. We have seen Mark's compulsion to write it and the inhibition that withheld him from working it out to an end. So now, I think, we may make some judgments. We have seen in fiction the shape of the imprint left on Mark Twain's mind and heart by the series of catastrophes I began by describing. For essentially they are the catastrophes that obsess him in these uncompleted stories, nor can there be any doubt what great personage is cast down from his high place, what beloved wife is maddened by despair, what beloved daughter dies in agony. But if we recognize all that, then we must also recognize the terrible accusation that had risen in his heart. I said, far back, that he walked the narrow edge between sanity and madness. How close he came to madness may be understood in this cry, "It must have been my fault!"

We need neither the anthropology of primitive religions nor the psychology of the unconscious mind to understand, for in all of us a similar fear and accusation hover about the margin of the mind, to come forward a little and lose some of their vagueness in moments when discouragement is on us or when the menace of living has suddenly sharpened. That primal guilt is of one tissue with our primal despair, but happily those are brief moments when we are in health. Yet we all know, of our own experience or experience near to us, that the shocks of life may sometimes prolong those moments, bring the accusation into the center of the mind, delay the healthy reaction from it—and then we have at best despair and at worst insanity. This close had Mark Twain come: that there had been set up in him a contention, an accusation he could not bear, a repudiation he could not make. In the yeasty darkness at the mind's base, he had, of his own fault, brought on himself this disgrace and degradation and humiliation. In the phantasy that underlay both his grief and his rebellion, he was the author of his own fall, and the author also of his wife's and daughters' illness, of his daughter's death, of the unabated agony that had come upon his family.

So now he had found the symbols of despair. Through stormy darkness and hemmed in by ice, directed by some unknown and malevolent will, a ship sails a terrible sea where no chart can be had and where monsters lurk that may strike and destroy at any moment. The ship sails there forever, there is no plan or sense to its voyage and no hope that the agony will end, and the helpless passengers are menaced not only by the Great Dark without but by mutiny and greed and maniac revenge within. And quite surely there will come to them bereavement, the death of their loved ones, the triumph of an idle and unmitigated malevolence whose terrible decoys are love and hope and human warmth, to lure humanity to destruction.

The artist is driven to make what he can of experience, and art is the terms of an armistice made with fate. Yet the compulsiveness he shows and above all his frustration make clear that here we are dealing with more than the comparatively simple way of art. The impact of calamity had been too great, he had taken one step too near the edge, and there is evident a struggle not only to make terms with his experience but also to vindicate himself. And not only to vindicate himself but, quite literally, by that vindication to integrate a mind that had been blasted and restore a talent that had been blown asunder.

We have seen his first attempt to still that accusation: the "It was not my fault" of the story where the major-general is betrayed by a trusted relative. That would not suffice: the excuse was too transparent. There followed the assertion in *What Is Man?* that no one can be blamed since the chain of circumstance holds him fast in a plan determined by a vindictive God. That would not move the judge's heart, nor could the voice be stilled by the argument of the cycle to which he returned so often (in the stories of the virtuous man turned murderer) that all men are weak and all men fall when tempted.

But important modulations had been made in the dream story. And let me add that at one time, as his notes show, he contemplated going back to the disgraced major-general and setting him out also on the dreambound ship in the eternal ice, together with a company of fellow-victims living out their diverse fates in the same predestined anguish and despair. He did not write it. If he had begun it, he would not have finished it. For though this addition to the idea had hope in it, he had not yet found the reconciliation.

But he had come close to it. There was a grotesque hope, or at least an alleviation, in the position he had now reached. For this dream idea has two parts, one that dreams are brief though their agony may seem to last forever, and the deeper one that the reality may fade into the dream, that one may not be sure, that as one wakes from dream so perhaps one may wake from a lesser to a greater dream. Here the perturbed spirit finds comfort, though not quite enough, in the simple thought, so direct and inevitable, so characteristic of the helplessness of our deepest selves: "It may not be true after all. It may be a dream. Maybe I have dreamed the whole agony. Maybe loss and suffering and despair are false, are only a dream."

Remember that this compulsive writing had produced other manuscripts, apparently at random and without relation to this bitter debate. Among them was a story about Tom Sawyer and Huck Finn, which I briefly described. But that story could not have been altogether aimless and at random. It was, in a way, a premonition. For in his winnowing of his own books and his lost years, he happened upon a mysterious stranger in the town of Hannibal. I do not know much about this man, for he takes various forms, but the important thing is his secret, the fact that there is noble or perhaps royal blood in his veins. This made him kin to Mark Twain, in whose veins ran the blood of an English earldom as well as that of a regicide. And was not Mark, besides, that most mysterious of strangers on this earth, a genius, a man born unlike other men, to a strange destiny? Somehow the image of this unrecognized nobleman blends with another image that has fascinated Mark all his life long, the figure of Satan. And this was a fruitful time to remember Satan, for Satan is an angel and angels are exempt from loss and pain and all mortal suffering, they are exempt from guilt and conscience and self-condemnation also, and temptation has no meaning for them and they have no moral sense, and neither humiliation nor death nor the suffering of anyone affects them in the least. Moreover, of the angels who were all that Mark needed most to be, he felt nearest to Satan, the one who had revolted against the inexorable laws of the universe stated in *What Is Man?* and the one whose insatiable curiosity about the ways of man kept him going up and down on the earth and to and fro therein.

So it is not surprising when, presently, young Satan, a son of the fallen angel, comes to Hannibal and falls in with Tom Sawyer and Huck Finn. This first manuscript is not remarkable, being little more than a succession of marvelous works done by the young angel for the admiration and stupefaction of the village. It was fumbling and tentative and it frayed out. But in it and in the notes made for carrying it on Mark found the vital clues, the seeds that were to bear fruit at last. At first young Satan was no more than a vehicle for Mark's derision of the God whose vengefulness creates human pain and for his scorn of the ant-like race pain is inflicted on, and an identification, infantile at base, with a supernatural being who can perform wonders that make him distinguished and envied, a being also of irresistible strength. But he became more than that, and the way out of the basic frustration was his miracles. So another manuscript begins with Tom and Huck and young Satan in Hannibal, but this soon breaks off and a longer, better, and more deeply wrought one begins. The same story has been transferred to Eseldorf, in Austria, centuries ago —but if we needed any clue by now, note that this story includes a printshop such as young Sam Clemens worked in when he was the age of these boys. I will say nothing of this manuscript except that it led directly to the one that came through to triumph at last, the book which, after it had been painfully written over and changed and adjusted and transformed, was to achieve the completion denied its many predecessors, the book which we know as *The Mysterious Stranger*.

In those tortured revisions and adjustments, which are part of the same desperate effort to make the story go somehow that I have traced in other sequences, we see the thing finding expression at last. Or, if I may so phrase it, we see the psychic block removed, the dilemma solved, the inhibition broken, the accusation stilled, and Mark Twain's mind given peace at last and his talent restored. The miracles, which at first are just an idle game for the amusement of the boys and the astonishment of the villagers, become finally a spectacle of human life in miniature, with the suffering diminished to the vanishing point since these are just puppets, unreal creatures moving in a shadow-play, and they are seen with the detachment of an immortal spirit, passionless and untouched. And so from a spectacle they become a dream—the symbolic dream of human experience that Mark had been trying to write in such travail for so many years.

So an unrecognized purpose had dominated the chaos of those efforts, after all, and out of it had come *The Mysterious Stranger,* a minor masterpiece, with its clear, subdued colors, its autumnal pity and compassion, its fine, silvery echo of mortality and of hope destroyed and of man's pettiness somehow given the nobility of suffering, the thread of pain binding all living things together. But what is it? Eseldorf—Assville—is just Hannibal, seen far away, softened by the mist of centuries. The boys who are eager and cowardly, aspiring and cruel, are just Tom and Huck once more, which is to say they are what Mark had found best in himself and his long phantasies. The villagers, the human race in little, are just his friends and neighbors, his detractors and enemies and those who had undone him. The deaths died, the injuries suffered and agonies endured

—we do not need to inquire what they are, after the innumerable times he had tried to give them meaning in art. Nor can there be any doubt who the immortal Antagonist is, the enemy of God, which is to say the rebel against law—and so against responsibility. Here the dreadful things alleged against mankind, and so made as a confession, in *What Is Man?* are said again, but now they are tolerable, conformable, acceptable, for they have been removed far away, over them broods the peace of distant dream. And now we know that the dream had closed the arc and permitted him to say what he must say and enabled him at last to live at peace with himself.

> You perceive, *now* [Satan says, just before he vanishes and the book ends] that these things are all impossible except in a dream. You perceive that they are pure and puerile insanities, the silly creations of an imagination that is not conscious of its freaks—in a word, that they are a dream, and you the maker of it. . . .
>
> It is true, that which I have revealed to you; there is no God, no universe, no human race, no earthly life, no heaven, no hell. It is all a dream—a grotesque and foolish dream. Nothing exists but you. And you are but a *thought,*—a vagrant thought, a useless thought, a homeless thought, wandering forlorn among the empty eternities!

The dream, that is, was the answer and the proof. He had tried to say: it was not my fault, I was betrayed. But the accusation could not be stayed so easily. He had tried to say: it was not my fault, for the fixed universe of inescapable law intended from the beginning that this should happen. But that was too easily exposed as subterfuge. He had tried to say: it was not my fault, for anyone would have done the same, but the remorseless feet that follow, follow after had driven him from that refuge. He had tried to say: it is just a delusion, a dream I will wake from—and that had almost served, but not quite. Susy's delirium was not his delusion and there could be no waking from it—and if that was so, then the terrible accusation still held.

But there was still an answer. If nothing existed but a homeless thought wandering forlorn among the empty eternities, then his smaller agony and his personal guilt were also a dream. If everything was dream, then clearly the accused prisoner might be discharged. The accusation begotten by his experience could be stilled by destroying all experience. It was possible to uproot terror and guilt and responsibility from his little world, by detonating the universe. He could end his contention with the vengeful God and put away remorse forever by reducing all contention, vengeance, pain, degradation, guilt, sin, and panic to a lonely dream.

That was the price he paid for peace. It seems a high price. But art is the terms of an armistice signed with fate, and the terms one makes are the terms one can make. At this cost the fallen angel of our literature, the mysterious stranger who seemed only a sojourner in the cramped spaces of our mortal world, saved himself in the end, and came back from the edge of insanity, and found as much peace as any man may find in his last years, and brought his talent into fruition and made it whole again.

The Lost America—The Despair of Henry Adams and Mark Twain

by Tony Tanner

Henry Adams and Samuel Clemens are often considered to represent the polar extremes of their age. Yet, however divergent their careers seem to be, it is absorbing to watch them approaching, each in his different way, a final mood of total despair that argues concurrence rather than coincidence. Personal tragedies might be adduced to explain this: the heart-breaking death of Susy Clemens and the long drawn out agony of Livy, the suicide of Adams' wife Clover, even the humiliation of bankruptcy, which Clemens suffered personally and Adams witnessed in his family, these certainly are contributory causes. But as one examines the conspicuous modes of this despair—a compound of comminatory denunciation and brooding, intense pessimism—one is compelled to search further afield for the prime causes. Such an investigation reveals that this despair is in a slow process of incubation from their earliest work, and that it is finally hatched by the growing discords, conflicts, and problems of the age. It is not a despair of personal bereavement but of country— ultimately of man.

Much of Adams' despair, to say nothing of his wounded pride, is the negative residue of a constantly diminishing faith in American politics, which seemed progressively to abandon all the moral idealism that he felt that he and his family preeminently represented. His bitterness increases as it becomes increasingly apparent that such a person as himself has no part to play in the politics of his age: that such a stage of affairs should have come about clearly indicated an intolerable debasement of the whole political scene. His two early novels and the nine-volume history really have a common theme: they ask the question: What is the fate of idealism in American politics, is there any longer any meaning in the way things are going, is life moving towards any ideal end?

"The Lost America—The Despair of Henry Adams and Mark Twain" by Tony Tanner. From *Modern Age*, V (Summer 1961), 299-310. Copyright © 1961 by The Institute for Philosophical and Historical Studies, Inc. Reprinted by permission of the author and *Modern Age*.

The Life of Albert Gallatin, as well as being a simple biography, is also an examination of political aspiration that results in failure, and it points out the fact that republican idealism failed to establish its ideally conceived society. *Democracy,* written almost immediately after 1879, is an excoriating analysis of contemporary American democratic administration. The heroine, Mrs. Madeline Lee, sets out to understand Senator Radcliffe who is made to represent the contemporary American politician in all his naked power. He proves to be selfish, hypocritical, and unscrupulous, "a naked will operating under convictions of moral lunacy." Mrs. Lee comes to consider him "diseased" and the disease is diagnosed as "atrophy of the moral sense." She had been searching for some meaning in life and had focused on the senator as a possible provider of an ideal end for which she could work. His failure to furnish her with such an ideal induces in Mrs. Lee a mood of complete despair: for her, life is "emptier than ever now that this dream was over." She decides to "quit the masquerade" and sets out on a voyage to the Mediterranean and the Nile. The voyage, we feel, is but the first of many meaningless meanderings and it aptly prefigures Adams' own restless existence. These two novels about the futile search for some form of idealism were written while Adams was engaged in research for his great *History.* This work, published between 1889 and 1891, is a massive demonstration of the inevitable failure of idealism. The ideals governing Jeffersonian republicanism are set out in the chapter called "American Ideals" and the rest of the work records the attempt to achieve these ideal goals. As George Hochfield observes in *Henry Adams: An Introduction and Interpretation:* "The failure of that attempt—for failure it obviously was—is thus the conclusion to which the whole work tends." The attempt to establish an ideal society leads eventually to the horrors of war: this is the mute, sinister portent of the work. To phrase it thus is to slight its greatness but for our purpose it is interesting to note that Adams chose to study exactly that portion of history which would provide him with a pessimistic conclusion. Even here, long before *The Education,* there are hints of an incipient determinism, a determinism justified by this great failure of the past. As Hochfield writes: "the necessitarianism that tinctures the *History* is a response to the failure of idealism; it signifies Adams' conclusion that idealism must have been doomed from the start by the very nature of history." It is as though Adams unconsciously chose just that period in American history which would most warrant his inchoate pessimism. The odd thing is that Clemens chose to do exactly the same.

Clemens of course was not so articulate or painstaking in his political opinions. He was an admirer and later a friend of Grant, and Grant's regime did not fill him with the same deep disgust that afflicted the more perspicacious Adams. Nevertheless, he is far from being blithely unaware of an unpleasant drop in the tone of American politics after the Civil War. In *The Curious Republic of Gondour,* written in 1871, he satirizes an aspect of American politics that we might have expected to annoy Adams rather than Clemens, for the curious thing about Gondour is that "for the first time in the history of the republic, property, character, and intellect were able to wield a political influence." In this strange land an education entitles a man to more votes than the unlettered hod-carrier, and the ignorant are not allowed to swamp the intelligent with their greater numbers. The tone is more that of an alienated aristocrat than that of a supporter of the great American dream of government by the people. Three years later Clemens gave the definitive title to his times with *The Gilded Age.* The book is by no means the unrelieved attack on democracy that Adams' novel was to be, but the satirical intent is clear and Senator Dilworthy invites comparison with Senator Radcliffe. Clemens was no stranger to Washington, and his stay there during the winter of 1867 was sufficient to give him as low an opinion of American politics as Adams held. However, it is in that strangely confused book *A Connecticut Yankee,* published just before the *History,* that Clemens comes so close to echoing Adams' despairing conclusions. The book actually starts out from a point of view very distant from the omniscient retrospection of Adams the historian: the novel, as Professor Henry Nash Smith has shrewdly pointed out, is a *roman expérimental* and the question at issue is whether republican idealism and nineteenth century technology can redeem society. This in turn poses the question of whether or not man can improve his lot if offered an ideal opportunity; whether, indeed, man is perfectible. Thus, it is asking the same question answered negatively by the *History,* for the ideals that are tested in that book are man's natural capacity to develop morally and intellectually, and the possibility of intelligent economic expansion. Frequently before the writing of this book Clemens exhibits a belief in natural goodness, the innately decent proclivities of the "heart" that has not been corrupted by inherited prejudice and the coercions of established institutions. Huck Finn is his supreme assertion of such a belief, and Hank Morgan is in some ways a grown-up Huck who instead of being in passive flight *from* society is in aggressive conflict *with* it. To the dark ages of sixth century England he brings these two great gifts—a theory of amelioration based on a belief in the goodness and perfectibility of man, and the economic principles and technological means to implement a beneficent alteration of the age. But all his efforts prove wasted: the initial philanthrope gradually becomes misanthropic; the idealistic democrat shades into a scornful tyrant; hoping to bring light he ends by concentrating on destruction: people are unapt for improvement—idealism is bound to fail. As the faith in man falls, so a savage authorial anger intrudes itself: the undertaken project of reconstruction ends in a foul holocaust just as the *History* shows idealism leading inevitably to the "bloody arena" of war. Adams never had Clemens' belief in the perfectibility of man: he called it "this doubtful and even improbable principle" and proved the point by his *History*. Clemens' anger and dismay are the greater for his having once believed but the conclusions he reaches are identical. Yet we may note, as we noted of the *History,* that Clemens chose a situation in which idealism was bound to fail: established historical fact precludes all possibility of success and surely it is not excessive to see in this choice of situation a lurking, if unacknowledged, pessimistic determinism such as we discerned in Adams. (A similar unconscious fatalism clearly dictates his preoccupation with the Joan of Arc story; she is another idealistic person who comes to redeem a "sick age," and her ultimate rejection by society is even more inflexibly determined than Hank Morgan's.) It might here be argued that *A Connecticut Yankee* was an anti-English polemic stimulated by the patronizing contempt of America exhibited by Matthew Arnold, but the satiric barb of the book is aimed at contemporary America—the "dark ages" become the corrupt post-Civil-War years in which the great American dream was so glaringly betrayed. The Round Table, for instance, comes to have an uncanny resemblance to the stock exchange and the final civil war is precipitated by a shady deal reminiscent of the railroad frauds of the Seventies: the slavedriver in the illustrations, which were executed by the radical Dan Beard with Clemens' approval, is clearly meant to be Jay Gould; in a word, the degradation and misery of the sixth century is America's own. The years from 1873 to 1879 were years of great economic distress; the small farmers were badly off and in the cities there was widespread unemployment, while in 1877 the first nation-wide strike led to a sinister outburst of labor rioting. In 1879 Henry George published his *Progress and Poverty*. The book opens with a statement of the expectations and opportunities of the early nineteenth century: its theme is "disappointment has followed disappointment," a theme re-echoed in Adams' historical work and Clemens' novels. If the ideals on which America was founded were being rapidly stained by political practice, so also was the paradisaical surface of the continent suffering a comparable degradation from the rapid urbanization and industrialization of the period. One would not have expected a nostalgia for the unspoiled wildness of an earlier America to have had much effect on the urbane temperament of Adams, yet it clearly does. Several amazingly passionate passages in the *Education* reveal that for Adams "the vast maternity of nature" always "showed charms more voluptuous than the vast paternity of the United States senate." And this is not to be discounted as the urban man's genteel indulgence in the country from a safe distance—this is not an age of pastoral poetry. It is definitely the profligate waywardness of an untamed nature that arouses his sympathies. When he first sees the South he is most distressed by the fact that it is "unkempt, poverty-stricken, ignorant, vicious" and yet certain aspects of it draw him as though he were hypnotized by them against his better, civilized, judgment. "The want of barriers, of pavements, of forms; the looseness, the laziness; the indolent southern drawl; the pigs in the streets, the negro babies and their mothers with bandanas; the freedom, openness, swagger of nature and man soothed his Johnson blood"—a passage that Clemens would have applauded. What disappoints Adams in his later travels is that "the sense of wildness had vanished" and *Huckleberry Finn* embodies a similar lament, lyrically developed, for some lost "wildness" that is Huck's natural element. We should remember that Adams, when talking of the visible nature of trees and mountains, never calls it a chaos: the wildness of this nature gratified some deep instinct in him and he was saddened to see it vanishing from the continent. The nature he came to consider as pure chaos was an intellectual system. To maintain the comparison with Clemens we may recall the passage in which he speaks of changes on the Mississippi. "Ten years had passed since he last crossed the Mississippi, and he found everything new. In this great region from Pittsburgh through Ohio and Indiana, agriculture had made way for steam; tall chimneys reeked smoke on every horizon, and dirty suburbs filled with scrap iron, scrap paper and cinders, formed the setting of every town." In *Life on the Mississippi* Clemens records his feelings as he witnesses the changes along the river he knew so well as a youth, and the great quality of the work is a controlled nostalgia for a lost era. And yet here we must point to a difference. Just as Clemens had believed in the perfectibility of man while Adams doubted, so he was initially optimistic about the beneficence of industrialization, an optimism never shared by Adams. When Clemens sees some of those tall chimneys on the horizon he expresses great delight at the "changes uniformly evidencing progress, energy, prosperity": it was only later that, sickened by the corruptive powers of materialism, he gravitated to a mood of cynical despair.

More specifically let us cite the machine and the mob as two phenomena that served to alienate these men from their age. There is a significant moment when Adams visits the great Chicago Exposition in 1893. The extended exposure to mechanical novelties of which he has no understanding completely immobilizes him. Before the array of steam engines, electric batteries, telephones, etc., he "had no choice but to sit down on the steps and brood as [he] had never brooded on the benches of Harvard College. . . . The historical mind can only think in historical processes, and probably this was the first time since historians existed, that any of them had sat down helpless before a mechanical sequence." The word "mechanical," so neutral to us, should be noted, for it gradually acquires an ominous weight of meaning as Adams discovers that the world is being increasingly administered by mechanical forces of one kind or another. (His attitude is comparable to that of the writer of the Erewhonian "Book of the Machines"; "Is it not plain that the machines are gaining ground upon us, when we reflect on the increasing number of those who are bound down to them as slaves, and of those who devote their whole souls to the advancement of the mechanical kingdom?") There is an irony in this since the eighteenth century rationalism that was so dear to Adams was based on the Newtonian conception of Nature as a divinely ordered machine. But the Great Watchmaker had decreed a mechanistic universe which was rational and explicable. As the scrap heaps and the cinders came increasingly into view mechanism gradually ceased to exemplify a rational principle and seemed to become a hideous principle of blind force. Mechanism had turned on the class and way of life that initially upheld it. Adams talks of "the whole mechanical consolidation of force, which ruthlessly stamped out the life of the class into which Adams was born." Again in the Exposition: "As he grew accustomed to the great gallery of machines he began to feel the forty-foot dynamo as a moral force, much as the early Christian felt the cross." But at least there had been a Christ on the cross: the dynamo is completely impersonal in its divine power. It is non-human and therefore inhuman, non-moral and therefore immoral, or rather amoral. And it is that dynamo which really unfixes Adams' mind. Clemens' career affords us a comparable symbol although his antipathy to the machine is the result of a long process of disillusionment rather than the sudden bewilderment felt by Adams. His relationship with the Paige typesetter symbolically foreshortens this disillusionment. An initial enthusiasm gradually gives way to a profound despair as the machine heartlessly robs him of a fortune and mockingly refuses to arrive at the hoped-for perfection.

A concomitant of Adams' reaction to the dynamo is a feeling that just as the world is coming to be dominated by impersonal forces so also are the inhabitants of this world becoming as impersonal, mechanical, and

inhuman as the forces that guide them. The mob was making its appearance in America and although in many ways these people were the
victims of the machines that Adams deprecated, their impersonal violence disturbed him as much as did the dynamo. In his youth, he recalls,
he was once involved in a snow-ball fight: the sides were the Latin school
versus the rest of the local boys. The account of the fight reads like a
parable. At first the Latin school dominate the others, but then as night
comes on the tide turns. "A dark mass of figures could be seen below,
making ready for the last rush, and rumor said that a swarm of black-
guards from the slums . . . was going to put an end to the Beacon Street
cowards forever. Henry wanted to run away with the others, but his
brother was too big to run away, so they stood still and waited immola-
tion. The dark mass set up a shout, and rushed forward." It ends as all
children's games should, but throughout the extended description one
feels the terrible threat of the dark forces who come swarming up against
the Latin school (which very easily can be made to represent the aristocratic element in society) threatening total annihilation. In its way it is
like a small Dunciad and the idea that "universal darkness" will eventually "cover all" is a theme which grows throughout the book until that
last apocalyptic description of New York in 1905 which ends: "A traveler
in the highways of history looked out of the club window on the turmoil
of Fifth Avenue, and felt himself in Rome, under Diocletian, witnessing
the anarchy, conscious of the compulsion, eager for the solution, but
unable to conceive whence the next impulse was to come or how it was
to act. The two-thousand-years failure of Christianity roared upward
from Broadway, and no Constantine the Great was in sight." Although
Clemens had a ready sympathy for the strikers so brutally suppressed under Cleveland, he also came to hate "the mob." Colonel Sherburn's scornful arraignment of the brutality, pusillanimity, and cowardice of the
lynching crowd is an overt piece of authorial intrusion: Hank Morgan
who came to save the people finds himself admiring their king and de-
spising them as "muck," and it is the ungrateful mob that allows Joan to
be burned after she had devoted herself to their liberation. Adams' patrician heritage helped to enforce his antipathies on him and although
Clemens certainly enjoyed no comparably cultured environment as a
child yet he also recalls that "the aristocratic taint was in the air." His
Virginian father, John Marshall Clemens, was a type of aristocrat in his
insistence on the proud, austere, dignified bearing proper to "a man";
an Andrew Jackson, perhaps, rather than a John Quincy Adams. If
Adams inherited an aristocracy of class, then Clemens certainly inherited
an aristocracy of character, and this must not be ignored in any attempt

to account for their disaffiliation from the age of the common man. Mobocracy, like "dollarocracy" and "machineocracy" (if we may coin a word) aroused bitterness, contempt, and despair in both men. It remains to examine this despair.

The *Education* is an account of a life dissolving into chaos. Adams construes his life as a series of false starts—a continual failure to learn anything. Everywhere he looks he can only see a world "both unwise and ignorant" and full of contradictions among intelligent people: "from such contradictions . . . what was a young man to learn." Continually he says "the horizon widened out in endless waves of confusion," and we should note that sea image: it is one that will recur. On the moral level he never finds anything he can trust. In London diplomatic circles he loses all confidence and when Russell, Gladstone, and Palmerston seem to be double-dealing he makes it a crucial test: "could one afford to trust human nature in politics . . . for education the point was vital. If one could not trust a dozen of the most respected private characters in the world . . . one could trust no mortal man." When they fall short of his idealistic standards he just gives up, blaming it all on "the sheer chaos of human nature." Such moments recur: as he makes his way through political life he seeks out something he can hold fast to, some one facet of human nature that will never let him down. He is almost adolescent, almost child-like in his search for goodness in the world. One can see him as conducting on an international urban level the search that Huck carried out down the Mississippi, and in the course of this search he confesses "he had wholly lost his way." He is always making another "leap into the unknown" and after working near the Grant administration for a while he emerges with the comment by now only to be expected from him. He "had made another total misconception of life—another inconceivable false start." Like Huck he is lost and always passive. He "drifted into the mental indolence of history" and wherever he goes he says that knowledge absorbs him—"he was passive." Like Huck he often appears as "a helpless victim" with no defense or means of attack and he feels "at the mercy of fools and cowards": even when he takes a job as a teacher his morbid comment is: "he went on, submissive." Again like Huck he is continually on the move. Feeling unfitted for Boston "he had to go": shocked by McKinley's ways he says "once more, one must go!" He is well aware of this nomadic aspect of his life since he adds: "Nothing was easier! On and off, one had done the same thing since the year 1858, at frequent intervals." Very early on in the book he recalls: "Always he felt himself somewhere else . . . and he watched with vague unrest from the Quincy hills the smoke of the Cunard steamers stretching in a long line to the horizon . . . as though the steamers were offering to take him away, which was precisely what they were doing." It is important to note how purposeless Adams makes all his voyaging seem—both the actual travel and the larger voyage towards knowledge. He is always "drifting" with some unspecified current. The sea imagery is prolific throughout the book. It starts when he is writing of the Civil War: "On April 13 the storm burst and rolled several hundred thousand young men like Henry Adams into the surf of a wild ocean, all helpless like himself, to be beaten about for four years by the waves of war." But there was no ebb of the tide for Henry Adams. As the end of his first year in England approaches he writes: "His old education was finished; his new one was not begun; he still loitered a year, feeling himself near the end of a very long, anxious tempestuous successful voyage, with another to follow, and a summer sea between." Success would seem to consist merely in keeping afloat—a success not always permitted him since he elsewhere talks of "sinking under the surface." In 1871, he writes, "his course had led him through oceans of ignorance" and the ocean seems limitless. In the chapter entitled "The Abyss of Ignorance" the final stage of passivity is reached. "After so many years of effort to find one's drift, the drift found the seeker and slowly swept him forward and back, with a steady progress oceanwards." He doesn't let go of the image even when talking of smaller matters, of his attempt to study "race and sex" he writes: "Even within these narrow seas the navigator lost his bearings and followed the winds as they blew." That he sometimes wishes this sea of ignorance to turn into something more soporific, something to rock him back to unconsciousness again, is shown by one remarkable passage. "Adams would rather, as choice, have gone back to the east, if it were only to sleep forever in the trade-winds under the southern stars, wandering over the dark purple ocean, with its purple sense of solitude and void." Images of the sea as a fearful void are supported by images of darkness. He refers to himself as being "lost in the darkness of his own gropings" and after King's death "Adams could only blunder back alone, helplessly, wearily, his eyes rather dim with tears, to his vague trail across the darkening prairie of education, without a motive, big or small, except curiosity to reach, before he too should drop, some point that would give him a far look ahead." This "darkening prairie" later becomes "mountains of ignorance" where the "weary pilgrim . . . could no longer see any path whatever and could not even understand a signpost." One tends to forget the almost phantasmagoric nature of his accounts because of the tempered, elegant detached tone, but the accounting voice is a neutral, almost blank, one and its purpose is to direct attention to the pitiful figure struggling down on earth.

"Never had the proportions of his ignorance looked so appalling. He seemed to know nothing—to be groping in darkness—to be falling forever in space." The images of sea, space, and darkness blend for one moment when he tells of the significance for him of Karl Pearson's writing: "At last their universe had been wrecked by rays, and Karl Pearson undertook to cut the wreck loose with an axe, leaving science adrift on a sensual raft in the midst of a supersensual chaos" and now Adams finds himself "on the raft." He might have found two companions on the raft—Huck Finn, and that hapless narrator of *The Mysterious Stranger,* Theodor Fischer. In one sense the voyages of these two boys complement each other. Huck is afloat in America in search of a destination. He is an Odysseus without an Ithaca. Like Odysseus he is "never at a loss" and knows how to disguise himself or manufacture a tale in order to get himself out of trouble and continue on his way; but that way is no longer clear. The frontier to which he finally heads is too vague to be a definite destination—it is the geographical location of the great unknown. But still, there is a feeling that out there all things are possible. Huck, we feel, stands a chance. But not Theodor. The ending of *The Mysterious Stranger* reads like a more hysterical and total version of Adams' own despair. Here is a part of Satan's last speech. "In a little while you will be alone in shoreless space, to wander its limitless solitudes without friend or comrade forever. . . . It is true, that which I have revealed to you; there is no God, no universe, no human race, no earthly life, no heaven, no hell. It is all a dream—a grotesque and foolish dream. Nothing exists but you. And you are but a *thought*—a vagrant thought, a useless thought, a homeless thought, wandering forlorn among the empty eternities!"

One can add comparable evidence from Clemens' last period that he became increasingly preoccupied with images of chaos, darkness, purposelessness, the passivity of man before the dark forces of the world, and the complete lostness of man. In some of his late, unfinished scraps of fiction there is a measure of unwarranted horror which one might expect from a writer more devoted to symbolism than Clemens at any time showed himself to be: there is a feeling of living in a symbolic universe to which man has lost the interpretative key, thus leaving the writer with an accumulating emotion that finds no satisfactory deciphering expression. Just to mention the three sea stories among these late papers will reveal something of this process, and the preoccupation with purposeless voyages which end in horror is one which seems to mirror something that was going on in Adams' mind. (It is interesting to recall that Emerson employed images of voyaging and water to enforce his optimistic view of man's effortless relationship with a benign nature. "Place yourself in the middle

of the stream of power and wisdom which animates all whom it
and you are without effort impelled to truth, to right and a perfect
tentment." And again: man "is like a ship in a river . . . he swe
serenely over a deepening channel into an infinite sea.")

For Twain and Adams that "infinite sea" turned into pure nightmare.
The Enchanted Sea Wilderness is the story of a ship which wanders into
a great area of the ocean where the compass suddenly goes berserk and
loses all value as a means of steering and plotting direction. First it runs
into a terrible nine-day storm which the sailors nickname "the devil's race
track" and then it emerges into a deadly calm or "the everlasting Sunday." Here they slowly drift until they see what they take to be a fleet on
the horizon: full of hope they row towards it but it turns out to be a dead
fleet which rotted away years ago leaving only the deceptive shells on the
surface to mock all who find them with an image of their irrevocable fate.
In all this "universal paralysis of life and energy" the only active thing is
the compass which is whirling around "in a frenzy of fear." Out of this
morbid but pregnant predicament Clemens makes nothing and we are
left to wonder how the narrator lived to tell the tale.

A more suggestive story is *An Adventure in Remote Seas,* where once
again a ship gets lost but this time arrives at a strange island. Half the
crew go ashore to catch penguins and find, implausibly enough, a vast
hoard of gold: this turns the captain's mind and the men are employed
in weighing and counting it. Strikes and labor disputes arise and there are
some satirical references to the question of adopting the silver standard,
on which William Jennings Bryan was campaigning at the time. All
thought of the original purpose of the voyage is given up, and those on
shore start to forget the ship and cease to worry about their location.
Suddenly they realize the ship has gone—and here the story breaks off.
This has all the inchoate lineaments of an allegory. The unknown island
which they discover could be America and the penguins (who are so
docile and friendly while the sailors cut their throats) might well be the
original inhabitants, the Indians. The frenzy aroused by the money is
Clemens' comment on what the Industrial Revolution was doing to men
and the final situation seems to symbolize contemporary America: busy
scrambling for money while the one chance of salvation, the ship, is
finally lost, leaving the men abandoned in a nameless ocean with only a
meaningless wealth for consolation. Again this is not brought to anything;
it remains formless and crude, merely indicating a desire to express a
bitter comment on the crisis of mankind.

The long story to which DeVoto applied Clemens' phrase "The Great
Dark" is a more prolonged, though scarcely more successful, attempt to

find a fitting parable to carry his feelings. A man named Henry Edwards dreams that he embarks on a long trip across the drop of water that he had been studying under the microscope shortly before falling asleep. The "blind voyage" across this unknown ocean moves from dream to nightmare. At first it is constantly dark: no one knows where they are but they try and conceal the fact from others; the charts and compass prove to be utterly useless since none of the expected landmarks seem to exist; fantastic animals flounder in the sea, occasionally attacking them giving the impression of a Bosch-like apocalyptic chaos. Hideous surreal incidents multiply and the story spirals to a pitch of phantasmagoric insanity: the sea dries up, fighting and brawling (again over a useless treasure) gradually account for all the characters except Edwards who, like Theodor Fischer, is left alone in an arid eternity. The terrible dream turns out to be the true reality—a favorite theme of the aging Clemens.

This unrelenting vision of life as chaos is, in essence and conclusion, not very different from that of Henry Adams. Whence this similarity of vision? Both of them had ceased to believe in God but both retained something of that Calvinistic intensity of vision common to believers of previous ages. It is their inability to disburden themselves of the mental framework which accompanied belief that makes both determinists of one kind or another. God had either fled or been diminished to a thing— a *deus absconditum,* but the feeling of predestination lingered on just beneath the surface of the conscious mind. To this we can trace the persistent image of the voyage in so much nineteenth century American literature, but now what was the destiny to which man had been predestined? The compasses were not functioning, the chart of infallible absolutes was completely useless on these novel seas of dissolving belief. It seems that without the one all-solving deity the world collapsed into an amorphous, inexplicable mess before which the only reaction was one of sterile horror. Not that either man wanted the old God back, but they were equally dismayed at America's failure to provide any substitute ideal purpose or explanation: (they are both, at one time or another, extremely sardonic about evolutionary optimism).

At first both Clemens and Adams had credited man with some degree of free will: in the *History* there is such a thing as moral responsibility and decision, while Huck is a superb example of man's ability to argue with, challenge, and finally rebuff the circumpressure of environment and heredity. By the end of their lives they were both convinced that free will was completely illusory. In the *Education* Adams decides that people involved in politics are simply "forces as dumb as their dynamos" and this interpretation gradually extends over all mankind. One sentence intimates the large shift in conviction. "Adams never knew why, knowing nothing of Faraday, he began to mimic Faraday's trick of seeing lines of force all about him, where he had always seen lines of will." Very quickly man becomes "a feeble atom."

1898 was a bad year for Clemens, a year in which he sought some relief from Susy's death and his bankruptcy, in a prolonged spell of uninterrupted work. He not only wrote *The Mysterious Stranger* but he also completed a work which he had been toying with for eighteen years— *What Is Man?* It is entirely apt that the very first sub-title should read: "a. Man the Machine." This book has been almost entirely ignored by subsequent generations and for good reason: yet Clemens was so apprehensive about the scandal he thought it would cause that he would only print it anonymously and privately for a few friends in 1906. It is a jumble of half-pursued thoughts and improperly defined terms the whole upshot of which is that man is "an impersonal machine . . . he is moved, directed, COMMANDED by exterior influences—solely. He originates nothing, not even a thought." And then there follows that notorious simile —Shakespeare is merely a "Gobelin loom" compared with the sewing machine which is the average man. Of course it wasn't subsequent generations who were shocked—it was Clemens himself. He was terrified by his own conclusion (and note how his "exterior influences" have taken over the imperious authoritarianism of the Calvinist God). There is something unnerved and frenzied about his insistence that man is a completely irresponsible object at the mercy of forces that he cannot understand and he is almost vengeful in his efforts to humiliate and degrade mankind.

It is interesting that he seeks out the most ignoble animals with which to compare man (in personal dignity, for instance, man is on the same level as a rat) for Adams continually chooses to compare himself to animals: and such animals—the small, the helpless, the ones that crawl. For example he likens himself at various times to a mosquito, a maggot, a worm, a firefly, and a horseshoe crab. More interesting is his simile for Jefferson, Madison, and Monroe. In a letter to Tilden in 1883 he wrote: "they appear like mere grasshoppers kicking and gesticulating on the middle of the Mississippi River . . . they were carried along on a stream which floated them, after a fashion, without much regard to themselves." One can see here an unconscious preparation for his later attitude toward the predicament of man: this image conjoins just those two themes which later he consciously exploited. Man is as helpless as a trivial animal: his life is a brief floating on the endless waters of chaos.

As a boy Adams was impregnated with truths that were rigid, absolute, and transcendent: it is only natural that when he embarks on his search for some new truth he should search for some inflexible, theoretic, and timelessly true principle. His search for unity is actually a yearning for some inviolable, transcendent principle of unification such as Aquinas had postulated. But along with everything else the philosophic climate was changing. Absolute systems of philosophy tended to be reactionary, to justify the old *status quo* that brought them into being; they inhibited reform, they imposed a mental vise on a world which was breaking its boundaries in every direction. A new philosophy was needed to control and discipline the new directions man was taking without closing off any avenues to him—the philosophy was pragmatism. Pragmatism kept truth open and searched for useful instruments rather than final answers; it turned away from "a priori reasons, from fixed principles, closed systems, and pretended absolutes": it turned towards facts and was not dismayed by their improvident multiplicity.

William James, attacking a conservative professor, writes in a way that seems almost like a direct answer to the morbid despair of Adams and Clemens with all their images of oceans of chaos and fruitless voyages. He writes: "These critics appear to suppose that, if left to itself, the rudderless craft of our experience must be ready to drift anywhere or nowhere. Even tho there were compasses on board, they seem to say, there would be no pole for them to point to. There must be absolute sailing directions, they insist, decreed from outside, and an independent chart of the voyage added to the 'mere' voyage itself, if we are ever to make a port. But is it not obvious that even tho there be such absolute sailing-directions in the shape of pre-human standards of truth that we *ought* to follow, the only guarantee that we shall in fact follow them must lie in our human equipment. . . . The only *real* guarantee we have against licentious thinking is the circumpressure of experience itself, which gets us sick of concrete errors, whether there be a trans-empirical reality or not."

As the recurrent imagery of their late work reveals, both Adams and Clemens felt profoundly uneasy without a set of "absolute sailing directions."

It is strange that Adams and Clemens never seem to have met. They had many mutual friends—Clarence King, John Hay, and most notably William Dean Howells, and they both spent many years in New England, yet we have no record of a meeting. There is a strange moment in *What Is Man?* when Clemens suddenly cites one "Henry Adams" as a (presumably fictional) example of the unhappiest man he knows: he must certainly have known too much about Adams to have used the name quite innocently and perhaps this is a covert way of intimating that he considers himself at an extreme temperamental remove from such a man. Had they met they would probably have found themselves at odds, yet they are two of the most notable alienated figures of their age. They never felt quite at home anywhere, never quite settled down, never really found themselves. At one point Adams imagines describing himself to his father and finds that all he could say of himself would be: "Sir, I am a tourist!," and when he later calls himself "a historical tramp" we are reminded of that habitual tourist who punningly names himself in *A Tramp Abroad*. Both these international hobos spent many years of their lives wandering around the world and beneath the successful exterior of the one and the cultured veneer of the other one can indeed discern the lineaments of that recurrent American image—the tramp. Devious and unpremeditated as their wanderings may seem they were both on the same road, not *to* anywhere but *away from* a society with which they could no longer identify themselves and which seemed to offer no answering image to their own deepest hopes and ideals.

If these two were alone in their disillusion and despair one might be inclined to put it down to a personal perversity of vision. But the evidence is all the other way. One can trace a spectrum of complaint throughout the age. Whitman, although he had faith in democracy—"the unyielding principle of the average"—conceded "the appalling dangers of universal suffrage in the United States." Committed to loving all men he was yet sufficiently offended by the progress of post-Civil-War America to write that "society," despite or because of "unprecedented materialistic advancement . . . is canker'd, crude, superstitious and rotten." A man less like Adams than Whitman never lived and yet the former would have supported Whitman's complaint that "the element of the moral conscience, the most important, the vertebrae to State or man, seems to me either entirely lacking, or seriously enfeebled or ungrown."

Brooks Adams, in his significantly titled *The Law of Civilization and Decay*, developed an adventurous cyclical interpretation of history and the lesson he reads in the past is the inevitable disintegration of a society in which the economic type had gained total supremacy. As determinist as his brother Henry he maintained that Nature operates on the human mind "according to immutable laws"—a theory which endorses pessimism but slights man's ability to learn from the past. Consequently he saw in the exaltation of the new materialistic middle class a portent of inevitable doom. Henry James fled to England to avert his eyes from the new generation of Americans dedicated to the "great black ebony God of business": in the last scene of *The Bostonians* Basil Ransom dismisses the middle class mob at the lecture hall as "senseless brutes" and it is difficult not to feel that he speaks with the author's approval.

Near the turn of the century Henry Adams, perspicacious enough to see that the future of society might lie in the direction of state-socialism, pronounced it a "future with which I sincerely wish I may have nothing to do." Clemens, more angry because more humane, composed this "salutation speech from the 19th century to the 20th" (subsequently withdrawn) in which he bitterly arraigns the imperialistic greed of the West.

> I bring you the stately matron named Christendom, returning bedraggled, besmirched and dishonored from pirate-raids in Kiao-Chow, Manchuria, South Africa and the Philippines, with her soul full of boodle, and her mouth full of pious hypocrisies. Give her soap and a towel, but hide the looking glass.

But middle-class America was to receive a more disturbing turn-of-the-century salutation. In 1899 Thorstein Veblen published *The Theory of the Leisure Class* in which the pecuniary fanaticism of the *nouveau riche* received its most mordant, sardonic analysis. His evidence must be taken as conclusive. It remained for later scholars such as Vernon Parrington to clarify the phenomenon which had so distressed men like Clemens and Adams: namely, "the emergence of a new middle class" which in the second half of the nineteenth century subdued America "to middle class ends."

Chronology of Important Dates

1885	*Adventures of Huckleberry Finn* and **Grant's** *Memoirs* published by the Webster Company
1888	Honorary M.A. degree conferred by Yale
1889	*A Connecticut Yankee in King Arthur's Court*
1891-1895	Residence in Germany, Italy, and France, with occasional business trips back to the United States
1894	Paige typesetter pronounced a failure; Webster Company in bankruptcy
1894	*Pudd'nhead Wilson*
1895-1896	Lecture tour through Southern hemisphere
1896	*Personal Recollections of Joan of Arc*
1896 (August)	Favorite daughter, Susy, died of meningitis
1897-1900	Residence in Vienna and London
1897	*Following the Equator*
1900	*The Man That Corrupted Hadleyburg and Other Stories*
1900	Took house in New York; active with Howells in anti-imperialism campaign
1901	Litt.D. conferred by Yale
1902	LL.D. conferred by University of Missouri
1903	Took family to Italy for his wife's health
1904	Olivia Langdon Clemens died in Italy
1907	Litt.D. conferred by Oxford
1908	Took up residence at Stormfield, near Redding, Connecticut
1909 (December)	Daughter, Jean, died
1910 (April 21)	Died at Stormfield; buried at Elmira

Notes on the Editor and Authors

HENRY NASH SMITH, the editor, is Professor of English in the University of California, Berkeley. He is author of *Virgin Land* (1950) and *Mark Twain: The Development of a Writer* (1962), and editor (with William M. Gibson) of *Mark Twain-Howells Letters* (1960).

VAN WYCK BROOKS, author of more than a score of books of criticism and biography, is best known for his five-volume literary history of America, which includes *The Flowering of New England* (awarded the Pulitzer Prize in 1937).

MAURICE LE BRETON is Professor of American Literature and Culture in the University of Paris and Director of the Institute of English and American Studies.

KENNETH LYNN is Associate Professor of English in Harvard University. In addition to *Mark Twain and Southwestern Humor* (1959) he is author of *The Dream of Success* (1955) and editor of *The Comic Tradition in America* (1958).

LEO MARX is Professor of English and of American Studies in Amherst College.

WALTER BLAIR, Professor of English in the University of Chicago, is author of *Horse Sense in American Humor* (1942) and *Mark Twain & Huck Finn* (1960); co-author (with Franklin J. Meine) of *Mike Fink* (1933); and editor of *Native American Humor 1800-1900* (1937).

DANIEL G. HOFFMAN, Associate Professor of English in Swarthmore College, is author of *Paul Bunyan* (1952), *The Poetry of Stephen Crane* (1957), and *Form and Fable in American Fiction* (1961).

W. H. AUDEN, the celebrated poet, after beginning his career in England became an American citizen in 1946.

JAMES M. COX is Associate Professor of English in Indiana University. He edited the volume on Robert Frost in this series.

LESLIE FIEDLER, author of *An End to Innocence* (1955), *Love and Death in the American Novel* (1960), and *No! in Thunder* (1960), is Professor of English in Montana State University.

BERNARD DeVOTO, who died in 1955, was author of many books of fiction, criticism, and history. His best known work is the sequence dealing with the early West: *The Course of Empire* (1952), *Across the Wide Missouri* (1947), and *The Year of Decision: 1846* (1943).

TONY TANNER, a Fellow of King's College, Cambridge, is currently studying in this country on an ACLS Fellowship in American Civilization.

Bibliographical Note

An exhaustive bibliography of Mark Twain criticism during the first half of the twentieth century is contained in Roger Asselineau's *The Literary Reputation of Mark Twain from 1910 to 1950* (1954), which lists more than 1300 books, articles, reviews, and unpublished theses. Professor Asselineau's judicious fifty-page introductory essay traces all the main trends of interpretation during this period. Among the thirty-four essays and reviews reprinted in Arthur L. Scott's *Mark Twain: Selected Criticism* (1955) are twenty-four published between 1901 and 1951. The controversy over Van Wyck Brooks's *The Ordeal of Mark Twain* is amply documented in the collection edited by Lewis Leary under the title *A Casebook on Mark Twain's Wound* (1962), which includes, in addition to a selection of passages from Brooks's *Ordeal,* twenty-three items by other critics published between 1920 and 1961. Professor Leary's introduction deals fully with the prolonged debate, and his ten-page bibliography is especially useful for the past decade. Convenient access to articles about Mark Twain is provided by Professor Leary's *Articles on American Literature 1900-1950* (1954); by the supplementary *Index to Articles on American Literature 1951-1959* prepared by the Reference Department of the University of Pennsylvania Library (1960); and by the list of "Articles on American Literature Appearing in Current Periodicals" in each issue of *American Literature.* All significant books dealing with Mark Twain are reviewed in this journal as they appear.

General bibliographies are contained in Harry Hayden Clark's essay on Mark Twain in Floyd Stovall, ed., *Eight American Authors: A Review of Research and Criticism* (1956) and E. Hudson Long, *Mark Twain Handbook* (1957).

TWENTIETH CENTURY VIEWS

Other Titles